CONCENTRATE Q&A
EQUITY AND TRUSTS

FREE online study and revision support available at **www.oup.com/lawrevision**

Take your learning further with:

- Multiple-choice questions with instant feedback
- Interactive glossaries and flashcards of key cases
- Tips, tricks and audio advice
- Annotated outline answers
- Diagnostic tests show you where to concentrate
- Extra questions, key facts checklists, and topic overviews

unique features

student-focused online support

CONCENTRATE Q&A
EQUITY AND TRUSTS

Rosalind Malcolm

Barrister, Professor of Law, University of Surrey

THIRD EDITION

OXFORD
UNIVERSITY PRESS

Great Clarendon Street, Oxford, OX2 6DP,
United Kingdom

Oxford University Press is a department of the University of Oxford.
It furthers the University's objective of excellence in research, scholarship,
and education by publishing worldwide. Oxford is a registered trade mark of
Oxford University Press in the UK and in certain other countries

First edition 2016
Second edition 2018

Public sector information reproduced under Open Government Licence v3.0
(http://www.nationalarchives.gov.uk/doc/open-government-licence/open-government-licence.htm)

Published in the United States of America by Oxford University Press
198 Madison Avenue, New York, NY 10016, United States of America

British Library Cataloguing in Publication Data

Data available

Library of Congress Control Number: 2020942195

ISBN 978–0–19–885321–3

Printed in Great Britain by
Bell & Bain Ltd., Glasgow

For Margaret Wilkie

Contents

Guide to the Book

Every book in the Concentrate Q&A series contains the following features:

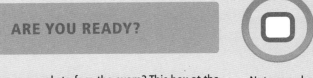

Are you ready to face the exam? This box at the start of each chapter identifies the key topics and cases that you need to have learned, revised, and understood before tackling the questions in each chapter.

Not sure where to begin? Clear diagram answer plans at the start of each question help you see how to structure your answer at a glance, and take you through each point step-by-step.

Demonstrating your knowledge of the crucial debates is a sure-fire way to impress examiners. These at-a-glance boxes help remind you of the key debates relevant to each topic, which you should discuss in your answers to get the highest marks.

What makes a great answer great? Our authors show you the thought process behind their own answers, and how you can do the same in your exam. Key sentences are highlighted and advice is given on how to structure your answer well and develop your arguments.

Each question represents a typical essay or problem question so that you know exactly what to expect in your exam.

Don't settle for a good answer—make it great! This feature gives you extra points to include in the exam if you want to gain more marks and make your answer stand out.

Don't fall into any traps! This feature points out common mistakes that students make, and which you need to avoid when answering each question.

Really push yourself and impress your examiner by going beyond what is expected. Focused further reading suggestions allow you to develop in-depth knowledge of the subject for when you are looking for the highest marks.

Guide to the Online Resources

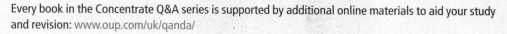

Every book in the Concentrate Q&A series is supported by additional online materials to aid your study and revision: www.oup.com/uk/qanda/

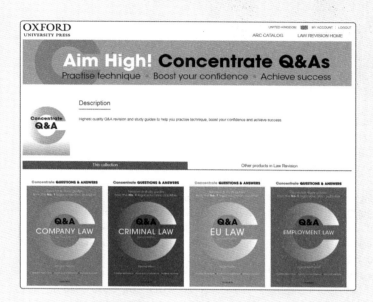

- Extra essay and problem questions with guidance on how to approach them.
- Video guidance on how to put an answer plan together.
- Audio advice on revision and exam technique from Nigel Foster.

Table of Cases

Table of Primary Legislation

Exam Skills for Success in Equity and Trusts Law

1

During the Module

- The first thing is: attend all your lectures and tutorials. Do the work for the tutorials and go to each of them prepared to engage in the discussion. Don't be shy. This is your chance to test out whether you have understood and this is where you get the best feedback available. So, put your hand up and have a go. You might be told you are wrong—well, best to know now than in the exam room (or on results day). And if you get a brisk tutor—really that's going to be nothing to what it will be like standing up in front of a county court judge on your first day in court. If you can't face a tutorial, then ask yourself: am I really looking for a career as a lawyer? The best tutors are those who give you a run for your money; who don't allow free riders to sit in the class; and, who demand the highest standards from you. Give thanks for them and, if your pride gets a bit dented, then put it down to experience.

- Your module will likely end with a revision lecture. It is always astonishing how many students view this as an optional extra (especially when they are in the week before Christmas or a vacation). What do you think a revision lecture means? It means revision for the exam. Don't expect to be told what is in the exam (unless it is that sort of exam). There is nothing more frustrating than the question—so is that going to be in the exam? Or, should I practise essay or problem questions on this topic? You will just irritate your lecturer with those questions when they are trying to do the best by you—which is to turn you into a decent lawyer. An unseen exam is what it says—it is unseen before you sit down at the desk in the exam room. It is an important test for a lawyer, training you to think under pressure. But you will run through topics in this lecture which will enable you to focus your mind for that final push before the exam and, as such, it is unmissable.

The Revision Period

- Having worked your socks off during the module then the next key stage is the run up to the exam after all the lectures have ended. Get hold of previous exam papers. Unless your lecturer is new (or a new teacher on this module) then it is likely that your exam will follow the pattern in previous papers. Have a look through them to get the feel and style of the questions. If you have worked for all your tutorials then it is likely that you will find you have already prepared some of these questions as module leaders usually use them for tutorial practice. Another reason for attending and preparing for tutorials—they are exam practice as well as feedback.

● Check the length of your paper and the number of questions you are required to complete during that time. This enables you to be able to practise under exam conditions. Basic arithmetic applies here: divide the length of the paper by the number of questions you have to do and then you know how long on average you have to write each answer. Then sit in your room with a timer on and tackle questions from past papers.

● Have you done any writing by hand recently? Most of us type and word process now. The most handwriting we do may be to sign a Valentine's Day card. There are two points to be made here: is your handwriting legible and can you actually write fast enough to complete what is necessary within the time allowed for the exam? If legibility is your problem then get a copy book and practise handwriting. And do those test exam questions in the privacy of your study under exam conditions until you have had enough practice at simply writing so that is not a barrier in the exam.

● Question spotting: a very dangerous strategy. You might think that being required to answer three (or however many it is) questions means that if you revise four topics or, worse—past questions on a topic—then you will be safe. But the danger here is that you may get that topic, but in a form you were not expecting. Or, only two of your revised topics might crop up. Do not limit your chances of success in this way. Basic arithmetic again applies. If you have to answer three questions and only one or two of them are what you have worked for, your chances of succeeding well (or at all) are tragically limited. Further, some students revise a topic on the basis that they will only answer an essay question on that topic. And then, horror of horrors, a problem question crops up for the first time in five years. Revise a topic from all angles. Be ready to answer either a problem or an essay question on it.

In the Exam Room

● There are four key pieces of advice which can be offered: (1) read the question; (2) read the question; (3) read the question; then (4) answer the question set—not the one you wish had been set.

● You will be marked on whether you have spotted all the issues. So, in a problem question read it slowly and carefully. List the issues in your plan. There is unlikely to be anything in the question which is not important so you need to ask yourself—what is that point about? Why is that fact included?

● Be careful about reading what you think is there. For example, if you are told that the will states: 'a respectable income to Uncle Uglow' your mind may jump to 'reasonable income' (**Re Golay**). I have seen this happen where students have assumed the word is 'reasonable' and have answered on that basis thus missing the analysis which is required from discussing whether **Re Golay** will apply or not. So be careful to read the question and don't assume anything. Working under exam conditions does odd things to the mind so you need to look carefully and weigh each word in the exam paper. Your examiner is unlikely to give you the exact words from a case but ones which require you to discuss whether that case would apply to this point or whether it is distinguishable.

● In a problem, are you asked to advise a trustee or some named person? Write your answer on that basis: 'the trustees are advised that this gift is likely to fail so they will be required to hold the property on resulting trust for XYZ'.

- In an essay, what is the instruction? Are you asked to comment or to compare or discuss? For example, if you are asked to discuss whether the law relating to certainty of objects is in a fair and rational state then you are being asked to critique this area of law. So, if you set out to explain it you will only achieve so many marks (if you are accurate) but if you use that knowledge to critique this area of law then you will be doing what the examiner wants and your mark will improve. Throughout the essay you will need to comment on this as you go along and then your conclusion will address this precise point: 'In conclusion, while the general principles for certainty of objects for a private trust are rational, the status of non-charitable purpose trusts, lacking as they do the requirement for a human beneficiary, introduce irrationality into this area of law.' It means you have to think yourself into the question. You might have revised and practised questions on this topic but this particular angle might be new. Don't be fazed by it but think yourself into it. Use your knowledge and turn it round to address the question.

- You already know how long you have got and how many questions you need to answer so you know how long you have for each one. Make sure you have a working watch with you and that it is synchronised with the exam room clock. Give yourself time to read the paper and choose your questions then set yourself a time limit for each answer. Don't be caught out at the end by running out of time and having to write sad billets-doux to your examiner—'sorry, out of time'. No marks for that.

- Don't worry about saving the planet when writing your answers. The answer book is all yours to use so write on one side only and start each answer on a new page. That way, when you have a last moment inspiration you will have room to go back and add it in without sending your examiner on a hunt for that tiny asterisk.

- Write the question number clearly at the beginning of each answer and also write numbers clearly for sub-sections within each answer. Leave a space between sub-sections.

- Don't be afraid to use headings and underline them as you go along. E.g. (a) Aunt Jemima's emerald ring.

- Underline cases and statutes as you go along. Rulers are not required—just draw a freehand line under the relevant name.

- Always include the date of a statute. If you can, do the same for cases but that is less of a demand than for statutes.

- Memory matters. Learn the case names. Use memory techniques that work for you—post-it notes round the house; card indexes; fancy software packages—whatever works for you. And if, despite all that, in the exam room your mind goes blank then identify a case by giving a few of its key facts 'in a case where the young man was befriended by the gentleman farmer who made promises to him that if he worked for him then the estate would be his …'.

The Structure and Approach to Problem Questions

- All the books in this series have adopted the IRAC structure (Identify the Issues, Relevant Law, Apply the Law, and Conclusions). This has the advantage of imposing a clearly remembered structure on you. The I (the facts or factual issues) is the issue spotting bit. You need to pick up all the issues to earn all the marks which are going. Miss one and you miss earning marks. The R is the law. In Equity and Trusts this is usually case law except in the rare areas where Parliament has stuck its nose in. The A is really the core of getting top marks—the trick with a problem question is applying the law to the problem. Stating the law is one thing—the clever bit is to do what lawyers do—apply it to the problem and become a problem-solver. The C is (obviously) the conclusion. A word of warning about the IRAC approach. It helps to get a structure into your answer—or more importantly into your thoughts in the first place. But in the answer plans I have often summarised the points quite extensively—so you will find that the suggested answers do go into quite a bit more detail than the answer plans. It is probably fair to say that the answer plan gives you the basics. But if you want to do better than that and get into the heady and utterly desirable upper second and first class answers then study the suggested answers where I have attempted to give you the full monty.

Last Word

● Do you write well? Lawyers are wordsmiths. Words are our tools and we must use them precisely to convey what we mean. Writing well is an essential requirement and if you have been pulled up about this in formative coursework, or, if you know that this is not your strong point, then do something about it. It may be that your university offers classes for writing skills. Go to them. Practise writing. Write letters to friends and relatives. Write a short story and ask someone to read it over and critique it. Learn basic grammar from an English grammar book. Read how others write. Read a judgment and see how judges construct their sentences. I would like to urge you to write beautifully but clarity will suffice. Clarity comes from writing grammatically and coherently. You will not be marked on whether you have good grammar. But you will be marked on whether you have made clear what you are arguing. That comes from good writing skills.

Online Resources   www.oup.com/uk/qanda/

Go online for extra essay and problem questions, a glossary of key terms, online versions of all the answer plans and audio commentary on how selected ones were put together, and a range of podcasts which include advice on exam and coursework technique and advice for other assessment methods.

Nature of Equity and the Law of Trusts

2

ARE YOU READY?

In order to attempt the questions in this chapter you will need to have covered the following topics:

- The nature of equity
- The development of equity and its relationship to the common law
- The maxims of equity
- The nature of the trust

 ## KEY DEBATES

Debate: The fusion argument.

Have the rules of common law and equity fused? This argument deals with the historical foundations of equity and raises the challenging question as to whether it has fused with common law. The **Judicature Acts 1873** and **1875** are at the heart of the argument insofar as it relates to administrative questions. But of more interest is the substantive side. There is a lot written about this such as: Burrows, 'We do this at Common Law but this in equity' (2002) 22 OJLS 1; Lord Millett, 'Proprietary Restitution' in *Equity in Commercial Law* (Degeling and Edelman, eds), Law Book Co of Australasia, 2005, chapter 12; Worthington, *Equity*, Oxford University Press, 2006, chapter 10; Martin, 'Fusion, fallacy and confusion: a comparative study' [1994] Conv 13—to name just a few. The area requires wide reading.

(Q) | **QUESTION** | **1**

The innate conservatism of English lawyers may have made them slow to recognise that by the **Judicature Act 1873** the two systems of substantive and adjectival law formerly administered by courts of law and courts of equity . . . were fused. As at the confluence of the Rhône and the Saône, it may be possible for a short distance to discern the source from which each part of the combined stream came, but there comes a point at which this ceases to be possible. If Professor Ashburner's fluvial metaphor is to be retained at all, the confluent streams of law and equity have surely mingled now.

(Lord Diplock in **United Scientific Holdings Ltd v Burnley Borough Council [1978] AC 904**)

Discuss.

(!) **CAUTION!**

- The structure of your answer is critical here to avoid an overly discursive approach. Strict observance of the PEA approach will help to keep your structure tight.

- You need to have covered all the literature in order to engage fully with this question—the answer needs to have full referencing to the various statements made by the judiciary and academics.

- If, when you are in the exam room, this is the first time you have come across the quote, or indeed any quote in a question (it is a key one on this topic), then you may want to consider whether this is the question for you.

- Some students tend to address equity as though it is a 'free-for-all' so don't fall into that trap. When answering any general questions on equity show you understand that it is as rule-bound as the common law!

(O) **DIAGRAM ANSWER PLAN**

Set out the source of the quotation and the issues in the case

▼

Show the extent of agreement with the proposition in the quotation

▼

Establish the background and history culminating in the key statutes

▼

Set out the arguments going either way

▼

Conclusions

[1] Start with the source of the quotation. A weakness is to ignore the source of the quote and to go straight into the arguments.

The statement by Lord Diplock was accepted unanimously by the judges in the House of Lords.[1] The case concerned the timing of the service of a notice triggering a rent-review clause which had been served late. The question arose as to whether time was of the essence. The **Law of Property Act 1925, s. 41** provides that 'stipulations in a contract, as to time or otherwise, which according to rules of equity are not deemed to be or to have become of the essence of the contract, are also construed and have effect at law in accordance with the same rules'. The section clearly states that a rule of equity is to be adopted within the body of legal rules. Lord Diplock proclaimed that **the systems had become fused and no distinction was to be drawn between law and equity.**[2]

[2] It is good to make reference to the judge in this way to show familiarity with the argument.

This view is at the most extreme, yet it is one apparently shared by other eminent judges. Lord Denning, in *Landmarks in the Law*, states that 'the fusion is complete'. Sir George Jessel MR in ***Walsh* v *Lonsdale* (1882) 21 ChD 9**, one of the first cases on this issue to be heard subsequent to the **Judicature Acts 1873** and **1875**, said 'there are not two estates as there were formerly, one estate at common law by reason of the payment of rent from year to year, and an estate in equity under the agreement. There is only one court, and the equity rules prevail in it.' Carnwath LJ concurred in ***Halpern* v *Halpern (No. 2)* [2007] EWCA Civ 291** when relying on the **Senior Courts Act 1981** to conclude that '130 years after the "fusion" of law and equity . . . an argument based on a material difference in the two systems would have faced an uphill task' [70]. The approach of Lord Goff in ***Napier and Ettrick (Lord)* v *Hunter* [1993] AC 713** is in accord with this:[3] 'No doubt our task nowadays is to see the two strands of authority, at law and in equity, moulded into a coherent whole.'

[3] Although this looks a bit like listing—often hated by examiners—it actually shows wide reading and support for the proposition made in the quotation.

The Development Phase

[4] This paragraph sets out the historical background which helps to give depth and context to the arguments about fusion.

The difficulty originates from the early development of equity as a separate system from the common law.[4] Intervention by the Lord Chancellor into the common law gradually developed into a separate body of law, known as equity, which, by the fifteenth century, become well established eventually through the Court of Chancery. The two systems were sometimes in conflict. Parties seeking common law relief would need to seek the jurisdiction of the common law courts. If they wanted equitable relief they would go to the Court of Chancery. The common law courts only had limited jurisdiction to grant equitable relief. The **Common Law Procedure Act 1854, s. 79**, gave the common law courts a limited power of granting injunctions; the **Chancery Amendment Act 1858** gave power to the Court of

Chancery to award damages instead of (or in addition to) injunctions or specific performance.

[5] The **Judicature Acts** need a paragraph to themselves—such is their importance in the story you are telling.

The Judicature Acts[5]

The problem became acute in the nineteenth century, and a series of Parliamentary reports led eventually to the **Judicature Acts 1873** and **1875**. These Acts amalgamated the superior courts into one Supreme Court of Judicature which consisted of the Court of Appeal and the High Court. The Supreme Court could administer both rules of common law and equity. Thus, there is no question as to the fusion of the courts.[6] The two distinct sets of courts fused on 1 November 1875. Sir George Jessel MR said in *Salt* v *Cooper* **(1880) 16 ChD 544**, that the main object of the Acts was not the fusion of law and equity, but the vesting in one tribunal of the administration of law and equity in all actions coming before that tribunal.

[6] This sentence sets out a strong viewpoint which is borne out by the preceding discussion about the **Judicature Acts**.

The Arguments

[7] This paragraph begins to set out the counter-argument.

Yet it is difficult to pursue Lord Diplock's dictum further to the point of saying that the substantive rules of law and equity are themselves indistinguishable.[7] In trusts there is a distinction between legal and equitable interests and the right to trace property in equity depends on the existence of a fiduciary relationship. Except where statute has intervened, legal and equitable interests are distinguishable in that legal interests are rights *in rem* that bind the whole world whereas equitable rights are lost against the bona fide purchaser of a legal estate for value without notice. In land with unregistered title, the **Land Charges Act 1972** made a number of equitable interests registrable (and one legal interest—the puisne mortgage) and had the effect of determining that such interests which are not registered are void against certain types of purchasers. Nevertheless, in land with unregistered title, a group of equitable interests still fall outside the ambit of this statute and are subject to the equitable doctrine of notice. Equitable interests behind a trust, pre-1926 equitable easements, and restrictive covenants fall into this category.

[8] This is a balancing paragraph showing the other side to the story.

It is possible to cite examples, however, where the distinction has become irrelevant.[8] In registered land, the categories of registered, minor and overriding interests (**Land Registration Act 2002**) cut across the distinction.

Remedies present some interesting examples of the distinction which has grown up between law and equity; a distinction which arose as 'an accident of history' according to Lord Nicholls in *A-G* v *Blake* **[2000] 3 WLR 625**, p. 634. In general, legal rights and remedies remain distinct from equitable ones. Some overlap does, however, occur; for example, an injunction, an equitable remedy, can be sought for an anticipatory breach of contract, or to stop a nuisance, both common law claims. In *A-G v Blake* **[2000] 3 WLR 625**, the House of Lords allowed the equitable remedy of account of profits for a claim for breach of contract where the common law remedy of damages would have been inadequate. The equitable remedy of account of profits is normally available where there is a fiduciary relationship but the House of Lords permitted its application otherwise in exceptional cases where it was the effective way to remedy a wrong. By contrast, in *Seager v Copydex Ltd* **[1967] 1 WLR 923, CA**, an action was brought for breach of confidence in respect of confidential information. Such a claim is equitable and normally the equitable remedies of injunction and account are available. However, an injunction would have been ineffective and the judge awarded damages. It would seem, therefore, that a common law remedy is available for an equitable claim for breach of confidence. See, for example, the *Spycatcher* case, **A-G v *Guardian Newspapers Ltd (No. 2)* [1990] 1 AC 109** (p. 286).

In *Tinsley v Milligan* **[1994] 1 AC 340**, which was, until the Supreme Court decision in *Patel v Mirza* **[2016] UKSC 42**, the leading case, the conflict between law and equity again became apparent. The principle that a litigant cannot rely on an illegal purpose to rebut the presumption of advancement was confirmed, but, in this case, the equitable presumption of the resulting trust was held to apply. Thus, the defendant did not need to rely on her own illegal conduct and the equitable maxim that 'he who comes to equity should come with clean hands' did not have to be invoked. This case, seeking to balance illegality and unjust enrichment, created difficulties in application. In *Tribe v Tribe* **[1996] Ch 107**, a case concerning a transfer of shares from father to son, the matter was complicated by the effect of the presumption of advancement. This area of illegal transactions has been the subject of a Law Commission consultation (see Law Com Consultation Paper No. 154, 1999, *Illegal Transactions: The Effect of Illegality on Contracts and Trusts* which resulted in 2010 in a final report: *The Illegality Defence*, Law Com No. 320). *Tinsley v Milligan* has unsurprisingly been much criticised and has since been overturned by the Supreme Court in *Patel v Mirza* **[2016] UKSC 42**—a case where the transaction between the parties involved insider dealing which amounted to a criminal conspiracy. The Supreme Court decided that the decision should rest upon a range of factors and that the court, when dealing with an instance of illegality, should make a more flexible assessment of whether the public interest would be harmed by enforcement of the illegal contract. Relevant factors included (a) the underlying purpose of the prohibition which was illegally contravened, (b) public policy, and (c) whether denial of the claim would be proportionate, bearing in mind that punishment was a concern of the criminal courts. In turn, of course, it is quite possible to criticise **Patel v Mirza** for introducing discretion and uncertainty into the mix. Nevertheless, it does provide a more rational basis for decisions as to property where it has passed on the basis of an illegal purpose. It also demonstrates the way in which the courts are able to deal equally within the same forum with matters concerning the common law and equity.

By contrast, Worthington argues that equity and the common law should now be fully integrated. But her arguments rest upon odd analyses of cases which introduce the concept of reasonableness such as **Donoghue v Stevenson [1932] AC 562**. The objective standard of reasonableness can hardly be equated with the use of discretion in equity. There is no need in practice for such an argument. The fusion of the courts was all that was necessary to enable the judges to use the full range of common law and equity.

Conclusion

[9] If you can reach a clear statement summarising briefly what you have reviewed and discussed then do so. This final paragraph does just that.

Thus, the systems are administered in the same courts, but in general the distinction remains relevant. While it may continue in some instances to produce conflicts, in general it enables the full use of remedies to be available.[9]

LOOKING FOR EXTRA MARKS?

- The statement is provocative—even controversial—so be prepared to argue for or against it. Don't be afraid to take and argue a position on the issue.

- Provide a clear analysis of the case mentioned in the question—some students ignore the source of the quote and that is nearly always a mistake.

- You could expand the reference to Worthington (Worthington, S., *Equity*, 2nd edn, Oxford University Press, 2006). There is, also, a nice discussion of illegality and cases such as **Patel v Mirza** in R. N. Nwabueze, 'Illegality and trusts: trusts-creating primary transactions and unlawful ulterior purposes' [2019] Conv 29–46 which could be incorporated into this answer for extra marks.

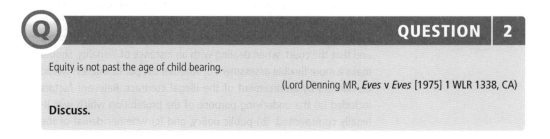

Q QUESTION | 2

Equity is not past the age of child bearing.

(Lord Denning MR, *Eves v Eves* [1975] 1 WLR 1338, CA)

Discuss.

CAUTION!

- This question may sometimes appear as an assessed essay. Confronted in the examination room, it may seem daunting. Take care to plan the points before you start writing.

- It may be difficult to decide what should be included. Take your cue from the source of the quotation and what your lecturer covered in lectures. You could take a broad approach and cover a range of examples here or focus on one example but address it in more depth. This suggested answer takes the broad approach.

- If you were taking a narrow approach here, i.e. focusing on one aspect in depth, you could include a broad list and then state that it is your intention to address one example to show in detail the operation of equity in the context of this question. That displays your broad grasp of the point made by the question.

DIAGRAM ANSWER PLAN

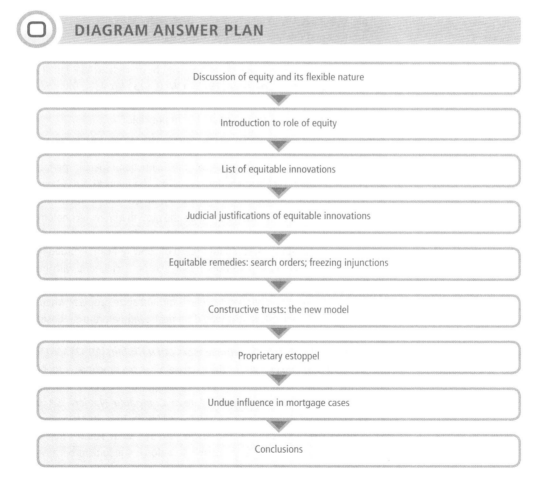

Discussion of equity and its flexible nature

Introduction to role of equity

List of equitable innovations

Judicial justifications of equitable innovations

Equitable remedies: search orders; freezing injunctions

Constructive trusts: the new model

Proprietary estoppel

Undue influence in mortgage cases

Conclusions

A   SUGGESTED ANSWER

Introduction: Equity and Its Flexible Nature

[1] There needs to be an explanation at the start of the development of equity—why did it develop? How did it develop?

[2] The maxims are sometimes thought to be a bit outdated but they do still underpin the operation of equity so make mention of them in the introduction.

[3] This ties in one of the maxims with the whole way in which it operates—discretion but not without rules. It is good to show you have grasped this early on.

[4] This listing can be used to establish the structure of your answer.

[5] The equitable remedies form a nice example so you can devote a good paragraph to them. You need to address the examples of search and freezing orders here as the latest developments.

When equity originally developed as a gloss on the common law it was innovative;[1] it developed new remedies and recognised new rights where the common law failed to act. The efficacy of equity was largely due to its ability to adapt and innovate, yet inevitably, this development itself became regulated in a similar way to the development of the common law. There are maxims of equity[2] which may determine the outcome of disputes. Although the judge has discretion in the granting of an equitable remedy, that discretion is exercised according to settled principles.[3] Thus, it might be said that equity can develop no further; the rules of precedent predetermine the outcome.

Yet, this is belied by various new developments in equity, for example: restrictive covenants, remedies, proprietary estoppel, contractual licences, and the new model constructive trust.[4]

There is an attempt, however, to justify these new developments, which are all examples of judicial creativity, by precedent. As Bagnall J said in *Cowcher v Cowcher* **[1972] 1 WLR 425** at p. 430: 'This does not mean that equity is past childbearing; simply that its progeny must be legitimate—by precedent out of principle.'

Development of Equitable Remedies[5]

Equity developed the remedies of the injunction, specific performance, account, rectification, and rescission. The injunction has been a growth area. The search order (*Anton Piller KG v Manufacturing Processes Ltd* **[1976] Ch 55**), reflects the growth of new technology and the need to protect ownership rights. Intellectual property can easily be lost before an action for breach of copyright can be brought. Confidential information can disappear leaving a claimant with no means of proof. The search order developed to allow a claimant to enter a defendant's premises to search for and seize property where there was a clear risk that it would be destroyed before trial. Cases such as *Columbia Picture Industries Inc. v Robinson* **[1986] 3 All ER 338** and *Universal Thermosensors Ltd v Hibben* **[1992] 1 WLR 840** laid down guidelines for the exercise of such a draconian order.

The freezing injunction is another example of a refined application of an established remedy (*Mareva Compañía Naviera SA v International Bulkcarriers SA* **[1975] 2 Lloyd's Rep 509** following *Nippon Yusen Kaisha v Karageorgis* **[1975] 1 WLR 1093**). While a claim may succeed, if it is impossible to enforce a judgment because there are no assets, then the judgment is worthless. In international disputes, assets may be transferred abroad to make the judgment debt impossible or, very difficult, to follow. Recognising this dilemma, the judges in *Mareva* were prepared to grant an order freezing the defendant's assets. Further cases have demonstrated that the courts are prepared to make this order available worldwide in certain circumstances (*Masri* v *Consolidated Contractors International (UK) Ltd (No. 2)* **[2008] EWCA Civ 303;** *Dadourian Group International Inc*. v *Simms* **[2006] EWCA Civ 399;** *Derby & Co. Ltd* v *Weldon (No. 3 and No. 4)* **(1989) 139 NLJ 11;** *Republic of Haiti* v *Duvalier* **[1990] 1 QB 202** and see **Civil Procedure Rules, r. 25.1(1)(f)).**[6]

[6] If this were coursework then you could develop these cases there. In general, you shouldn't set out lists of cases but it would be justified here—lack of space and time—yet still displays your knowledge—for 'extra marks'.

The Trust and Other Equitable Creations[7]

[7] This section groups the trust development which is the new model constructive trust plus other areas which go with that— proprietary estoppel and licences.

Equity initially recognised the trust. This was one of the original developments of equity. However, the protection granted to equitable owners behind a trust has developed significantly with the new model constructive trust, the contractual licence, and the doctrine of proprietary estoppel.

The constructive trust of a new model developed largely because of the creative activity of Lord Denning MR. In *Hussey* v *Palmer* **[1972] 1 WLR 1286, CA**, Lord Denning described the constructive trust as one 'imposed by law wherever justice and good conscience require it'. Cases such as *Eves* v *Eves* **[1975] 1 WLR 1338**, and *Cooke* v *Head* **[1972] 1 WLR 518**, took this development further. Several cases, including *Lloyds Bank* v *Rosset* **[1991] 1 AC 107**, sought to re-establish less flexible principles in this field relating to the existence of a common intention that an equitable interest should arise, and the existence of a direct financial contribution. Nevertheless, the House of Lords in *Stack* v *Dowden* **[2007] UKHL 17**, followed by the Supreme Court in *Jones* v *Kernott* **[2011] UKSC 53** and the Privy Council in *Marr* v *Collie* **[2017] UKPC 17**, have reintroduced some of the earlier flexibility into the constructive trust showing that equity is alive and well.

The new model constructive trust is notable in the field of licences. Equitable remedies have been used to prevent a licensor breaking a contractual licence and to enable a licence to bind third parties. It has been accepted that certain licences may create an equitable proprietary interest by way of a constructive trust or proprietary estoppel. In *Binions* v *Evans* **[1972] Ch 359, CA**, purchasers were bound by a contractual licence between the former owners and Mrs Evans, an occupant. A constructive trust was imposed in her favour as the purchasers had bought expressly subject to Mrs Evans's interest and had, for that reason, paid a reduced price. In *Re Sharpe* **[1980] 1 WLR 219**, a constructive trust was imposed on a trustee in bankruptcy in respect of an interest acquired by an aunt who lent money to her nephew for a house purchase on the understanding that she could live there for the rest of her life.

The fluidity of these developing areas is shown in case law which appears to hold back from a development which may have pushed the frontiers too far. Obiter dicta by the Court of Appeal in *Ashburn Anstalt* v *W. J. Arnold & Co.* [1989] Ch 1, approved in *Habermann* v *Koehler* (1996) 73 P & CR 515, suggest that a licence will only give rise to a constructive trust where the conscience of a third party is affected. It will be imposed where their conduct so warrants. Judicial creativity in equitable fields is thus made subject to refinements by judges in later cases.

Proprietary estoppel is another example of an equitable doctrine which has seen significant developments in the interests of justice since its establishment in the leading case of *Dillwyn* v *Llewelyn* (1862) 4 De GF & J 517. Its application was further enhanced in *Gillett* v *Holt* [2001] Ch 210, where a broader approach was taken that depended, ultimately, on the unconscionability of the action. Two House of Lords' decisions in *Yeoman's Row Management* v *Cobbe* [2008] UKHL 55 and *Thorner* v *Major* [2009] UKHL 18 also injected new approaches into the doctrine with later decisions in *Crossco No. 4 Unlimited* v *Jolan Ltd* [2011] EWCA Civ 1619 and *Herbert* v *Doyle* [2010] EWCA Civ 1095, evaluating the use of the equitable doctrine in commercial contexts. Again, it is a development which stands outside the system of property rights and their registration established by Parliament.

Cases such as *Jennings* v *Rice* [2002] EWCA Civ 159, [2003] 1 P & CR 8, *Matharu* v *Matharu* (1994) 68 P & CR 93, *Costello* v *Costello* (1995) 70 P & CR 297, and *Durant* v *Heritage* [1994] EGCS 134 show that the doctrine of proprietary estoppel and the protection of licences by estoppel remain an effective method used by the judges for the protection of licences and equitable rights. The degree to which the right receives protection is variable depending on the circumstances of the particular case. For instance, in *Matharu* v *Matharu*, the licence did not confer a beneficial interest but gave the respondent a right to live in the house for the rest of her life. In *Durant* v *Heritage*, the court ordered the house to be transferred to the applicant under the doctrine of proprietary estoppel. In *Jennings* v *Rice*, by contrast, the equity was satisfied by monetary compensation.

[8] It is possible that you didn't cover this area in lectures. But this paragraph is an example of another illustration of the point. If you omitted this paragraph you would still have enough for a good answer.

Undue Influence in Mortgages[8]

Another development in equity resulted from the decisions in *Barclays Bank plc* v *O'Brien* [1994] 1 AC 180 and *CIBC Mortgages plc* v *Pitt* [1994] 1 AC 200. These two cases heralded the re-emergence in a broad sense of the equitable doctrine of notice. They provide that, where there is undue influence over a co-mortgagor or surety, this may give rise to a right to avoid the transaction. This right to avoid the transaction amounts to an equity of which the mortgagee may be deemed to have constructive notice. This resurrection of the equitable doctrine of notice in a modern context demonstrates the flexibility of equity. This was followed in *Royal Bank of Scotland v Etridge (No. 2)* **[2001] 4 All ER 449** (eight conjoined appeals), where the House of Lords laid down general guidelines for the application of the doctrine of notice in this context.

So, although there may be setbacks and refinements in the development of new doctrines when later judges seek to rationalise and consolidate new principles, nevertheless it is clear that equity maintains its traditions.

[9] A tight conclusion. There is no point in repeating what you have said. In an essay question your conclusion is a concise summary to round off the argument.

Conclusion[9]

So equity is still developing and forms an important aspect of the legal system providing new remedies and rights where no established route to satisfy the demands of good conscience and order exists.

LOOKING FOR EXTRA MARKS?

- In the context of the quotation, the judge is seeking to justify a new development in equity, that is, in the particular case cited, the new model constructive trust. Be prepared to critique that justification to get extra marks.

- Be topical. If there is a new case or area of development which signals a new direction then show how this ancient area of law is vibrant and modern.

QUESTION | 3

Explain and discuss the maxim, 'equity looks upon that as done which ought to be done'. To what extent (if any) does this maxim operate to impose a trust on any person?

CAUTION!

- Some aspects of this answer are esoteric, for example the rule in *Lawes v Bennett* (1785) **1 Cox 167**. Many lecturers do not cover this rule in their courses. If that is the case then you may not be expected to deal with it in a question of this sort. The guidance on the suggested content of the answer offered here must be tempered by what you have been expected to cover in your syllabus.

- As ever, plan your points before starting writing.

DIAGRAM ANSWER PLAN

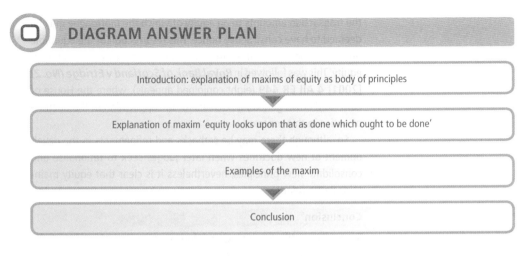

Introduction: explanation of maxims of equity as body of principles

↓

Explanation of maxim 'equity looks upon that as done which ought to be done'

↓

Examples of the maxim

↓

Conclusion

SUGGESTED ANSWER

Introduction: The Maxims of Equity[1]

The maxims of equity[2] operate as guidelines for the exercise of judicial discretion. Although equity did not acquire the rigidity of the common law, it did develop a body of principles. An equitable remedy is available at the discretion of the judge. The judge is assisted in the exercise of this discretion by these principles. They provide, for example, that for claimants to be granted equitable remedies, they must come to court with clean hands; they must have behaved equitably; and must not have delayed in seeking the intervention of equity.[3] These principles, known as maxims, do not operate as binding precedent but provide a basis for the development of equity. Some of them have, however, formed the basis for certain rules which are binding. There are 12 maxims in addition to some general principles.[4]

'Equity Looks Upon That as Done Which Ought to Be Done'

The maxim 'equity looks upon that as done which ought to be done' demonstrates the principle that,[5] where there is a specifically enforceable obligation, equity will enforce it as though the obligation had been carried out. The common law is rigid in that, if the proper formality has not been carried out (for example, the execution of a deed for the transfer of an interest in land) then it will not recognise the interest. Equity is prepared, nonetheless, to enforce the obligation as though all due formalities are present.

For example,[6] a contract for the sale of land is specifically enforceable if it has been effected in accordance with the rules laid down in the **Law of Property (Miscellaneous Provisions) Act 1989, s. 2**. It is

---

[1] Start with a straightforward explanation as to what the maxims are, what they do, and why they developed.

[2] Don't start by going straight into an explanation of the particular maxim as you need to set it in context.

[3] You can choose any example of the maxims.

[4] Don't list them all! That would be a waste of words. It is better to explain some of the key ones as in the earlier part of this paragraph.

[5] This paragraph starts the explanation of the subject maxim.

[6] Now give some examples of how this maxim works.

an estate contract which creates an equitable interest in favour of the purchaser, and is binding on third parties if protected by registration. Until completion, the vendor holds the legal estate upon constructive trust for the purchaser.

It is arguable, on the authority of *Oughtred* v *IRC* **[1960] AC 206, HL**, and *Re Holt's Settlement* **[1969] 1 Ch 100**, that, once an agreement has been entered into which is specifically enforceable, then the equitable interest passes without the need for formalities, as provided by the **Law of Property Act 1925, s. 53(2)**. This view was held to be sound in *Neville* v *Wilson* [1997] Ch 144, CA.

A contract for a lease, provided it complies with the contractual requirements, is enforceable in equity under the rule in *Walsh* v *Lonsdale* (1882) 21 ChD 9. Although the due formality of a deed required at law has not been complied with, equity sees as done that which ought to be done, and enforces the contract for the lease.

The Doctrine of Conversion

The maxim underlies the doctrine of conversion. Before the implementation of the **Trusts of Land and Appointment of Trustees Act 1996**, this doctrine stated that where there was a trust for the sale of land, equity assumed that the sale had already taken place. This meant, therefore, that the beneficiaries' interests were deemed to have been converted into personalty already, even if the land had not been sold. Since many trusts for sale arose where couples purchased a home for their joint occupation, their interests were frequently held in this manner long before the property was sold. The problem was considered in *Williams & Glyn's Bank Ltd* v *Boland* **[1981] AC 487, HL**. Mrs Boland was deemed to have an interest behind a trust for sale. The contest arose between her equitable interest and the interest of the bank, as mortgagee of the legal estate. If Mrs Boland had an interest in land then she would have an overriding interest under the Land Registration Act 1925, s. 70(1)(g) (now repealed and replaced by the **Land Registration Act 2002**). However, if her interest had already been converted into personalty, she would not have an overriding interest since the sub-section only protects rights in land. It was held that the purpose of the doctrine was to simplify conveyancing in cases where the intention was to sell the land immediately. The doctrine should not be extended beyond that to a case where it was clearly a fiction.

The **Trusts of Land and Appointment of Trustees Act (TLATA) 1996** provides that trusts for the sale of land are replaced by trusts of land with the power of sale. This means that the interest behind the trust is an interest in land until the power is exercised (**s. 3(1)**). This applies to trusts for sale arising before or after the commencement of the **TLATA 1996**, except in relation to trusts created by will where the testator died before commencement (**s. 3(2), (3)**).

[7] You may not have covered this— but, its inclusion would be quite impressive in any event and might earn extra marks.

A more obscure application of the doctrine is the rule in *Lawes v Bennett* **(1785) 1 Cox 167**,[7] which applies to the exercise of an option. If a leaseholder is granted an option to purchase the freehold and the freeholder dies before the option is exercised, then the disposition of the rents pending the exercise of the option, and the eventual purchase price, must be determined. The rents will go to the person entitled to the freehold. This would be either a residuary or a specific devisee. The proceeds of sale, however, which are payable when (and if) the option is exercised, pass to the residuary legatee as conversion into personalty is deemed to have taken place.

The maxim was applied to conditional contracts in *Re Sweeting (deceased)* **[1988] 1 All ER 1016**. A contract for the sale of land, subject to conditions, was not completed until after the vendor's death. It was held that the proceeds of sale went to the residuary legatee as the interest had already been converted into personalty.

The maxim also underlies the rule in *Howe v Earl of Dartmouth* **(1802) 7 Ves 137**, which relates to the duty to convert (*inter alia*) wasting assets. The rule is limited in that it only applies to residuary personalty settled by will in favour of persons with successive interests. The duty is that, where there are hazardous, wasting, or reversionary assets they must be converted into authorised investments. Where there is a duty to convert, there is also a duty to apportion between the life tenant and remainderman until sale. The scope of the rule in *Howe v Earl of Dartmouth* is now of more limited significance, however, as the **Trustee Act 2000** has greatly widened the range of investments that are available to trustees.

[8] A summarising conclusion to an essay question.

Conclusion[8]

So, the maxim applies to a variety of cases where equity is prepared to act as though the common law requirements had been fully complied with, or to convert property where it is equitable to do so.

LOOKING FOR EXTRA MARKS?

■ This discussion question requires an examination of the various applications of the maxim. It touches upon a number of different fields. In relation to trusts of land, its operation was affected by the **Trusts of Land and Appointment of Trustees Act 1996**. Showing your knowledge of how it was affected by this statute will earn extra marks.

■ For extra marks, when dealing with the application of the doctrine in the context of *Williams & Glyn's Bank Ltd v Boland* **[1981] AC 487, HL**, see the arguments made by Stuart Anderson (1984) 100 LQR 86.

QUESTION | **4**

What is equity?

CAUTION!

- This question requires an historical and jurisprudential analysis of the meaning and position of equity in the legal system. Being fascinated by this concept will help in answering the question.

- It is tricky to structure an answer to a question of this sort. The approach suggested here is to deal with the historical side first, using this as a vehicle for a discussion of the contribution which equity has made to the legal system.

DIAGRAM ANSWER PLAN

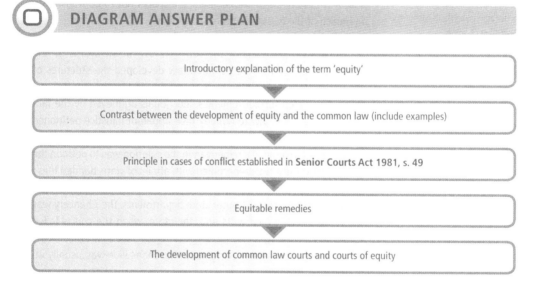

Introductory explanation of the term 'equity'

Contrast between the development of equity and the common law (include examples)

Principle in cases of conflict established in **Senior Courts Act** 1981, s. 49

Equitable remedies

The development of common law courts and courts of equity

SUGGESTED ANSWER

The Meaning of 'Equity'

[1] It is worth drawing this contrast between the lay meaning of equity and the legal one so as to show your understanding of the distinction.

Equity to the layman means fairness and justice, but in the legal context its meaning is much more strictly defined.[1] There are rules of equity: it must obey the rules of precedent as does the common law, and its development may appear equally rigid and doctrinal.

Yet, because of its historical development and the reasons underlying this, there does remain an element of discretion and the potential for judges to retain some flexibility in the determination of disputes.[2]

There are well-established principles which govern the exercise of the discretion but these, like all equitable principles, are flexible and adaptable to achieve the ends of equity, which is, as Lord Selborne LC once remarked, to 'do more perfect and complete justice' than would be the result of leaving the parties to their remedies at common law: *Wilson v Northampton and Banbury Junction Railway Co.* **(1874) LR 9 Ch App 279**, p. 284 (and see Lord Hoffmann, *Co-operative Insurance Society Ltd v Argyll Stores (Holdings) Ltd* **[1998] AC 1**). Principles of unconscionability underpin much of equity in its modern context. In *Westdeutsche Landesbank Girozentrale v Islington LBC* **[1996] AC 669**, Lord Browne-Wilkinson described the operation of equity in relation to the trust as working on the conscience of the legal owner. Likewise, in *Pennington v Waine* **[2002] 1 WLR 2075**, Arden LJ based her decision on the grounds that it would be unconscionable for the shares not to be transferred in breach of the testatrix's promise (at pp. 66, 67).[3]

Equity developed as a result of the inflexibility of the common law;[4] it 'wiped away the tears of the common law' in the words of one American jurist. When the common law developed the strictures of the writ system through the twelfth and the thirteenth centuries and failed to develop further remedies, individuals aggrieved by the failure of the common law to remedy their apparent injustice petitioned the King and Council. The King was the fountain of justice and if his judges failed to provide a remedy then the solution was to petition the King directly. The King, preoccupied with affairs of state, handed these petitions to his chief minister, the Chancellor. The Chancellor was head of the Chancery, amongst other state departments. The Chancery was the office which issued writs and, therefore, when the courts failed to provide a remedy, it was appropriate to seek the assistance of the head of the court system. Originally the Chancellor was usually an ecclesiastic. Receiving citizens' petitions, the Chancellor adjudicated them, not according to the common law, but according to principles of fairness and justice; thus developed equity.

Early on, each individual Chancellor developed personal systems of justice giving rise to the criticism that equity had been as long as the Chancellor's foot. The Lord Chancellor did indeed sit alone in his court of equity, or Chancery, as it became known. It was not until 1813 that a Vice-Chancellor was appointed to deal with the volume of work. Equity began to emerge as a clear set of principles, rather than a personal jurisdiction of the Chancellor, during the Chancellorship of

[2] This introductory paragraph opens out the discussion which follows.

[3] This paragraph focuses on what might be described as the modern approach where unconscionability is deemed to be the basis for the operation of equity.

[4] By contrast to the preceding paragraph, the next few paragraphs deal with the historical development.

Lord Nottingham in 1673. By the end of Lord Eldon's Chancellorship in 1827 equity was established as a precise jurisdiction.

But the development of a parallel yet separate system of dispute resolution was inevitably bound to create a conflict. An individual aggrieved by a failure of the common law to remedy a gross injustice would apply to the court of equity. The Chancellor, if the case warranted it, would grant a remedy preventing the common law court from enforcing its order.

The catharsis occurred in the *Earl of Oxford's Case* **(1615) 1 Rep Ch 1**, where the court of common law made an order which the court of equity was prepared to reverse.

The clash was eventually resolved in favour of equity; where there is a conflict, equity prevails. This rule is now enshrined in the **Senior Courts Act 1981, s. 49**.

A series of maxims underlies the operation of equity, establishing a series of principles: 'equity looks upon that as done which ought to be done'; 'he who comes to equity must come with clean hands'; 'equity will not allow a statute to be used as a cloak for fraud', are all examples of the maxims. Equity's operation can be well observed in the decision in *Rochefoucauld v Boustead* **[1897] 1 Ch 196** where the courts determined that, despite the absence of written evidence of a declaration of trust in compliance with statutory requirements, the trust would take effect as intended. Equity's intervention could override the will of Parliament.

The remedies developed by equity, such as injunctions and specific performance, are, unlike the common law remedy of damages, subject to the discretion of the judge. Thus a judge may decide that, although a breach of contract has been established, the conduct of the claimant is such that an equitable remedy should not be granted. In addition, if damages are an adequate remedy, then there is no need to substitute an equitable remedy.

[5] This paragraph introduces the trust.

In substantive law, equity has frequently reflected the reality of transactions between private citizens.[5] It recognised the trust when the common law had refused to acknowledge the existence of a beneficiary and provide remedies for breach of trust against a defaulting trustee. The concept of the trust has been the vehicle for much creative activity on the part of the courts of equity. The trust has developed from an express agreement between parties to situations where the conduct of parties has led the courts to infer or to impose a trust.

[6] This section covers the structural and institutional position of equity.

Structural Questions[6]

So, equity remains a separate system of rules operating independently of the common law. Until the late nineteenth century it operated in a separate set of courts. So, a plaintiff seeking both legal and equitable remedies would be obliged to pursue an action in separate courts. Much delay and expense ensued. The position was eventually resolved in the **Judicature Acts 1873** and **1875** which established a system of courts in which both the rules of equity and common law could be administered. The position had already been ameliorated to some degree by the **Common Law Procedure Act 1854**, which gave the common law courts power to grant equitable remedies, and the **Chancery Amendment Act 1858 (Lord Cairns' Act)**, which gave the Court of Chancery power to award damages in addition to, or in substitution for, an injunction or a decree of specific performance. A claimant can, therefore, seek both damages and an injunction in the same court.

The equitable jurisdiction is, in fact, a personal jurisdiction operating against the conscience of the individual, whereas the common law jurisdiction operates against real property. Thus, an order from a court based on equitable principles preventing a legal order being enforced operates against the conscience of the defendant. In theory, therefore, there is no clash between the jurisdictions. In practice, there is a significant constraint on the common law jurisdiction. The historical distinction does remain, however, in the existence of separate divisions of the High Court, viz., the Chancery Division (which deals primarily with matters which involve equitable rights and remedies) and the Queen's Bench Division (which deals primarily with matters involving rights and remedies at common law).

Conclusion

So, equity represents a later development of law, laying an additional body of rules over the existing common law which, in the majority of cases, provides an adequate remedy: 'Equity, therefore, does not destroy the law, nor create it, but assists it'[7] (per Sir Nathan Wright LJ in *Lord Dudley and Ward* v *Lady Dudley* (1705) Pr Ch 241 at p. 244).

[7] This rounding up paragraph ends with a nice quote which neatly summarises the role of equity.

LOOKING FOR EXTRA MARKS?

■ Take a specific area of development and use it to demonstrate your points.

■ Include strong academic references.

■ A discussion of 'unconscionability' as the modern descendant of the maxims would make for an unusual approach. It would need to be supported by an effective analysis of the cases where this has been discussed as the underlying principle. These could include cases on proprietary estoppel as well as cases such as *Westdeutsche Landesbank Girozentrale* v *Islington LBC* [1996] AC 669 and *Pennington* v *Waine* [2002] 1 WLR 2075.

TAKING THINGS FURTHER

- Lord Denning, 'The need for a new equity' (1952) 5 CLP 1.
- Lord Denning, *Landmarks in the Law*, Butterworths, 1984.

  A chapter on equity would not be complete without reference to some of Lord Denning's many works in this field.

- Lord Evershed MR, 'Reflections on the fusion of law and equity after 75 years' (1954) 70 LQR 326.

  A classic article from a leading judge on the fusion debate.

- Macnair, M., 'Equity and conscience' (2007) 27 OJLS 659.

  This article discusses the role of conscience in equity.

- Martin, J. E., 'Fusion, fallacy and confusion' [1994] Conv 13.

  This article argues there is confusion around this topic and sets out the arguments.

- Mitchell, C. and Mitchell, P. (eds), *Landmark Cases in Equity*, Hart Publishing, 2012.

  This is a good text to read which covers some leading cases which usefully raise the issues covered by the key topic in this chapter covering the nature of equity.

  The next two articles consider cases such as **Patel v Mirza** *where the trust arose from ulterior activities which were unlawful.*

- Nwabueze, R. N., 'Illegality and trusts: trusts-creating primary transactions and unlawful ulterior purposes' [2019] Conv 29–46.

- Virgo, G., '*Patel* v *Mirza*: one step forward and two steps back' (2016) 22(10) Trusts & Trustees 1090.

Online Resources   www.oup.com/uk/qanda/

For extra essay and problem questions on this topic, as well as advice on revision and exam technique, please visit the online resources.

Debate: should a trust be created to prevent money paid to a company for a particular purpose being available for distribution generally to its creditors?

The cases on this point have been criticised in academic articles (see, for example, Goodhart and Jones, 'The Infiltration of Equitable Doctrine into English Commercial Law' (1980) 43 MLR 489 and P. J. Millett, 'The Quistclose Trust: Who Can Enforce It?' (1985) 101 LQR 266). They are, however, defensible on the practical grounds that if potential customers or lenders who are helping a company to survive are not allowed to protect their property, they will not be prepared to deal with the company at all. In *Re Kayford Ltd* [1975] 1 WLR 279, where Megarry J found that a trust had been created, he made the point in his judgment that, although it was quite proper for the mail order company to have done what it did with money received from members of the public, he was not so sure that the same considerations should apply to commercial creditors. The distinction has not been drawn in subsequent cases, however, where the courts have found trusts in favour of commercial creditors also (see *Carreras Rothmans Ltd* v *Freeman Matthews Treasure Ltd* [1985] Ch 207 and *Re Lewis's of Leicester* [1995] 1 BCLC 428).

Q **QUESTION** **1**

Lucien, who died recently, left a will appointing Bill and Ben his executors and trustees. The will contained the following dispositions:

a   'My freehold house to my wife Harriet absolutely in full confidence that she will hold it for either my daughter Tessa or my son James as she sees fit.'

b   'The income from my blue-chip shares to my trustees Bill and Ben from which they must ensure that my old Uncle Tom has a reasonable standard of living.'

c   'Three of my five Van Gogh paintings to my trustees to hold one of them in trust for my sister Pearl, whichever she may choose, and the other two in trust for my sister Jewel.'

Pearl died before the testator.

Advise Bill and Ben as to the validity of these dispositions.

Would your answer in (c) differ if Pearl had survived the testator but died before choosing?

! **CAUTION!**

- This question is an example of how two parts of a question, (a) and (b), may both include different examples of uncertainty as to words or intention. You should therefore state the general law on this subject fairly fully in your answer to (a), but merely refer to it briefly and apply it in your answer to (b).

- Both parts (b) and (c) include uncertainty as to subject-matter, and again any general statement of law on this should be made under (b) and avoid repetition of this under (c).

- It may be appropriate to mention some cases briefly in (a) and discuss them further in (b) and (c), but make sure that they are relevant ones, e.g. *Mussoorie Bank* **v** *Raynor* **(1882) 7 App Cas 321**. However, as well as looking for an understanding of the requirement of certainty of intention, the examiner will be looking for a proper application of the law to the problem set and not a general discussion of cases which are dissimilar.

- Sometimes there is a trap in these apparently straightforward questions. If the question seems to fit very obviously into a particular precedent (as in part (a) of this question), look out for a later precedent which may distinguish it.

- Frequently, parts of the question may appear to be based directly on one case. Avoid the temptation to start your answer with a reference to the case. Establish the general principle, apply it to the particular problem, and then support it with a reference to the particular case.

DIAGRAM ANSWER PLAN

Identify the issues	(a) Certainty of words (b) Certainty of subject-matter (c) Certainty of subject-matter
Relevant law	■ Requirements of certainties derived from case law from *Knight* v *Knight* onwards
Apply the law	(a) Do the words 'in full confidence' impose a trust or are they merely precatory? (b) Possible uncertainty as to subject-matter again as to which three of the five Van Gogh paintings; possible that uncertainty as to Uncle Tom's share may be resolved by *Re Golay*, where the court said that 'reasonable income' was capable of objective determination (c) Possible uncertainty as to subject-matter as to which two paintings Jewel is to have as Pearl, with the power to choose, has died before choosing (*Boyce v Boyce, Re Knapton*) ■ If Pearl survives the testator but dies without choosing, there is still uncertainty of subject-matter. There are possible, but untried, arguments which might persuade the court to decide differently
Conclude	■ Advise Bill and Ben

SUGGESTED ANSWER

(a) Freehold House

[1] You could separate this as an introduction to all that follows. But it is a single sentence and works just as well as part of the answer to part (a).

In *Knight* v *Knight* (1840) 3 Beav 148, Lord Langdale MR said that three certainties were required to establish a valid trust, namely, certainty of words (or intention), subject-matter, and objects.[1] The essence of a trust is that it imposes a binding obligation on the trustees, and the question to consider here is whether the words used are sufficiently obligatory to impose a trust. Until the **Executors Act 1830**, courts were very ready to find a trust, as property to which a trust was not attached would remain in the hands of the executors. The **Executors Act 1830** changed this, however, and from then on the courts were less willing to find a trust where the words used could be construed as merely precatory. *Lambe* v *Eames* (1871) 6 Ch App 597 is generally regarded as the turning-point, where the court refused to construe merely precatory words as creating a trust. In *Re Steele's Will Trusts* **[1948] Ch 603** it was said that the exception to this would be where a testator had used identical wording to that previously held to create a trust. This case has been criticised, however, for replacing a search for the testator's intention with a mechanical application of legal rules; furthermore it ignores the fact that the meaning of words can change over time.

There are two conflicting cases where words used were similar to those found here. In *Re Adams & Kensington Vestry* **(1884) 27 ChD 394** a gift 'to the absolute use of my wife . . . in full confidence that she will do what is right as to the disposal thereof between my children' was held not to impose any trust upon the wife but was construed by the court to be an absolute gift to her. In *Comiskey v Bowring-Hanbury* **[1905] AC 84**, however, the House of Lords (Lord Lindley dissenting[2]) considered a bequest to the testator's wife of 'the whole of my real and personal estate absolutely in full confidence that she will make use of it as I should have made myself and that at her death she will devise it to such one or more of my nieces as she may think fit and in default to my nieces equally'. This was held to create a trust for the widow for life, remainder to the nieces as she might by will appoint, but otherwise equally between them, as the testator had shown a clear intention to benefit his nieces in any event.

In *Re Hamilton* **[1895] 2 Ch 370** it was said by Lindley LJ that each disposition must be construed on its own merits. So, in *Suggitt v Suggitt* **[2011] EWHC 903 (Ch)**, the court considered it quite clear that a trust was not intended where the words used were: 'And I express the wish (without imposing a trust)'. The disposition in this problem appears to be nearer to *Re Adams & Kensington Vestry* than to *Comiskey v Bowring-Hanbury* on the ground that there is no gift over in default. Nevertheless it may be possible to distinguish the disposition in (a) from *Re Adams & Kensington Vestry* on the specificity of the ultimate beneficiaries—in which case it could be construed as imposing a trust.

If there is a trust, it is a discretionary trust for either Tessa or James, and there is therefore no uncertainty of objects. If the words are held not to impose a trust, then the disposition operates as an absolute gift to Harriet.[3]

(b) Income From Blue-Chip Shares[4]

For a trust to be valid, the subject-matter must also be certain. This includes both the property and the beneficial interests which the beneficiaries are to take. If either of these is uncertain, the trust will fail. In this case, it is possible that both are uncertain.

---

[2] See 'Looking for Extra Marks?' later. You could take this dissenting opinion further for extra marks. But if you do that—be judicious and don't devote too much space to a lengthy discussion for fear of going off-point.

[3] Students often forget to add this part focusing just on the discussion of certainty of intention.

[4] Never come across this expression? That means you have not come across *Re Kolb* which might make answering this question difficult.

In *Re Kolb's Will Trusts* **[1962] Ch 531** it was said that a reference to stocks and shares 'in the blue-chip category' was insufficiently certain because the term 'blue-chip', whilst used to indicate a very good share, has no precise meaning. If so, the trust will fail for uncertainty of subject-matter, which means that all Lucien's shares (and the income therefrom) not otherwise validly and specifically bequeathed, will form part of Lucien's residuary estate. If, however, the reference to blue-chip shares is held sufficiently certain it becomes necessary to consider other parts of this disposition.

The wording 'they must ensure' might well be sufficiently obligatory to impose a trust on the income in the hands of the trustees, as it indicates that the trustees were not intended to enjoy the whole of the income beneficially. It would appear, however, that they are not to use the whole of the income for Uncle Tom. Sufficient income for a reasonable standard of living might appear to be uncertain, but in *Re Golay's Will Trusts* **[1965] 1 WLR 969** it was held that 'a reasonable income' was capable of being quantified objectively in relation to a person's lifestyle. Presumably, therefore, a sufficient income relating to Uncle Tom's lifestyle could be ascertained.

If the gift fails for lack of certainty of subject-matter then it will fall back into the estate and be disposed of in accordance with the provisions of the will regarding residue (or, failing that, fall to be determined according to the rules of intestacy).

(c) Van Gogh Paintings

The problem in this part of the question is again to determine the subject-matter of the trust. There is an initial uncertainty as to the subject-matter of the trust as a whole, that is, as to which three of the five Van Gogh paintings are to be held on trust for Pearl to choose from. This is similar to *Palmer* v *Simmonds* **(1854) 2 Drew 221**, where a gift of 'the bulk of my estate' failed for uncertainty. Additionally, the interests of Pearl and Jewel are uncertain until Pearl has made her choice; death means that no choice can now be made. In *Boyce* v *Boyce* **(1849) 16 Sim 476**, a testator left three houses in his will, 'one to Maria, which she may choose; the others to Charlotte'. Maria predeceased the testator, and the trust for Charlotte, which was dependent upon Maria's choice, was held to fail for certainty of subject-matter. Pearl having predeceased the testator, it is impossible to determine which paintings should be held in trust for Jewel. All three paintings will therefore fall into residue. In the absence of a residuary gift, they will pass, as on intestacy, to Lucien's next-of-kin.

If Pearl survives the testator but died before choosing?

If Pearl had survived the testator but died before making a choice, although prima facie there is still an uncertainty of subject-matter, it is possible that this would enable the circumstances to be distinguished from *Boyce* v *Boyce*. The *Boyce* v *Boyce* situation has an element of ademption about it as the testator is presumed to know that Pearl has predeceased him and is therefore unable to make a choice. However, if the testator has no reason to suppose that Pearl will not choose and dies in the belief that he has set up a valid trust, it might be possible for equity to intervene, although it is not clear how. The maxim 'Equity is equality' would not reflect the testator's intentions. In *Re Knapton* [1941] 2 All ER 573, the gift was saved by the complete absence of a mechanism to make a selection. It involved a number of houses which were to be distributed among identified relatives and friends. It was held that the beneficiaries could choose the house they wanted in the order in which they appeared in the will as the judge concluded that the intention was that they were to have one each. This sensible conclusion might well be applied to a situation where Pearl survives the testator but then dies without making a selection. It could be argued in reliance on *Re Knapton*, that the intention had been that Pearl would have one painting and Jewel the other two.

One tenuous argument might be that Lucien intended to make Pearl a trustee of the power of selection, i.e. that it is a trust power to select. This would mean that the maxim 'Equity will not allow a trust to fail for want of a trustee' could be applied, and someone else (or even the court) could make the choice. On the wording of the disposition, however, there seems little to favour such a construction.[5]

[5] No overall conclusion as each part is self-contained. To repeat would be a waste of words.

LOOKING FOR EXTRA MARKS?

■ Generally, these problem questions are gifts to the reasonably well-prepared examinee. No such person should get less than a 2(ii) on such a question. Conversely, it is quite difficult to get a first. You would really need to impress the examiner with a detailed knowledge of the cases, perhaps even referring to distinguishing judgments (as in question 1(a) with the reference to *Comiskey* v *Bowring-Hanbury* [1905] AC 84).

QUESTION | 2

Clockwise Ltd is a mail order company selling a particularly popular line of talking alarm clocks. It received numerous orders with accompanying cheques but, because of difficulties with the suppliers of certain components, was unable to dispatch the orders. On the advice of the company's accountants, the cheques were paid into a separate bank account which the bank was instructed to call the 'Customers' Trust Deposit Account'. Owing to an error by the bank clerk, the account was called instead 'Clockwise No. 2 Account'.

Clockwise Ltd also wished to purchase some new machinery, and one of its business associates, Ticktock plc, agreed to lend the company the sum of £10,000 solely for this purpose. This money was paid into

◀ another separate account called 'Clockwise No. 3 Account'. Clockwise Ltd signed an agreement for the purchase of the machine and paid a deposit of £3,000 from this account, leaving in it £7,000.

Unfortunately, the problems with Clockwise's suppliers became more acute and Clockwise Ltd has now gone into liquidation. The bank (which is owed money by the company) and the liquidator are claiming the monies in the No. 2 and No. 3 accounts.

a Advise the bank and the liquidator.

b Would your answer differ if the monies paid by the customers, and lent by Ticktock plc had, by an error of Clockwise Ltd, been paid instead into Clockwise Ltd's general trading account?

! CAUTION!

■ This is quite a complex question—especially with the addition of the rider at the end (a sting in the tail). It is a good example of a question which assumes you have the whole course at your fingertips linking certainties and tracing.

◯ DIAGRAM ANSWER PLAN

Identify the issues	■ Certainty of intention
Relevant law	■ *Barclays Bank* v *Quistclose*; *Re Kayford*: Megarry J said that a 'manifestation of an intention' to establish a trust is sufficient, and held on similar circumstances to this that money received by a mail order company was held on trust for the customers; *Re EVTR*; *Hunter* v *Moss*; Rule in *Clayton's Case*
Apply the law	■ If there is a trust, then the money at no time belongs to Clockwise Ltd and cannot be claimed by the liquidator ■ The fact that the account was not called 'trust account' is probably not fatal to establishing a trust ■ Was the money lent by Ticktock plc solely to purchase the new machinery? If so, then it is stamped with a trust for this purpose, and on failure of the trust will go on a resulting trust back to Ticktock plc ■ It does not matter whether the purpose fails initially or subsequently. The £7,000 held by Clockwise Ltd and any of the £3,000 deposit retained will go on a resulting trust back to Ticktock plc
Conclude	■ Advise Bank and Liquidator

A SUGGESTED ANSWER

Part (a)

One of the three certainties essential to establish a valid trust is the certainty of words or intention. Words are not themselves necessary: the person in whom the property is vested may manifest a clear intention to create a trust by actions. In *Paul v Constance* **[1977] 1 WLR 527**, a man said on several occasions that funds in a deposit account in his name belonged both to himself and his mistress. **Section 53 of the Law of Property Act 1925** does not require any formality for the creation of a trust of personalty, and these oral statements were held to be sufficient to create a trust for his mistress of half of the money in the account.

In *Re Kayford Ltd* **[1975] 1 WLR 279**, a mail order company, which was experiencing financial difficulties, paid cheques received from customers into a separate dormant account which only at a later date was called 'Customers' Trust Deposit Account'. Megarry J held that this appellation was a sufficient manifestation of intention to create a trust of the monies therein for the customers. Being a trust of personalty, no written formalities were required by the **Law of Property Act 1925, s. 53**, for its creation. The monies having been kept separately meant that there was certainty of subject-matter; the objects of the trust (the customers) were also certain.

Although in the question the account into which the monies have been paid does not bear the name 'Trust Account', the fact of segregation of the money received from the customers may be sufficient evidence of certainty of intention to create a trust.[1] As the money has been kept separately there is also certainty of subject-matter; the beneficiaries are the customers. The money would not therefore be available to the bank or the liquidator.

Similarly, where property is handed over for a particular purpose only, this may be sufficient to impress it with a trust for that purpose. In *Barclays Bank Ltd v Quistclose Investments Ltd* **[1970] AC 567**, Quistclose lent some £200,000 to Rolls Razor Ltd (which was in financial difficulties) for the sole purpose of paying a dividend on its ordinary shares. The money was paid into a separate bank account. Rolls Razor went into liquidation before the dividend was paid. It was held that the money was not available to the bank with whom the account was opened, nor for distribution by the liquidator to the general creditors of the company. It had from the start been impressed with a trust for a particular purpose (the payment of a dividend) and had therefore never belonged to Rolls Razor beneficially. When the trust failed because the liquidation prevented the payment of the dividend, the money was held on a resulting trust for Quistclose.

Applying these principles to the question, it would seem that the money paid by Clockwise Ltd into a separate account for the purpose of purchasing machinery would similarly be impressed with a trust for that purpose, and again would not be available to the bank or the liquidator.[2]

[1] Good example of referencing the exam question.

[2] This sentence provides an interim conclusion keeping the discussion anchored and structured.

In *Re Kayford Ltd* [1975] 1 WLR 279,[3] where Megarry J found that a trust had been created, he made the point in his judgment that, although it was quite proper for the mail order company to have done what it did with money received from members of the public, he was not so sure that the same considerations should apply to commercial creditors. The distinction has not been drawn in subsequent cases, however, where the courts have found trusts in favour of commercial creditors also (see *Carreras Rothmans Ltd* v *Freeman Matthews Treasure Ltd* [1985] Ch 207 and *Re Lewis's of Leicester* [1995] 1 BCLC 428).

Does the fact that part of this money has already been appropriated for the purpose affect the trust as to the remainder?[4] In *Re EVTR Ltd* [1987] BCLC 646, money lent for the purchase of a machine was paid to the borrower company's solicitors. When the borrower company went into liquidation, it had already paid part of the money to the suppliers under a contract of purchase. The Court of Appeal found no reason to distinguish between the resulting trust, which would have arisen if the purpose for which the money was paid had failed initially, and the failure of the purpose only subsequently. Money returned by the suppliers was held to go on a resulting trust for the lender. In the question it is likely that the £7,000 still held by Clockwise Ltd, and any money repayable to them from the £3,000 deposit paid, will go on a resulting trust for Ticktock plc.

Part (b)

What if the monies in either case are paid into Clockwise Ltd's general trading account by error?

In such circumstances, although the necessary intention to create a trust might be there, there would be no certainty or segregation of the subject-matter and it would almost certainly be impossible to find a trust. In the case of the customers' cheques, presumably if a trust were intended, it would affect only funds paid into the designated account. Payment into a different account would therefore prevent the trust being constituted. In the case of Ticktock's money, although the money would be impressed with a trust from the start, there would be the practical problem that money paid into the general trading account might not be traceable. The case of *Hunter v Moss* [1994] 1 WLR 452[5] suggests that segregation of the subject-matter of a trust is not essential if the subject-matter is all identical and the Court of Appeal in *Lehman Brothers (Europe) (in Administration)* v *CRC Credit Fund Ltd* [2010] EWCA Civ 917 stated that certainty is achieved provided that the source of the assets is identified. It might be argued on behalf of the customers of Clockwise Ltd that Clockwise Ltd has done everything in its power to constitute a trust so that the principle in *Re Rose* [1952] Ch 499 (as approved in *Zeital v Kaye* [2010] EWCA Civ 159) should apply. If it is possible to establish a trust in favour of the customers and Ticktock plc then they may be able to trace the trust monies into Clockwise Ltd's general trading account. They will only have a claim, however, to the

[6] For a more detailed explanation of the rules relating to tracing, see Chapter 13.

extent that their monies are still in the account and not deemed to have been paid out under the rule in *Clayton's Case* (*Devaynes* v *Noble* (1816) 1 Mer 572).[6] If the account has been overdrawn at any time since the monies were paid in, then their claim will be defeated.

LOOKING FOR EXTRA MARKS?

- The section dealing with the debate on the use of **Quistclose** is an example of 'extra marks'. You could also consider adding in some of the academic literature on this point although beware of losing sight of the problem question.
- Likewise the reference to the rules of tracing and **Clayton's Case**.

QUESTION 3

Consider whether a trust has been created in the following circumstances:

a Eliza orally declared herself a trustee of her house, Dunroamin, for her son Percy. She subsequently wrote a letter to Percy informing him that she had done so.

b Oliver, on visiting his only niece, Alison, aged ten, handed her an emerald ring which had belonged to his grandmother. As he handed it over, Oliver told Alison that she was to have the ring. When Oliver left, he took the ring with him, and when he died shortly afterwards, it was found among his effects.

c Simon, who died recently, made a will leaving, *inter alia*, 'the residue of my estate to my dear wife Sarah trusting that she will dispose of whatever she does not want between such of my relatives and friends as she shall select'.

d One Friday, Paul bought ten tickets in the National Lottery. He immediately declared himself a trustee of nine of them for his son Steve, and of the remaining one for his girlfriend Gladys, but without indicating which of the ten was to be held for Gladys. The following day, when the draw was made, one of Paul's tickets won the top prize of £40 million.

Advise Gladys.

CAUTION!

- This is a certainty question mixed with other areas of trust law. In (a) all three certainties are satisfied, but you are required to consider whether the necessary formalities for the creation of a trust of land have been complied with. Part (b) raises the question of the constitution of a trust and the difference between a trust and a gift. Part (c) raises doubts about all three certainties, but also requires a knowledge of the test for certainty of objects for discretionary trusts and powers, and some of the cases on this. In part (c) you will probably consider certainty of words and subject-matter first. If you come to the conclusion that the trust would fail on either or both of these, do not of course be deterred from discussing certainty of objects also. The examiner will undoubtedly be looking for a discussion of all three certainties. Part (d) deals with certainty of subject-matter in the light of **Hunter v Moss** [1994] 1 WLR 452.

■ When dealing with different parts of the question, avoid repeating yourself. The examiner will not give you marks for regurgitating the same law again. Make sure you spot the new topic in the other part and deal with this at more length. If you think both parts are on certainty of intention and nothing else, then you are probably in trouble and should choose another question.

DIAGRAM ANSWER PLAN

Identify the issues	(a) Formalities for the declaration of trust of land; constitution of trust (b) Declaration and constitution of trust of chattel and difference between trust and gift (c) Three certainties (d) Certainty of subject-matter
Relevant law	(a) **Section 53(1)(b) LPA 1925** (b) Case law—especially *Hunter v Moss*
Apply the law	(a) Is letter sufficient? Legal title already in Eliza (b) Oliver takes ring back—so gift not complete. Does wording indicate a trust? (c) 'Trusting' may be a precatory word not sufficiently obligatory to impose a trust on Sarah. Although 'residue' is certain as the subject-matter of the trust, 'whatever she does not want' is uncertain, and any trust would therefore fail for uncertainty of subject-matter. If it had been a valid trust, it would have been a discretionary one. The test for certainty of objects of a discretionary trust is individual ascertainability. 'Relatives' satisfies this test but 'friends' would fail it. (d) *Hunter v Moss* is authority for the point that identical items are certain (subject-matter) but can it apply to lottery tickets?
Conclude	■ Advise Gladys

SUGGESTED ANSWER

(a) Dunroamin

[1] This brief reference is enough to explain the certainties point.

The three certainties for a trust are satisfied,[1] but the **Law of Property Act 1925, s. 53(1)(b)**, requires that 'a declaration of trust respecting any land or any interest therein must be manifested and proved by some writing signed by some person who is able to declare such trust or by his will'. Although the oral declaration of trust by Eliza is therefore ineffective, the subsequent letter testifying to the oral declaration signed by Eliza would be sufficient for the purpose of **s. 53**. The section does not require that the trust should be created in writing, but merely that its creation should be evidenced in writing.

(b) Emerald Ring

If Oliver had declared himself to be a trustee of Alison's ring, this would have been effective as it is possible to create a trust of personalty by words alone. As the ring is still in his possession, he would have held it as trustee and the trust would have been fully constituted. His words would have had the effect of severing the beneficial ownership in the ring, thereby creating the duality of ownership essential to a trust. However, Turner LJ stated in *Milroy v Lord* **(1862) 4 De GF & J 264** at p. 274 that the court will not allow a purported gift which is ineffective because there is no delivery of the subject-matter to take effect as a trust. In *Jones v Lock* **(1865) LR 1 Ch App 25**, a father put a cheque into the hand of his nine-month-old son saying, 'I give this to baby for himself'. When he later died and the cheque was found among his effects, it was held that there had been no effective gift; nor had any effective trust of the cheque been created. Similarly, in *Richards v Delbridge* **(1874) LR 18 Eq 11** where a grandfather endorsed a lease of property he had with the words 'This deed and all thereto belonging I give to [his grandson] from this time forth', it was ineffective to transfer the lease by way of gift as a deed was required to transfer a legal estate in land. But neither could the words of gift be construed as an intention to create a trust.

If Oliver's words on handing over the ring to Alison indicate an intention to make a present gift, the gift is thereby perfected and his taking back the ring cannot recall such gift. In such circumstances, he would, at most, be a bailee of the ring for Alison.[2] On the other hand, Oliver's words on handing over the ring might indicate merely an intention to make a gift of it in the future. In these circumstances, Alison has merely custody or bailment of the ring, and Oliver is free to take it back (which he does).[3] If Oliver had made it clear when he left that he was taking the ring with him for safekeeping but he regarded it as belonging to Alison, this might have been sufficient intent to create a trust of it for Alison with himself as trustee, or else merely a bailment with himself as bailee. However, there is no evidence to support such interpretation, and it is therefore probable[4] that there will be an ineffective gift and an ineffective trust.

[2] This is an 'extra mark' comment answering the question: if not owner then what is he?

[3] This is an example of a discussion around the question—'on the one hand . . . this . . . on the other hand . . . that . . .'.

[4] Good word to indicate what degree of certainty there is in your answer.

(c) Residuary Gift

First,[5] it might be argued that the word 'trusting' in this context is a more colloquial expression than the legal words 'on trust for', implying merely reliance upon Sarah's integrity rather than imposing an obligation on her. If this is argued successfully, then the words are precatory in nature and fail to satisfy the certainty of words necessary to create a trust.

Secondly, 'the residue of my estate' is sufficiently capable of ascertainment to form the subject-matter of a trust (the residue being the remainder of a person's estate not specifically disposed of). Nevertheless, there is uncertainty of subject-matter here because the share which the friends and relatives are to receive ('whatever she does not want') is necessarily uncertain. In *Sprange* v *Barnard* (1789) 2 Bro CC 585, a gift to the testatrix's husband with a provision that 'at his death, the remaining part of what is left, that he does not want for his own wants and use' was to be divided between the testatrix's brother and sisters, failed as a trust for uncertainty of subject-matter.

The third certainty, that of objects, also has to be considered here. If the requirements of certainty of words and subject-matter were satisfied, there might still be a problem with regard to certainty of objects. This would be a discretionary trust and the test for certainty of objects is that laid down by the House of Lords in *McPhail* v *Doulton* [1971] AC 424, namely, can it be said of any given postulant that they are, or are not, within the scope of the discretion? When the Court of Appeal considered the application of this test to the word 'relatives' in *Re Baden's Deed Trusts (No. 2)* [1973] Ch 9, the Court of Appeal decided that the expression 'relatives' was conceptually certain enough to satisfy the test, although the judges had differing reasons for deciding this. We therefore have high judicial authority that the word 'relatives' is conceptually certain.

In *Re Barlow's Will Trusts* [1979] 1 WLR 278, the testatrix directed that 'any friends of mine' might buy a painting from her collection at a reduced price. This was held valid, but only because the court interpreted this as a series of individual gifts to apply conditionally to anyone who was able to satisfy the trustees that he or she was a friend. The test for certainty of objects of conditional gifts is, however, more relaxed than that applicable to certainty of objects of discretionary trusts. Had the provision been construed as a discretionary trust (or fiduciary power) to select amongst the testator's friends, it would not have satisfied the test in *McPhail* v *Doulton*. As part (c) involves a discretionary trust, the disposition might well fail the *McPhail* v *Doulton* test for conceptual certainty.[6]

(d) Lottery Tickets

A declaration of trust relating to property other than land may be made orally, so that the declaration of trust made by Paul does not offend the **Law of Property Act 1925, s. 53**.[7] It would seem, however, that the purported declaration of trust is void for uncertainty of subject-matter, in that the interests of the intended beneficiaries, Steve and Gladys, have not been specified. In other words, Paul has not indicated which tickets he is holding for which beneficiary.

In *Hunter v Moss* **[1994] 1 WLR 452**, the Court of Appeal held that a declaration of trust of 50 shares from a holding of 950 did not fail for uncertainty of subject-matter, even though the settlor had not specified which particular shares out of his holding were to be subject to the trust. A different result had been reached in the earlier decision of *Re London Wine Co. (Shippers) Ltd* **(1975) 126 NLJ 977**, where a purported allocation of some bottles of wine in a wine cellar was held insufficient to confer a property interest, since no bottles had actually been segregated and set aside for a particular customer. *Re London Wine Co.* was applied by the Privy Council in *Re Goldcorp Exchange Ltd* **[1995] 1 AC 74**, where it was affirmed that on the purchase of unascertained goods, there was no fixed and identifiable bulk created by a deemed appropriation, and therefore no property to which any tracing claim could apply. The purchasers of unascertained goods (as in *Goldcorp*) may now have a better claim as against creditors in a liquidation under the **Sale of Goods (Amendment) Act 1995**, which provides that purchasers who have paid for such goods acquire property rights as tenants in common in them. This would not of course affect a declaration of trust of identifiable and ascertained goods.

The *London Wine Co.* case was distinguished in *Hunter v Moss* on the ground that the bottles of wine might not be of equal quality, whereas the shares were all of the same class and carried the same rights. This is not true of tickets in the National Lottery, since the particular number selected for each ticket is an intrinsic part of its potential value. *Hunter v Moss* is therefore distinguishable.[8] The suggestion in *Hunter v Moss* that the tracing remedy could be used to cure uncertainty of subject-matter has been criticised:[9] Luxton, 'Certainty of subject-matter: a problem shared?' (1994) 28 Law Teacher 312. In any event, it is difficult to see how the tracing rules could be used to identify which beneficiary is entitled to the winnings.

Therefore, the only way in which certainty of subject-matter could be satisfied would be if the declaration could be construed as creating not one trust for Steve of nine tickets and another for Gladys of one ticket, but rather a single trust of all ten tickets under which Steve and Gladys, as tenants in common of the whole, share the beneficial interest in the ratio of 9:1 in Steve's favour. Such an approach was approved in the Australian case of *White v Shortall* **[2006] NSWSC 1379** where beneficial co-ownership over the shares in question was the solution. This approach was also approved in *Lehman Brothers*

[8] If the answer is clear then be clear in your answer.

[9] This is an 'extra marks' point.

[10] You can prevaricate in your answer when it is genuinely not free from doubt.

[11] Don't forget to say this—if the trust fails where does the subject-matter go?

(Europe) (in Administration) **v** *CRC Credit Fund Ltd* [2010] **EWCA Civ 917**. The winnings would then be held in trust for them both in the same ratio. This does not seem, however, to be what Paul intended. The trust is therefore probably void[10] for uncertainty of subject-matter, and Paul is entitled to keep the winnings for himself.[11]

LOOKING FOR EXTRA MARKS?

- Raise contentious issues contained in secondary references. *Hunter v Moss* is much criticized so reference to the literature here to show that you understand the critique would raise the mark. The article by Chung (2019) (see 'Taking Things Further') is also worth including as it criticises *Re Goldcorp Exchange Ltd (In Receivership)* **(PC)** on whether an alleged trust of gold bullion held for customers was ineffective for lack of certainty about the subject-matter of the trust. You don't have to agree with it but showing that you appreciate the critique will earn marks.
- Note the comments boxes for extra marks points.

QUESTION | 4

Last year, as part of his estate planning, Wurzel, a wealthy farmer, wished to dispose of some of his property for the benefit of his family. His first step was to set up a family trust, of which his friends, Oats and Rye, agreed to be the trustees and to hold any property which Wurzel might transfer to them upon any trusts that Wurzel might declare.

Wurzel transferred the freehold title to six holiday cottages in Wales into the names of Oats and Rye, and sent them the deeds. Upon Wurzel's recent oral instructions, his solicitor wrote to Oats and Rye directing them to hold the cottages and the shares in trust for Wurzel's two grandchildren, Turnip and Carrot, in equal shares.

Two years ago, Wurzel transferred his holding of 5,000 shares in Racine Ltd into the name of the Cube Bank plc as security for a loan which the bank made to him. Six months ago, Wurzel repaid all sums due under the loan, and at the same time wrote to the bank instructing it to transfer the shares into the names of Oats and Rye.

Last month Wurzel orally declared himself a trustee for his son, Spinach, of his (Wurzel's) beneficial interest under the Root Trust.

Consider the validity and consequences of Wurzel's actions.

CAUTION!

- The **Law of Property Act 1925, s. 53**, has been interpreted on a number of occasions in the House of Lords, namely in *Grey v IRC* [1960] AC 1, *Vandervell v IRC* [1967] 2 AC 291, and *Oughtred v IRC* [1960] AC 206, and, in the Court of Appeal, in *Re Vandervell's Trusts*

(No. 2) **[1974] Ch 269**. In each of these cases it fell to be determined whether a particular transaction attracted *ad valorem* stamp duty or income tax. Stamp duty is a tax on documents only; it has in recent years been restricted in scope, but it still applies to transfers of land and to sales of shares. The consequence of failure to have a document stamped is that it cannot be produced as evidence in court. In general, you will not need to recount the facts of these cases but apply them strictly to your problem. If necessary, give a very brief account.

DIAGRAM ANSWER PLAN

Identify the issues	■ Formalities for the declaration of trusts

Relevant law	■ S. 53(1)(b) LPA 1925; s. 53(1)(c) LPA 1925; s. 53(2) LPA 1925; bare trusts; sub-trusts

Apply the law	■ The cottages are held on a resulting trust for Wurzel. Wurzel's solicitor's letter would probably satisfy **LPA 1925, s. 53(1)(b)** for the creation of a trust in land. But the instructions may be a transfer of Wurzel's interest, in which case the formality requirement is **s. 53(1)(c)**, which may or may not be satisfied. **Section 53(2)** will not operate to exempt the transfer from writing (*Grey v IRC*)
	■ The Cube Bank hold the Racine shares for Wurzel on a bare trust. The transfer of the legal title by the bank on the instructions of the owner of the equitable interest (Wurzel) will operate to transfer the equitable interest without any separate disposition in writing.
	■ If Wurzel's oral declaration of trust creates a sub-trust, it is valid; if it is a transfer of Wurzel's interest, it is void as it falls within **s. 53(1)(c)**

Conclude	■ Advise Wurzel

SUGGESTED ANSWER

Six Cottages

When Wurzel transferred the legal title to the six cottages to his trustees without informing them of the names of the beneficiaries, the trustees would have held the legal title to the cottages on a resulting trust for Wurzel: *Grey v IRC* **[1960] AC 1**. A resulting trust arises whenever there is a gap in the beneficial ownership: as there was with the option to purchase back the shares given to the Vandervell Trustee Co. in **Vandervell v IRC [1967] 2 AC 291**.

Wurzel's declaration of the trusts of the cottages is subject to the **Law of Property Act 1925, s. 53**.

Section 53(1)(b) applies if Wurzel's equitable interest under the resulting trust ranks as an interest in land. It requires a declaration of a trust of land or any interest in land to be manifested and proved by some writing signed by some person who is able to declare such trust or by his will. The expression 'some person who is able to declare such trust' must be intended to include some person other than the settlor.

The question is whether the letter that Wurzel's solicitor sent to Oats and Rye could satisfy para. (b). There is no authority on this point;[1] but the express inclusion of signature by an agent in paras (a) and (c) of **s. 53(1)** might suggest that signature by agent does not satisfy para. (b): *expressio unius exclusio alterius*.[2] It would appear, however, that the transferee can sign: **Gardner v Rowe (1828) 5 Russ 258**. It would also appear that, unlike paras (a) and (c), para. (b) is merely an evidential requirement, i.e. non-compliance does not invalidate the declaration but merely means that, without signed writing, it cannot be proved: **Gardner v Rowe**. On this basis, Oats and Rye hold the cottages on a valid trust for the grandchildren, and are therefore, as trustees, obliged to provide the signed writing of the trusts in accordance with para. (b).

It is more likely, however, that the interest of which Wurzel is disposing is not an interest in land but a beneficial interest under a resulting trust. It was held by the House of Lords in **Grey v IRC**, that an instruction by a beneficiary to the trustee to hold his interest in trust for a third party is in substance a disposition, and must therefore comply with **s. 53(1)(c)**. Paragraph (c) states that a disposition of an equitable interest or trust subsisting at the time of the disposition must be in writing and signed by the disponor or by his agent thereunto lawfully authorised in writing. As the solicitor is Wurzel's agent, provided his letter to Oats and Rye complies with para. (c), there is a valid disposition of the beneficial interest.

If the solicitor's letter does not comply with para. (c) (if, for example, it is not signed), there is probably no valid disposition. It is not exempted from para. (c) by **s. 53(2)**, i.e. it does not involve the 'operation of a resulting . . . trust': see **Grey v IRC**, which itself concerned a direction to trustees to hold for a third party an interest under a resulting trust. Lord Denning MR's statement in **Re Vandervell's Trusts (No. 2) [1974] Ch 269** that a resulting trust dies without the need for any writing at all is difficult to reconcile with **Grey v IRC**, but is perhaps distinguishable on the special facts: the option to purchase

[1] You need to be sure before you can make this point—if you are wrong and have missed a case this is a major mark loser.

[2] The use of Latin is not fashionable (it will come back) but this expression is used by judges. Translation: 'using the expression in one place implies that it is omitted by design from the other'.

(which was the subject-matter of the resulting trust) ceased to exist when exercised, and a new beneficial interest arose in respect of the shares which were thereby purchased.

Racine Shares

Wurzel's repayment of sums due under the loan from the Cube Bank plc means that the bank's legal mortgage of the shares comes to an end, and the bank holds the legal title to the shares on a bare trust for Wurzel. In **Vandervell v IRC**, Vandervell's bank held the legal title to shares on a resulting trust for him and, upon his instructions, transferred them to the Royal College of Surgeons. The House of Lords held that Vandervell's beneficial interest passed to the College contemporaneously with the legal title without the need for compliance with para. (c).

The decision in that case means that a direction by a beneficiary under a bare trust to the trustee to transfer the trust property beneficially to a third party is not a disposition within para. (c) because the direction does not itself dispose of the beneficiary's interest. Furthermore, the trustees' transfer pursuant to such direction, although effective to vest a full title (both legal and equitable) in the third party, is not a disposition for the purposes of para. (c) either. The explanation seems to be that, when the legal and equitable titles pass together, the equitable interest is not separately disposed of, but is subsumed in the passing of the legal title. There is, therefore, no disposition of a 'subsisting equitable interest'.

For these reasons, if the Cube Bank plc has transferred the shares in Racine Ltd to Oats and Rye, the gift is perfect both at law and in equity, and Wurzel cannot recall it. If, however, the bank has not yet effected the transfer, Wurzel can revoke his instructions to the bank and prevent the gift from being completed.

Oral Declaration of Self as Trustee

If the effect of Wurzel's declaration of trust in favour of Spinach would be that Wurzel would drop out of the picture (**Grey v IRC**) and the trustees of the Root Trust would hold the trust property in trust for Spinach instead (**Grainge v Wilberforce (1889) 5 TLR 436**), the declaration would rank as a purported disposition of a subsisting equitable interest. As such, because it is made only orally, it would be void for non-compliance with para. (c).

[3] Deal with both options—don't assume one is wrong and therefore should not be discussed.

If, however, the declaration gives rise to a sub-trust,[3] there is no disposition for the purposes of para. (c) because Wurzel retains his equitable interest under the Root Trust and a new beneficial interest is created in favour of Spinach.

It appears that the declaration will be treated as a purported disposition if no additional duties are imposed on the trustees; but otherwise, it will give rise to a sub-trust. Wurzel's declaration does not impose any express duties. If, however, Spinach is a minor, a sub-trust will be created because otherwise the trustees would be subject to additional duties, e.g. those imposed by the **Trustee Act 1925, s. 31**. If construed as a sub-trust, therefore, the declaration will be valid.

LOOKING FOR EXTRA MARKS?

■ Incorporate dissenting judgments, obiter remarks, or judgments going a different way in a lower court. In *Oughtred* v *IRC*, it was argued that no *ad valorem* stamp duty was payable on a transfer of shares (in that case an exchange) on the ground that the equitable interest had already passed under the prior contract for sale by virtue of a constructive trust, for which no writing was required because of **s. 53(2)**. The majority of the House of Lords held that, in any event, *ad valorem* duty was payable on the share transfer because it ranked as a transfer on sale. This was sufficient to dispose of the case, so that the views expressed on **s. 53** were obiter.

TAKING THINGS FURTHER

■ Chung, B. 'Challenging the orthodoxy: a critique of *Re Goldcorp* and the English law approach to the certainty of subject matter' (2019) 25(5) Trusts & Trustees 481–492.
This article contains a critique of **Re Goldcorp Exchange Ltd (In Receivership)**.

■ Emery, C., 'The most hallowed principle—certainty of beneficiaries of trusts and powers of appointment' (1982) 98 LQR 551.
This article breaks down the certainty of object requirement into four different constituent parts.

For differing critiques of **Hunter v Moss** *(certainty of subject-matter), see these two articles:*

■ Goode, R., 'Are intangible assets fungible?' [2003] LNCLQ 379.

■ Hayton, D., 'Uncertainty of subject matter of trusts' (1994) 110 LQR 335, and

■ Martin, J., 'Certainty of subject matter: a defence of *Hunter* v *Moss*' [1996] Conv 223.
There is also this article on the same topic:

Online Resources
www.oup.com/uk/qanda/

For extra essay and problem questions on this topic, as well as advice on revision and exam technique, please visit the online resources.

Constitution of Trusts

4

ARE YOU READY?

In order to attempt the questions in this chapter you will need to have covered the following topics:

- Constituting the trust (the requirements for transferring the legal title in the subject-matter of the trust into the hands of the trustee)
- Different modes of transfer for different types of property
- The statutory requirements under **s. 53 of the Law of Property Act 1925**
- The effect of the **Rights of Third Parties Act 1999**
- The rules relating to *donationes mortis causa*
- The rule in *Re Rose*

KEY DEBATES

Debate: is the issue of unconscionability a ground for perfecting an imperfect gift?

The decision in *Pennington v Waine* [2002] 1 WLR 2075 where the basis of the decision to allow the perfection of an imperfect gift on the ground of unconscionability has been controversial.

QUESTION 1

Equity will not assist a volunteer.

Explain and discuss.

! CAUTION!

- Since constitution of trusts is an aspect of the creation of trusts, this topic may well be combined in an examination question with one or more of the three certainties and with formalities. It would be wise to revise these topics as a single issue.

- Superficially this may appear a simple question, but there is considerable opportunity for you to draw on your knowledge and understanding of different parts of the subject. The area is vast, but the secret is in selecting the material which most directly addresses the question.

- Note carefully that you are required not merely to explain the maxim, but to discuss it.

◯ DIAGRAM ANSWER PLAN

Introduction to scope of maxim meaning of 'volunteer' and 'consideration'; relevance to imperfect gifts/incompletely constituted trusts; relationship to actions at common law

▼

Exceptions to the maxim rule **Strong v Bird**; *donationes mortis causa*; proprietary estoppel; unconscionability

Ⓐ SUGGESTED ANSWER

[1] Start with a brief introduction to set the scope.

Introduction to Scope of Maxim[1]

The quotation is one of the maxims of equity. It is a pithy way of stating that, where a trust is incompletely constituted or a gift is imperfectly made, equity will not give its remedy of specific performance to an intended beneficiary who is a volunteer, or to the intended donee. In the context of gifts, the maxim is often expressed in the form 'equity will not perfect an imperfect gift': see **Milroy v Lord (1862) 4 De GF & J 264**.

[2] This section sets out the meaning of the terms in use.

Who is a Volunteer? What is Consideration?[2]

A volunteer is a person who has not furnished consideration for the creation of the trust. Consideration in equity consists of both common law consideration (money or money's worth) and (in certain instances) marriage. It is clear that a covenant (although it may be enforceable at common law) does not comprise consideration in equity.

If marriage is to constitute consideration, the trust must be made either before and in consideration of a particular marriage, or (if made after the marriage) in pursuance of an ante-nuptial agreement to make such a trust. Furthermore, only certain persons within a marriage settlement are treated by equity as providing consideration: these are the spouses to the marriage and their issue. Issue of a former marriage and illegitimate children will prima facie fall outside the marriage consideration: *Re Cook's Settlement Trusts* [1965] **Ch 902**. But they may come within it if their interests are so closely intertwined with those of the issue of the marriage in question that they cannot be separated: *A-G* v *Jacobs-Smith* [1895] **2 QB 341, CA**. Next-of-kin are outside the marriage consideration: *Re Plumptre* [1910] **1 Ch 609**.

The quotation needs to be treated with care, as equity will protect a beneficiary's interest under a completely constituted trust even if that beneficiary is a volunteer (as in *Paul* v *Paul* (1882) **20 ChD 742**, where the settlor, having completely constituted the trust, was not permitted to reclaim the property on the ground that the beneficiaries were volunteers).

A gift is perfect in equity when the donor has done everything necessary to be done by him; it is therefore perfect in equity if the donor has put the intended donee into the position of being able to get in the legal title: *Re Rose* [1952] **Ch 499, CA**. The effect is that, until the legal title passes, the donor becomes a trustee for the intended donee. Although Arden LJ in *Pennington* v *Waine* [2002] **1 WLR 2075**, at para. 56, treated *Re Rose* as an exception to the maxim, other authorities explain it as an instance in which a gift is in equity already perfect, so equity's assistance is not required: see *Mascall* v *Mascall* [1984] **EWCA Civ 10**; *T. Choithram International SA* v *Pagarani* [2001] **1 WLR 1 at p. 11, PC**; and Luxton [2012] Conv 70.

[3] This next section deals with the main body of the question.

Implications for Incompletely Constituted Trust[3]

The maxim also means that where a trust is completely constituted in regard to certain items of property, but incompletely constituted in regard to other items, volunteer beneficiaries cannot compel the settlor to transfer the latter into the trust: *Jefferys* v *Jefferys* (1841) **Cr & Ph 138**. However, if some of the would-be beneficiaries under an incompletely constituted trust have provided consideration for its creation, they may obtain specific performance. The consequence will be that the trust becomes completely constituted, thus also benefiting the volunteers, who could not have sued personally: *Davenport* v *Bishopp* (1843) **2 Y & C Ch Cas 451**.

The modern approach has been expressed as being that 'Although equity will not aid a volunteer, it will not strive officiously to defeat a gift': *T. Choithram International SA* v *Pagarani* [2001] **1 WLR 1, PC** at p. 12, per Lord Browne-Wilkinson. However, in some older cases it appears that equity went further than merely not assisting a volunteer, and would frustrate an action brought at common law to aid a volunteer. Thus, the court has directed covenantees of a voluntary covenant not to sue the covenantor for damages at common law since this would give the volunteers indirectly what they were not entitled to obtain directly: *Re Kay's Settlement* **[1939] Ch 329**. In principle, however, such a claim should be denied the covenantees only when they hold the benefit of the covenant on a resulting trust for the covenantor. A claim by them ought to be available if the covenant is itself the subject-matter of the express trust, as it was in *Fletcher v Fletcher* **(1844) 4 Hare 67**. In such a case, the trust is completely constituted vis-à-vis the covenant, even though it is incompletely constituted as regards the property to which such covenant relates. Thus, although equity will not give specific performance vis-à-vis such property, it will not frustrate a claim brought by the trustee-covenantees for damages for breach of covenant at common law. Indeed, in such circumstances, equity will (if necessary) at the behest of the beneficiaries compel the covenantee to lend his name to a claim at common law against the covenantor. This problem does not arise in relation to covenants entered into at least six months after the passing of the **Contracts (Rights of Third Parties) Act 1999**, which enables a third party to enforce a contract in his or her own right, thus enabling the volunteer to sue for damages.

Exceptions[4]

[4] This section deals with the exceptions. Aim to set them out clearly and show how they exemplify the maxim. In other words—don't forget to link back to the question and explain how the exceptions connect to the status of the volunteer in equity.

Equity has for many years recognised three so-called exceptions to the maxim that it will not assist a volunteer. The first[5] is the rule in *Strong v Bird* **(1874) LR 18 Eq 315** whereby, if the intended donee of an *inter vivos* gift becomes the executor, or even the administrator, of the intending donor upon the latter's death, the legal title passes to him. This, together with a continuing intention to make a gift on the deceased's part, perfects the gift. Arguably, however, this is not so much an exception to the maxim as an illustration of the means by which a gift can be perfected. This principle has been extended to trusts: *Re Ralli's Will Trusts* **[1964] Ch 288**.

[5] You could number these or indent them for clarity. That says to the examiner—'look, I said there would be three exceptions and here they are'. A favourite of some examiners is to point out there is no 'secondly', or 'thirdly'.

The second exception is *donationes mortis causa*. Equity's assistance is not needed (and therefore the maxim is inapplicable[6]) if the subject-matter of the gift is transferred to the intended donee during the donor's lifetime, albeit subject to the usual conditions to which such gifts are subject. If, however, the intended donee's title remains imperfect at the donor's death, equity's assistance will be required, and this constitutes a genuine exception to the maxim. This will be the case, for instance, if the subject-matter of the *donatio mortis causa* is a chose in action, and the donor hands over merely the indicia of title: *Birch v Treasury Solicitor* **[1951] Ch 298**.

[6] Aim for the occasional nod to the question as here.

A third exception is proprietary estoppel. If A encourages, or even acquiesces in, B's acting to his detriment in the belief that he has rights in the property of A, equity may protect B should A act inconsistently with such rights. This is the principle which can be traced back to *Dillwyn* v *Llewelyn* (1862) 4 De GF & J 517. A modern (and perhaps startling[7]) instance is *Pascoe* v *Turner* [1979] 1 WLR 431, where the Court of Appeal held that the equity raised by the estoppel could be satisfied only by a conveyance of the fee simple. Equity was there assisting a volunteer by perfecting an imperfect gift. In other cases, however, the equity has been satisfied by a lesser remedy, as by the award of a licence (*Inwards* v *Baker* [1965] 2 QB 29) or merely monetary compensation: *Dodsworth* v *Dodsworth* (1973) 228 EG 1115 and *Jennings* v *Rice* [2003] 1 P & CR 8, CA.

Conscionability—a Fourth Exception?

A further exception[8] was apparently recognised by the Court of Appeal in the rather unsatisfactory decision in *Pennington* v *Waine*.[9] In that case, a purported gift of shares appeared to be imperfect because the intending donor, Ada, had not done everything necessary to be done by her in accordance with the rule in *Re Rose*. She had merely put the completed share transfer form into the hands of her agent, Mr Pennington (who had retained it): she had not thereby put her nephew, Harold (the intended donee), into the position of being able to take steps to obtain registration. The court nevertheless held that, in the circumstances, it would be unconscionable for Ada to go back on her gift.

This decision seems to cast into doubt principles that have been settled since *Milroy* v *Lord* (1862) 4 De GF & J 264. Furthermore, the notion of unconscionability is vague, and, with respect, smacks of palm-tree justice. This is why, whilst unconscionability no doubt underlies much equitable intervention, it finds expression only through settled principles. The result in *Pennington* v *Waine* might possibly have been explicable on the basis of proprietary estoppel, if it had been established that, by signing a consent form to act as a director, Harold had acted to his detriment in reliance upon a representation that the necessary qualification share was being transferred to him. The Court of Appeal, however, made no reference to estoppel. The result might also have been better (if rather shakily) founded on Arden LJ's alternative explanation: namely, that, when Mr Pennington wrote to inform Harold of the gift, Mr Pennington became Harold's agent for the purpose of submitting the transfer to the company. In any event, whilst *Pennington* v *Waine* treats unconscionability as a separate exception to the maxim 'Equity will not assist a volunteer', the Court of Appeal in *Kaye* v *Zeital* [2010] 2 BCLC 1 applied traditional principles; and in *Curtis* v *Pulbrook* [2011] 1 BCLC 638, Briggs J treated *Pennington* v *Waine* as a case of detrimental reliance.

[7] This comment might be considered by some to be pejorative or a throwaway remark. But it does suggest you have a view (and the capacity to be startled by a judicial decision).

[8] This is actually the fourth (see earlier comment about getting your numbering right) but it doesn't sit with the standard three exceptions so has been set out as a 'further' comment here.

[9] Don't be afraid to be critical. The judges don't always get it right and you are entitled to your view. Of course, if you think *Pennington* v *Waine* is the greatest thing since sliced bread, say so.

LOOKING FOR EXTRA MARKS?

■ This topic has produced a welter of academic discussion in articles and elsewhere and incorporating this secondary material into your answers will earn extra marks.

QUESTION | 2

In 2014, A secured B's undertaking to hold any property which A might thereafter transfer to B in trust for A's niece, N. In 2015, A showed B a painting which was hanging on the wall in A's home, and told B that this was to be held on the trusts which he (A) had declared. A was owed the sum of £20,000 by C, and in 2016, A wrote to B saying: 'I hereby assign to you the debt owed to me by C.' A was himself a beneficiary under the FGH Trust, and in 2016, A orally directed the trustees of that trust to hold his interest thereunder in trust for B. In 2019, A covenanted with B to transfer to B in trust for N any property which A might receive under the will of D, who was then still alive. D died early in 2020, bequeathing to A shares in XYZ Ltd.

A died last month, leaving all his property to E. At the date of his death, he had not transferred either the painting or the shares to B, and he had not notified C of the intended assignment of the debt.

Advise N which of the foregoing items (if any) are held in trust for her, and what steps (if any) she might take to enforce the covenant.

CAUTION!

■ In this question on volunteers and incompletely constituted trusts you need to identify the requirements for transferring different sorts of property into a trust. To make it manageable, separate out the different types of property into different headed paragraphs.

■ The last section relates to trusts of covenants which is tricky and involves apparently conflicting decisions upon which a variety of academic and judicial views have been expressed. If you are not familiar with this debate then avoid the question—this is too important a part to be given short shrift.

DIAGRAM ANSWER PLAN

Identify the issues	▓ Volunteers; incompletely constituted trusts; requirements for transferring different sorts of property into a trust ▓ Trusts of covenants
Relevant law	▓ *Milroy* v *Lord*; **LPA 1925, s. 136; LPA 1925, s. 53(1)(c); Contracts (Rights of Third Parties) Act 1999**
Apply the law	▓ Painting: deed or delivery ▓ Debt: statutory assignment under **LPA 1925, s. 136** ▓ Assignment of interest under the trust: **LPA 1925, s. 53(1)(c)** ▓ Shares: transfer in books of company ▓ Covenant to transfer?
Conclude	▓ Advise N

SUGGESTED ANSWER

Introduction[1]

[1] This intro shows you know there is a trust and have correctly identified the key issue.

Since A intended to create a trust by transferring property to another person, B, as trustee, a trust will arise in favour of the intended beneficiary, N, only if there is a valid declaration of trust and an effective transfer of the property to the trustee: *Milroy* v *Lord* **(1862) 4 De GF & J 264**, per Turner LJ. The terms of the undertaking which A secured from B are a clear declaration of trust. As regards transfer, however, it is necessary to take each item of property in turn.

The Painting[2]

[2] The question is one solid block. Separate out the issues by using headed paragraphs. It makes it more manageable for you and shows you have grasped the points.

The painting is a chattel, which is transferred either by delivery or deed. There is no evidence of a deed here. Delivery requires a physical handing over; merely showing the painting to B does not comprise a delivery: *Re Cole* **[1964] Ch 175**. The painting has therefore not been transferred into the trust, and will pass under A's will to E.

The Assignment of the Debt

[3] Be aware of this section—it is easily forgotten but awfully useful.

The benefit of the debt could not be assigned at common law, but under **s. 136 of the Law of Property Act 1925**,[3] the benefit of a debt can be assigned so as to enable the assignee to sue the debtor in his own name. For such a legal assignment to occur, the assignment must be in writing under the hand of the assignor, it must be absolute, and written notice must be given to the debtor. In the problem, it appears that the assignment was absolute, in that it was intended to be an unconditional assignment of the entire debt. Furthermore, it appears to have been in writing under the hand of the assignor, since A instructed B in a letter. There can be no statutory assignment, however, unless written notice (whether by A or somebody else) has been given to C. As A gave no such notice, it may be that no such notice has been received by C.

Even if C has not been notified, there will have been an assignment in equity. By executing an absolute assignment in writing, A has done all he needs to do; **s. 136** does not require that notice to the debtor be given by the assignor. The assignment is therefore perfect in equity as soon as A executes the assignment: *Holt v Heatherfield Trust Ltd* **[1942] 2 KB 1**. The benefit of the debt in equity is therefore held by B in trust for N. In these circumstances, even after A's death, the assignment can become a statutory assignment if a third party (e.g. B) gives notice to C: *Walker v Bradford Old Bank Ltd* **(1884) 12 QBD 511**.

Equitable Interest under the FGH Trust

An instruction by a beneficiary to trustees to hold his interest in trust for a third party comprises a disposition of a subsisting equitable interest for the purposes of **s. 53(1)(c) of the Law of Property Act 1925**: *Grey v IRC* **[1960] AC 1**. It must therefore be in writing signed by the disponor or his agent.[4] Since A's direction to the trustees of the FGH Trust was merely oral, the purported assignment is void.[5] A's beneficial interest under that trust will therefore pass to E under A's will.

Covenant to Transfer Property to be Received under Will of D[6]

Lastly, as A did not transfer the shares in XYZ Ltd to B, the shares are not subject to the trust in favour of N. Equity does not regard a voluntary covenant as consideration, so B cannot compel A's estate to transfer the shares to him. It might, however, be argued that, by covenanting with B to transfer any property he might acquire under D's will, A has vested the benefit of the covenant in B. If this is so, it would seem to follow that N would be the beneficiary of a fully constituted trust of the benefit of the covenant, so that B would have to sue to enforce the covenant by claiming damages for breach of covenant, or else be liable to compensate N for breach of trust.

Whether the benefit of a covenant can comprise the subject-matter of a trust has been the subject of some judicial and much academic debate. The courts have shown their unwillingness to permit covenantees to

[4] The rules for transfer of interests are significantly different as between **s. 52(1)(b)** and **(c)**. Know your statute.

[5] Know the difference between void and voidable.

[6] This is the most complex part of the problem. If you are not familiar with the cases and arguments—then maybe give this question a miss.

sue on a covenant for the benefit of volunteers: *Re Kay's Settlement* **[1939] Ch 329**; *Re Cook's Settlement Trusts* **[1965] Ch 902**. In the latter case, Buckley J suggested that there can be no trust of the benefit of a covenant concerning future property. If this is correct, B cannot be holding the benefit of the covenant on trust for N, and the only possibility would be that B holds the benefit of the covenant on trust for A's estate. On the other hand, it might be argued that the benefit of a covenant will be held on trust for the intended beneficiaries if the covenantor makes it clear that this is his intention. Such an intention might also be inferred, as where all the intended beneficiaries are volunteers, as in *Fletcher* **v** *Fletcher* **(1844) 4 Hare 67**, since otherwise there would be no point in entering into the covenant in the first place: Hornby (1962) 78 LQR 228.

[7] A tricky point really as we have no case authority on it.

Much of the significance of this argument would now appear to have been rendered obsolete by the **Contracts (Rights of Third Parties) Act 1999**,[7] which applies to contracts entered into (like the covenant in the problem) at least six months after its enactment. Even a purely voluntary covenant (such as that in the problem) is a contract, and, under **s. 1**, a person who is not a party to a contract (N) may enforce a term of the contract in her own right if the contract expressly provides that she may, or if the term purports to confer a benefit on her (unless it appears that the parties did not intend the term to be enforceable by the third party). For the purpose of enforcing a term of the contract, the third party has the same remedies as would have been available to her in an action for breach of contract had she been a party to the contract: **s. 1(5)**. Since the covenant was purely voluntary, N could not obtain specific performance to compel A's estate to transfer the shares to B, so that the shares would pass to E under A's will. However, N could sue A's estate for damages, the measure of the damages being the value of the shares that A failed to transfer.

Against this it might be argued that, even if N had been a party to the covenant, if the court were to follow the approach of Eve J in *Re Kay's Settlement*, she would not be entitled to damages. In that case, it appears that the court held that the benefit of a voluntary covenant was held on a resulting trust for the covenantor's estate. If the court took the same view in the problem, so that the benefit of the covenant was held in trust for A's estate, this circumstance might indicate that the parties to the covenant did not intend it to be enforceable by the third party. This would effectively remove purely voluntary covenants for the benefit of third parties from the scope of the **Contracts (Rights of Third Parties) Act 1999**, since the Act would be available only in the very circumstance in which it is not needed, i.e. when equity treats the third party as a beneficiary under a trust of the covenant.

[8] Here you are making an argument—don't be dogmatic about it though.

While this is a tenable argument,[8] it is more likely that the courts will reject it and will use the opportunity afforded by the 1999 Act to abandon these refinements of equity, which were essentially designed for the now outmoded era of marriage settlements. The modern approach was expressed by Lord Browne-Wilkinson (albeit in a different context), when he said 'Although equity will not aid a volunteer, it will not strive officiously to defeat a gift': *T. Choithram International SA v Pagarani* **[2001] 1 WLR 1, PC** at p. 12. Long before the 1999 Act was passed, it was held that where the third party volunteer was herself a party to the covenant, she could recover substantial damages for breach of covenant in respect of her own loss: *Cannon v Hartley* **[1949] Ch 213**. It would therefore appear that, unless the covenantor indicates otherwise, the effect of the 1999 Act is to put every intended beneficiary under a voluntary covenant into the position of the covenantee in that case. On this footing, N could sue A's estate for damages to the value of the shares.[9]

[9] No conclusion because each part contains its own concluding remarks.

➕ LOOKING FOR EXTRA MARKS?

■ To be honest this is such a complex and tricky question that if you got all the points contained in this suggested answer which has been written with the benefit of a calm, clear head—you would be doing really well!

Ⓠ QUESTION | 3

In 2019, Acute handed his share certificate in respect of his shareholding in Diacritical Ltd to Cedilla, together with a share transfer form which Acute had completed in favour of Cedilla. As he handed these documents over, Acute instructed Cedilla to hold the shares in trust for Acute's nephew, Grave. Cedilla agreed. Shortly after, Cedilla attempted to obtain registration of the shares in her own name, but was defeated by the exercise by the directors of Diacritical Ltd of a power contained in the company's articles to refuse registration.

In 2020, Acute received back the share certificate from Cedilla. He handed it to his cousin, Umlaut, informing him that the shares were a gift to him.

Last month, Acute died with the shares still standing in his name. In his will he appointed Umlaut his executor and gave all his property to Cedilla.

Discuss who is entitled to the shares.

! CAUTION!

▨ This is a complex question, both because the relevant law itself is difficult, and also because you need to sort out in your mind the priorities of several claimants—never the easiest thing in the examination room.

▨ There is a lot to write so you will need to be economical with the facts of the cases. Cases should be cited to support legal principle; facts can be given sparingly in order to distinguish one case from another. See, for instance, the treatment in the suggested answer of the authorities which support, or which appear to conflict with, the principle of *Re Rose* [1952] **Ch 499, CA**. If you have a good understanding and keep a clear head, this is the sort of question where you could score very heavily.

⊙ DIAGRAM ANSWER PLAN

Identify the issues	▨ Constitution of trusts; position of volunteers
Relevant law	▨ *Milroy v Lord*; *Re Rose*; *Re Fry*; *Re Ralli*; *Strong v Bird*
Apply the law	▨ Grave's trust completely constituted *inter vivos*? • *Re Rose* • effect of refusal of registration? • Grave's priority over purported gift to Umlaut • if not perfect, equity will not assist Grave (a volunteer) ▨ Grave's trust completely constituted on Acute's death? • by bequest of shares to Cedilla (intended trustee)? • *Re Ralli* ▨ Umlaut's purported gift perfected on Acute's death? • Umlaut's appointment as executor • *Strong v Bird*
Conclude	▨ Who is entitled to shares

Ⓐ SUGGESTED ANSWER

[1] This is sufficient as an introduction showing the issue in the problem.

[2] This second sentence sets out the law.

Grave is beneficially entitled to the shares if he can establish that he is a beneficiary under a fully constituted trust of them.[1] A trust is completely constituted only if there is compliance with the requirements laid down in *Milroy v Lord* (1862) 4 De GF & J 264.[2] Where, as here, the settlor seeks to confer the benefit of property on a person by vesting it in a trustee, two things must be done. First, there must be a clear declaration by the settlor of the terms of the trust. Here, the instructions to Cedilla suffice. Secondly, the settlor must do all he can to vest the property in the intended trustee. The legal title to the shares will not pass to Cedilla unless and until the company registers Cedilla's name in its register of members. Since this has not been done, the legal title to the shares has not passed. The share transfer may nevertheless be perfect in equity if, in accordance with **Milroy v Lord**, the settlor has done everything necessary to be done by him to transfer the shares. In **Re Rose [1952] Ch 499**, the Court of Appeal held that a gift of shares was perfect in equity as soon as the donor had put the donee into the position of being able to take steps to complete the transfer: i.e. when the donor had handed to the donee the share certificate and executed share transfer form. On this basis, the trust in favour of Grave would have been completely constituted from the date in 2019 when these documents were delivered to Cedilla. If so, from that date, Acute would have held the legal title to the shares in trust for Cedilla, who would herself have held the equitable interest thereunder on a sub-trust for Grave.[3] This makes Cedilla a trustee of a completely constituted trust for Grave. She is therefore under a duty to ensure that the trust property is safeguarded—by taking steps to bring in the legal title to the shares (as she did attempt to do), and (if necessary) by compelling Acute to transfer to her any dividends he receives in respect of that holding.

The transfers in **Re Rose** were registered, but there is nothing in the case to suggest a different result where registration is refused. The principle in **Re Rose** has been attacked for thus saddling an intended donor with an unintended and potentially permanent trusteeship: see McKay (1976) 40 Conv (NS) 139. This objection carries some force; moreover, a permanent trusteeship in this context contrasts sharply with a contract for the sale of shares where (if the company refuses to register the purchaser) the vendor cannot be fixed with a permanent trusteeship: see **Stevenson v Wilson** 1907 SC 445, considered (without criticism) by the House of Lords in **Scott Ltd v Scott's Trustees [1959] AC 763**.

A case difficult to reconcile with **Re Rose** is **Re Fry**[4] **[1946] Ch 312**; but that case may be considered, perhaps, to turn on the effect of relevant defence regulations. Apart from that decision, the principle of **Re Rose** is consistent with a range of authorities: see, particularly, **Mallott v Wilson [1903] 2 Ch 494** and **Mascall v Mascall [1984] EWCA Civ 10**. The principle was assumed correct by the House of Lords in **Vandervell v IRC [1967] 2 AC 291, HL** and it also operates in the case of equitable assignments of legal choses in action: **Holt v Heatherfield Trust Ltd [1942] 2 KB 1**.

[3] This point is often missed but it is an inevitable consequence of the decision in **Re Rose**.

[4] Don't be afraid to point out a difficulty in reconciling cases. It shows your analytical ability.

If *Re Rose* applies, Grave is a beneficiary under a trust of the shares, and is entitled to the dividends which Diacritical Ltd will continue to pay to Acute (and, after Acute's death, to Acute's personal representative). On this basis, the purported gift of the shares to Umlaut, even if ultimately perfected (as discussed in relation to the rule in *Strong* v *Bird* **(1874) LR 18 Eq 315**) is later in time, and is therefore subject to the rights of Grave. Similarly, Acute cannot by his will give to Cedilla property which he does not own beneficially. Thus the gift of all his property to Cedilla does not include the shares.

If, however, a court were to distinguish or overrule *Re Rose* and hold that the trust was incompletely constituted, then, unless Grave had provided consideration for the creation of the trust, he could not (as a volunteer) gain the assistance of equity: *Re Plumptre* **[1910] 1 Ch 609**. Since, however, Acute gave all his property in his will to Cedilla, the intended trustee of the shares, it is arguable that the trust in favour of Grave is completely constituted on Acute's death, as Cedilla then has a right as beneficiary under the will to see that the property is properly distributed: *Re Diplock* **[1948] Ch 465, CA**. She will ultimately obtain the legal title to the shares when the executor, Umlaut, transfers the shares into her name. It makes no difference that the legal title comes to Cedilla, the intended trustee, in a different capacity: *Re Ralli's Will Trusts* **[1964] Ch 288**.

Umlaut's Appointment as Executor[5]

There is, however, one further twist: Umlaut's appointment as executor. If it can be shown that Acute had a continuing intention to give the shares to Umlaut from 2020 until his death, the imperfect gift to Umlaut might be perfected under what is known as the rule in *Strong* v *Bird* **(1874) LR 18 Eq 315** (i.e. by the acquisition by Umlaut of the legal title to the shares as executor). In principle, this would seem to postpone the equity of the beneficiaries under the will to that of the executor. It was upon this basis that Walton J in *Re Gonin* **[1979] Ch 16** objected to the decision in *Re James* **[1935] Ch 449**, which had extended the rule to administrators.[6] This objection may carry

less weight where the intended donee becomes executor, since such appointment results from the testator's own voluntary act. The objection may not be entirely overcome, however, since an executor does stand in a fiduciary relationship to the beneficiaries under the will, and to permit him to have a prior claim seems to fly in the face of normal equitable principles designed to prevent a conflict of interest: cf. *Holder* v *Holder* **[1968] Ch 353, CA**. Nevertheless, the application of the rule to executors is well established: *Re Stewart* **[1908] 2 Ch 251**. Umlaut will therefore be permitted to bring evidence outside the will that Acute intended to give him the shares. Since such evidence derives from the intended donee, however, it will need to be treated with caution: cf. cases involving secret trusts: **Re Rees [1950] Ch 204, CA**, and **Re Tyler [1967] 1 WLR 1269**.

If, therefore, the intended trust in favour of Grave was not perfected in 2019, Umlaut may be able to satisfy the court that he is entitled to the shares under the rule in **Strong v Bird** in priority to both Cedilla and Grave.

LOOKING FOR EXTRA MARKS?

- Discussion and critique of a rule such as that in **Strong v Bird** will earn extra marks (see earlier comment).

- Clarifying the way in which the legal title is held on trust by the intended donor when **Re Rose** applies is a point which will earn extra marks (see earlier comment). Although this is a problem question and such questions do not normally lend themselves to a theoretical discussion, reference to academic commentary such as Ollikainen-Read (2018) (see 'Taking Things Further') would be a good addition to show the origins of the rule in **Re Rose**.

QUESTION | 4

Three months ago, Lear, a keen rambler, caught a chill after spending a stormy winter's night wandering lost on the moors. He was taken to hospital suffering from pneumonia. When his eldest daughter, Goneril, visited him, he handed her the key to a deed box which was in his study at home. Lear told Goneril that he did not expect to live much longer and that, if anything were to happen to him, Goneril was to have the contents of the box.

Shortly after, when Lear's middle daughter, Regan, was by his bedside, Lear handed to her the Land Certificate that he had been sent by the Land Registry in 1980 when he acquired the freehold title to his country cottage in Gloucestershire. He advised Regan that, if he did not pull through, Regan was to have the cottage.

Last month, during a visit by his youngest daughter, Cordelia, Lear wrote a cheque for £10,000 in her favour. He informed her that this was to be her share of his property on his death.

Last week Lear, who remained seriously ill in hospital, deliberately took an overdose of sleeping pills, from which he died.

Goneril has now opened the deed box, and finds that it contains the keys and vehicle registration document to Lear's car, and a bank pass book relating to Lear's deposit account with the Serpent's Tooth Bank plc. It is discovered that, a couple of weeks before his death, Lear had leased the country cottage to Edmund for a term of 21 years. In his will, Lear gave all his property to charity.

Advise Lear's daughters.

! CAUTION!

- Note that *donatio* is a noun meaning gift, so one can refer either to a *'donatio mortis causa'*, or to a gift *'mortis causa'*. The plural is *donationes mortis causa*. (Comfort may be sought from remarks of Lord Simon of Glaisdale in **Brumby v Milner [1976] 1 WLR 1096**, a tax case, where his Lordship deprecated the unnecessary use by lawyers of Latin terms. In the present case, however, the English equivalent is slightly more of a mouthful, and the Latin reminds us of the Roman Law origins of this principle, which finds its modern counterpart in the Civil Law.)

DIAGRAM ANSWER PLAN

Identify the issues
- *Donationes mortis causa*

Relevant law
- **Sen v Headley** and other case law

Apply the law
- Gifts *mortis causa*?
  - Conditional on death
  - In contemplation of death
  - Part with dominion
- Car:
  - delivery of evidence of ownership with physical possession
- Deposit account:
  - pass book as indicia of title
- Cottage:
  - **Sen v Headley**
  - can there be a *donatio mortis causa* of registered land post **Land Registration Act 2002**?
  - granting of lease shows no parting with dominion?
  - lease subject to interest of donee?
- Cheque:
  - Unpresented cheque cannot be a gift *mortis causa* (merely revocable order to banker)

Conclude
- Advise Lear's daughters

A SUGGESTED ANSWER

[1] This introduction sets the scene by establishing the issue and the application to the facts.

Lear evidently intended the gifts to the daughters to take effect only in the event of his death.[1] Such gifts would normally be testamentary in nature and valid only if made in accordance with the **Wills Act 1837** (as amended). Such formalities are absent here. Nevertheless, Lear's daughters will be able to take the property concerned if they can establish a valid *donatio mortis causa* in respect of each item.

[2] Here comes the law.

To constitute a gift *mortis causa*, three elements must be satisfied.[2] These have been affirmed by the courts many times (e.g. in *Cain* **v** *Moon* **[1896] 2 QB 283**, and, most recently, in *Sen* **v** *Headley* **[1991] Ch 425**).

[3] Great to enumerate your points— as long as there is a second, third . . .

First,[3] the gift must be intended to be conditional upon death, so that it is not perfect until death, before which time it can be revoked by the donor. The gift must also be intended to be automatically re-voked in the event of the donor's survival. Such conditions will be readily inferred where the gift is made in contemplation of death, which appears to be the case here.

Secondly, the gift must be made in contemplation of impending death, which must be more than a contemplation that the donor, like all living things, must some day die. This requirement is met where the donor is suffering from a life-threatening illness (*Saulnier* **v** *Anderson* **(1987) 43 DLR (4th) 19**). In *King* **v** *Chiltern Dog Rescue* **[2015] EWCA Civ 581** (overruling *Vallee* **v** *Birchwood* **[2013] EWHC 1449 (Ch)**) it was held that imminent death for a particular reason must be actually anticipated at the time of the gift and the gift will fail if the donor does not die as he anticipated. As Lear, in the problem, was suffering from pneumonia, the requirement that the gift be in contemplation of death would seem to be satisfied. In *Re Dudman* **[1925] 1 Ch 553**, however, it was held that a *donatio mortis causa* made in contemplation of suicide (at that time a crime) was not valid. Suicide is no longer a crime (**Suicide Act 1961**) and the present position is unclear. Such a purported *donatio* might still be invalid today on the ground that the requisite contemplation of death imports an element of uncertainty as to whether and when death will ensue. Such uncertainty is absent if the donor has the intention of taking his own life. In the problem, however, at the time he made the *donationes mortis causa*, Lear may have contemplated death by pneumonia, not by suicide. In *Wilkes* **v** *Allington* **[1931] 2 Ch 104**, it was held that it does not matter if death occurs from a disease other than that contemplated. A *donatio* might therefore not be invalidated if death occurs by suicide not contemplated at the time the *donatio* was made: see *Mills* **v** *Shields* **[1948] IR 367**.

Thirdly, the donor must part with dominion over the subject-matter of the *donatio*. Delivery to the intended donee of the only key to a locked receptacle which contains the subject-matter suffices, even if the subject-matter could have been handed over: *Re Mustapha* **(1891) 8 TLR 160**. It has, however, been stated obiter that there is no sufficient parting with dominion if the donor retains a duplicate key: *Re Craven's Estate* **[1937] Ch 423**. The statement in the question that 'the key' was handed over to Goneril implies that it was the only key, in which case this requirement is satisfied. Moreover, it does not matter if the box itself contains another key which opens a further box: *Re Lillingston* **[1952] 2 All ER 184**.

The Car[4]

[4] Next sub-part.

On this principle, since the deed box contains the key to Lear's car, it would appear that (unless Lear retained a duplicate key) a valid *donatio* has been made of the car. Although the passing of dominion over a chattel is usually effected by physical delivery, delivery of the key both enables Goneril to take possession of the car and (together with the delivery of the vehicle registration document, which evidences Lear's ownership) effectively puts it out of Lear's power to deal with it.

The Pass Book

[5] Setting out the law here.

Parting with dominion over a chose in action requires the donor to part with the essential evidence or indicia of title: *Birch* v *Treasury Solicitor* **[1951] Ch 298**.[5] There, the Court of Appeal held (*inter alia*) that a *donatio mortis causa* of a chose in action represented by a deposit pass book to Barclay's Bank was effected by delivery to the donee of the pass book. In such instances, equity will perfect the imperfect gift by treating the deceased's personal representatives as trustees of the chose in action for the donee: *Duffield* v *Elwes* **(1827) 1 Bli NS 497**. This principle would therefore apply to Lear's deposit account with the Serpent's Tooth Bank plc.

The Country Cottage

[6] Nice extra marks point here but could go straight to *Sen* v *Headley*.

Lear's country cottage is land and it used to be doubted, on the basis of dicta in *Duffield* v *Elwes*,[6] whether land could ever be the subject-matter of a *donatio mortis causa*. In *Sen* v *Headley*, however, the Court of Appeal held that it could. There was no difference in substance between the principle applicable to choses in action established in *Birch* v *Treasury Solicitor* and the parting with dominion over land by the delivery of the title deeds. Although the doctrine of *donationes mortis causa* is anomalous, it was preferable to avoid creating anomalies of anomalies.

Sen **v** *Headley* concerned unregistered land,[7] but at the time that case was decided it might have been argued that the same principle would appear to apply to the delivery of the Land Certificate in registered land. The problem, however, is that the **Land Registration Act 2002** made no provision for Land Certificates, which were therefore effectively abolished. Instead, the Land Registry now issues the registered proprietor only with a 'Title information document', which (unlike the former Land Certificate) is not a document of title, and should not be sent to the Land Registry on any subsequent application. Even though Lear still retained the Land Certificate that had been issued to him in 1980, it ceased to be a document of title on 13 October 2003, when the **Land Registration Act 2002** came into force. It is the case that a decision in the Singapore High Court, *Koh Cheong Heng* **v** *Ho Yee Fong* **[2011] SGHC 48** suggests that a *donatio* of registered land can take place but, although *King* only deals with unregistered land and does not consider this point, it now seems unlikely that such a document would be treated as the indicia of title for the purpose of making a *donatio mortis causa*. If this is correct, it is difficult to see how there can now be a *donatio mortis causa* of a registered title:[8] see Roberts [2013] Conv 113.[9]

Even if Lear could be treated as having handed over the indicia of his title to the cottage,[10] whether he has parted with dominion over the cottage is less clear. He did after all subsequently lease it out. Such a situation was hypothesised in *Sen* **v** *Headley* by the Court of Appeal, which opined that a retention by the donor of a power to deal with the subject-matter did not invariably preclude a parting with dominion. It was a matter of fact in each case. Although the donor in *Sen* **v** *Headley* retained a key to the premises, the donee had her own set and was in *de facto* control. The problem does not state how many sets of keys there are, or who has possession of them. If Regan has the only set of keys to the cottage, that might, in accordance with *Sen* **v** *Headley*, be a sufficient parting with dominion by Lear. Nevertheless, the legal principle is obscure. Mummery J at first instance could not see how the equitable interest of the donee, which arises only on the death of the donor, can be binding upon a tenant of a lease granted during the donor's lifetime. The Court of Appeal did not provide a satisfactory answer to this.

The Cheque

It is well established[11] that delivery of the donor's own cheque to the intended donee cannot constitute a valid *donatio mortis causa*: *Re Beaumont* **[1902] 1 Ch 889**, *Re Leaper* **[1916] 1 Ch 579**. A cheque is merely a revocable order to a banker to pay a sum of money.

The position may be otherwise if the cheque is presented and the donor's account credited during the donor's lifetime or before the bank has been informed of his death. Subject to these qualifications, Cordelia can derive no benefit from the cheque, which is mere waste paper.[12]

[12] No need for a conclusion—each item has been dealt with in the clearly labelled preceding paragraphs.

LOOKING FOR EXTRA MARKS?

- The Court of Appeal in *King* has clarified and narrowed the boundaries of *donationes* so further discussion of the way in which it has limited the doctrine overruling *Vallee* would be worthwhile for extra marks. You could refer to the interesting article by Charles Towl on this case and its implications (see 'Taking Things Further') where he argues that *donationes* are a necessary evil.

TAKING THINGS FURTHER

- Edelman, J., 'Two fundamental questions for the law of trusts', paper presented at the Western Australian Bar Association CPD Conference, 15 October 2011 (available online).
- Hornby, J., 'Covenants in favour of volunteers' (1962) 78 LQR 228.
  A useful article on this tricky topic of covenants.
- Luxton, P., 'In search of perfection: the *Re Rose* rule rationale' [2012] Conv 70.
- Ollikainen-Read, A., 'Assignments of equitable interests and the origins of *Re Rose*' [2018] Conv 63–73.
  Three papers on the rule in **Re Rose**.
- Roberts, N., '*Donationes mortis causa* in a dematerialised world' [2013] Conv 113.
- Towls, C., '*Donatio mortis causa* and suicide—an anomaly within an anomaly?' [2018] Conv 367–374.
  Perhaps surprisingly donationes *are popular exam topics and these two articles discuss the latest case law.*

Online Resources

www.oup.com/uk/qanda/

For extra essay and problem questions on this topic, as well as advice on revision and exam technique, please visit the online resources.

5

Trusts, Powers, and Discretionary Trusts

ARE YOU READY?

In order to attempt the questions in this chapter you will need to have covered the following topics:

- The difference between a power and a trust
- The definition of mere powers and fiduciary powers
- The definition of a discretionary trust

KEY DEBATES

Debate: what is the difference between a discretionary trust and a power?

Discretionary trusts and powers may look similar and they may be created for a similar purpose. A testator wishing to provide for the members of his family after his death may prefer to give the trustees a discretion in the allocation of the beneficial interests, so that account can be taken of the changing needs and circumstances of the objects after the testator's death. The appropriate machinery for this is the discretionary trust. Mere powers (whether fiduciary or non-fiduciary) result in different rights. An individual object of a power (whether fiduciary or non-fiduciary) has a right (a mere equity) to prevent any appointment being made outside the defined class of objects. Only an object of a fiduciary power, however, has equitable rights (mere equities) in relation to the exercise of the power. These rights are broadly similar to those enjoyed by an object of a discretionary trust; but the crucial distinction, which was emphasised by Lord Wilberforce in *McPhail v Doulton* **[1971] AC 424**, is that trustees of a discretionary trust are under a greater duty to survey the class than donees of a fiduciary power. That case repays careful study on a variety of grounds!

Adam, who has just died, made the following dispositions in his will:

a   £50,000 to my trustees on trust to apply the net income of the fund in making, at their absolute discretion, grants to or for the benefit of any of the employees or former employees of Abel & Sons, their spouses or dependants, or any others having a moral claim on me.

b   £5,000 to my trustees upon trust to be divided equally amongst my friends at the 'Paradise' public house, Edenton.

c   £100,000 to be applied by my trustees as they see fit for the benefit of the middle classes of my home town, Edenton.

d   The residue of my estate to my wife, Eve, absolutely, but I direct my trustees to allow such old friends of mine who wish to do so, to acquire any of my collection of stuffed reptiles at 50 per cent of market price.

Advise the trustees of the will as to the validity of these dispositions.

CAUTION!

- There usually appears in examination papers a question on certainty of objects dealing with the ramifications of the House of Lords' decision in ***McPhail v Doulton* [1971] AC 424** and its application by the Court of Appeal in ***Re Baden's Deed Trusts (No. 2)* [1973] Ch 9**. So a careful preparation of the case law will repay the effort.

- This question mixes fixed and discretionary trusts—watch out for that and make sure you are clear about which type you are dealing with. The rules for certainty of objects are very different.

DIAGRAM ANSWER PLAN

Identify the issues	■ Certainty of objects; fixed and discretionary trusts
Relevant law	■ *McPhail v Doulton*; *Re Baden* and relevant case law
Apply the law	**(a)** Test for certainty of objects of a discretionary trust is the individual ascertainability test adopted in *McPhail v Doulton* Application: • Employees, former employees, and their spouses would be conceptually certain and satisfy the test • The Court of Appeal decision in *Re Baden (No. 2)* is authority that relatives and dependants also satisfy the certainty test • But persons 'having a moral claim upon me' would fail the test **(b)** This disposition is a fixed trust and the test for certainty is therefore the complete list test (*IRC v Broadway Cottages*) • Friends at the 'Paradise' would not satisfy this test and would fail **(c)** This is a discretionary trust and the test for certainty of objects is the *McPhail v Doulton* individual ascertainability test • 'Middle classes' would not satisfy this test • Also, if this were a very large number of people, it would additionally fail for administrative unworkability, as the trustees of a discretionary trust should survey the whole class (*R v District Auditor, ex parte West Yorkshire Metropolitan County Council*; *Re Harding*) **(d)** 'Old friends' as a class gift would fail the individual ascertainability test • But in *Re Barlow*, this type of disposition was construed as a series of conditional individual gifts to persons able to prove that they were old friends, and so was valid
Conclude	■ Advise the trustees

[1] In a problem question go straight into the answers matching the numbering in the question. Never, never, never write it as an unnumbered continuous answer.

[2] This states the law and identifies the issue at the same time. This is the only way to answer a problem question with numbered points.

[3] Here is the application to this part of the problem.

[4] Part (a) has sub-parts to it. Take each in turn (you could use a sub-numbering system if you find that makes it clearer to read).

[5] Conclusion—you cannot be definitive so state the choices.

[6] This question mixes fixed and discretionary trusts. State clearly in the opening of each section which you are dealing with.

[7] The conclusion (which is clear) is stated here. The answer then goes on to discuss the case law around this point.

(a) Abel & Sons[1]

A trust must be for ascertained or ascertainable beneficiaries:[2] **Re Endacott [1960] Ch 232, CA**. The test to determine certainty of objects in a discretionary trust was decided by the House of Lords in **McPhail v Doulton [1971] AC 424** ('can it be said with certainty that any given individual is or is not a member of the class?').

Since this decision, therefore, it is no longer necessary to prepare a complete list of objects of a discretionary trust as is still required in a fixed trust (**IRC v Broadway Cottages Trust [1955] Ch 20, CA**). In **McPhail v Doulton** the House of Lords adopted the test for certainty of objects of powers established in **Re Gulbenkian's Settlement Trust [1970] AC 508**, and the two tests are now the same.

It is necessary, therefore, to apply[3] the test to the terms of Adam's will and ask: can it be said with certainty whether any individual is or is not an employee or former employee of Abel & Sons, or their spouse or dependant, or any other having a moral claim on Abel?

Employees or former employees would satisfy the test.[4]

In **Re Baden's Deed Trusts (No. 2) [1973] Ch 9, CA**, the terms 'relatives' and 'dependants' were subjected to the test. It was considered that the terms were conceptually certain and, therefore, sufficient to satisfy the test although all three judges gave different reasons for finding 'relatives' certain.

The term 'spouses' is clearly certain as a concept and this part of the gift would be valid.

However, the gift also includes a category of 'any others having a moral claim on me'. It was said in **McPhail v Doulton** that such an expression is conceptually uncertain.

It is not clear whether[5] this would cause the whole gift to fail for uncertainty or whether the courts could sever the offending part, thereby saving the valid parts (**Re Leek [1969] 1 Ch 563, CA**; **Re Gulbenkian's Settlements [1968] Ch 126 at p. 138, CA**).

(b) Paradise Public House

The gift upon trust to be divided equally amongst my friends at the 'Paradise' is a fixed trust.[6] The beneficiaries hold equitable interests under the trust in fixed shares. It is necessary to be able to draw up a list of all the beneficiaries in order for the division to be made. The older and stricter rule in **IRC v Broadway Cottages Trust** applies. The expression 'friends' is not a term that is sufficiently certain for such a complete list to be drawn up.[7] The expression 'old friends' was held to be certain in **Re Gibbard's Will Trusts [1967] 1 WLR 42** in relation to a power, but this case used the old test of whether it could be said of any one person that they were within the class (a test favoured by Lord Denning MR in his dissenting judgment in the Court of Appeal in *Re Gulbenkian*). This test was rejected by the House of Lords in *Re Gulbenkian*, however, and so is not now good authority for this point. A gift to 'friends' was upheld in *Re Barlow's Will Trusts* **[1979] 1 WLR 278**, but this was a series of gifts with a condition precedent. The size of the gift to each recipient did not alter according to the numbers answering the description, therefore it is not authority for certainty of the expression 'friends' in a class gift, whether a fixed (or discretionary) trust.

(c) Middle Classes of Edenton

This gift constitutes a purported discretionary trust.[8] It raises questions about certainty of objects and administrative workability.

The problem of certainty of objects is raised in respect of the definition of 'middle classes' (*McPhail v Doulton*). Again, it is necessary to decide whether such a concept is certain, applying the test in *McPhail v Doulton*. Although it may be possible to say definitely whether some individuals are or are not members of the middle classes, there may be a number of people who cannot be classified in this way. There was a difference of approach amongst the judges in *Re Baden's Deed Trusts (No. 2)*.

Megaw LJ accepted[9] that there may be a substantial number of persons about whom it could not be proved whether they are in or out. However, this may relate more to the question of evidential uncertainty. Conceptual certainty means that the class must be definable. Evidential certainty is the proof an applicant must supply to establish membership of the class. In the case of a gift to 'middle classes' it is difficult to define criteria for such a concept.

However, even if the gift is conceptually certain, then the question of administrative unworkability arises. In *McPhail v Doulton*, it was said that if the definition of 'objects is so hopelessly wide as not to form anything like a class', then the trust would be administratively unworkable. A discretionary trustee has duties to survey the class and this is impossible in a class of great width. This was the position in the case of *R v District Auditor, ex parte West Yorkshire Metropolitan County Council* **(1986) 26 RVR 24**, where a trust for the inhabitants of the county of West Yorkshire was held to be too wide and therefore void for administrative unworkability. In *Re Harding* **[2008] Ch 235**, it was considered that a trust for the black people of four London boroughs would have been administratively unworkable. If the trust could be construed as a power[10] this rule would not apply: *Re Manisty's Settlement* **[1974] Ch 17**.

[8] Make it clear that this is an example of a discretionary (rather than fixed) trust.

[9] It is good to display the fact that you have read the case and know the opinions of the individual judges.

[10] An easy point to forget so extra marks if you get it.

(d) Old Friends and Stuffed Reptiles

[11] Statement of the issue and law.

This gift must be distinguished from discretionary trusts.[11] It is not a trust for a class but a number of individual gifts to any person who is able to prove to the trustees that he or she qualifies as 'an old friend'.

[12] The concluding view.

Such a gift does not require conceptual certainty.[12] The gift will be valid if only one person seeking to take can be identified as an 'old friend' (**Re Allen [1953] Ch 810, CA**). In **Re Barlow's Will Trusts**, the direction to sell a painting at a preferential price to 'any friends of mine who may wish to buy one' was held to be a valid gift. A friend was a social acquaintance of long standing and anyone who satisfied this condition precedent could take the gift.

[13] Each section has its own conclusion so no need for final summary.

On the basis of this authority, this final disposition is therefore valid.[13]

LOOKING FOR EXTRA MARKS?

- For a high mark, some discussion of the issues going beyond a simple application of the cases to the problem is desirable. Some further discussion of the issues of conceptual certainty, evidential certainty, ascertainability, and administrative workability would be appropriate. If you can display your knowledge of the individual opinions of their Lordships in **McPhail v Doulton** that would be even better.

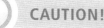

QUESTION | 2

But it is difficult in borderline cases to draw a dividing line between discretionary trusts and powers . . . The decision turns on the proper construction of the language of the instrument. The matter is made more difficult by reason of the fact that a discretionary trust may be 'exhaustive' or 'non-exhaustive'.

(Hanbury and Martin, *Modern Equity*, 18th edn, Sweet & Maxwell, 2009, at p. 66)

Discuss.

CAUTION!

- This essay question requires a discussion of the distinction between discretionary trusts and powers with reference to relevant literature; see, for example, Y. Grbich (1974) 37 MLR 643. In particular, such reference must be made where an essay of this type is set as an assessed essay. A straightforward explanation of the difference and the importance of the distinction between discretionary trusts and powers is required. The essay could be grouped under different headings to clarify the different aspects of the problem; for example, the different position of the trustees/donees, and the potential recipients.

- Be precise in your use of terminology. Confusion can easily arise because some terms are used by different judges or writers to mean different things; so, unless they define the sense in which they are using the terms, you will have to look to the context in order to determine what the meaning is. The term 'trust-power' is a dangerous one to use without any explanation of its meaning. A trust-power is a combination of a duty (a trust) and a power. For this reason, a discretionary trust is often called a trust-power, since it combines a duty to distribute with a power of selection.

- Unfortunately, the term trust-power can also be used to mean a fiduciary power, since this too combines a power and a trust obligation, i.e. a power to distribute and a duty to consider exercising it. In this chapter, the term trust-power is used to mean a discretionary trust.

- Another problem is with the term 'mere power'. This expression is used in contradistinction to a trust-power (in the sense of a discretionary trust). It is, in other words, a power which the donee or fiduciary is not obliged to exercise. In this sense, the term 'mere power' embraces both fiduciary and non-fiduciary powers. By contrast, a 'bare power' (sometimes called a 'personal power') means a non-fiduciary power.

DIAGRAM ANSWER PLAN

Both a discretionary trust and a power give a person the right to benefit members of a class whom they choose, and are the same in this respect

↓

A discretionary trust imposes an obligation to select beneficiaries, whereas a power is merely an enabling provision

↓

It follows that trustees must exercise their discretion under a trust, and the court will intervene if they do not, whereas the court will not generally intervene to exercise a power

↓

The donee of a power is not obliged to exercise it, although he should consider its exercise if it is a fiduciary power

↓

The test for certainty of objects of powers established in *Re Gulbenkian* was adopted in *McPhail v Doulton* for discretionary trusts—can it be said of any given postulant that they are, or are not, within the class of objects?

↓

Although no individual potential beneficiary under a discretionary trust has any interest in the property, collectively they own the property and the rule in *Saunders v Vautier* applies

↓

Although the objects of a power generally have no rights, the courts have taken the view in some pension fund cases that, as the objects have given consideration, the courts should have a right to intervene to protect them

↓

A disposition which contains a gift over if there is no selection will be a power, as selection is clearly not intended to be obligatory

▼

In the absence of a gift over, the court must decide if the settlor's intention was to benefit the objects in any event (a discretionary trust) or merely to enable someone to benefit them if he so wished (a power)

(A) SUGGESTED ANSWER

[1] These introductory paragraphs set out the basic aspects of the issue.

At first sight a discretionary trust and a power may achieve the same purpose.[1] A disposition is made which is available for a group of people but the selection of the recipients and the size of their shares is left to the decision of a third party. The purpose of such a disposition is not to benefit each member of the group equally regardless of their need, but instead, a power of selection is given to a trusted third party. That person is to make the selection according to criteria fixed by the settlor or at their absolute discretion. If the settlor wished each member of the group to benefit in any event, then this would have been achieved by creating a fixed trust in equal or other shares.

The person making the selection may be obliged to use up all the property or income in making a selection, as in an exhaustive trust, or there may be power to accumulate income and make no selection as in a non-exhaustive trust.

However, the basic difference that a trust imposes an obligation to distribute, whereas a power is merely an enabling provision, results in important differences in the duties of trustees of a discretionary trust and the donees of a power, and the position of the beneficiaries under each.

Duty of Trustees under Discretionary Trusts[2]

[2] In order to keep a structure to the essay set out the points to be made under headings as here.

A trustee is under a duty to perform the trust. If the trust is discretionary, the trustees are obliged to consider and exercise their discretion. If they fail to exercise their discretion, the court can order them to do so. If the trust is exhaustive, they must make an appointment even though the decision as to the recipient and the size of the distribution is at the trustees' discretion. The court will intervene and make an appointment if the trustees fail to act, or if the trustees predecease the testator—the trust will not fail for want of a trustee. If no appointment is made the property will normally be divided equally between the beneficiaries on the basis that equality is equity, as in the case of *Burrough* v *Philcox* **(1840) 5 My & Cr 72**.

[3] The structure proposed is
straightforward. First explain the
point in relation to a trust and then
to a power.

Duty of Donee of a Power[3]

There is an initial distinction to be drawn between fiduciary powers
and bare powers. A fiduciary power is a power of appointment
granted to a trustee or to a person in a fiduciary position (*Re Mills*
[1930] 1 Ch 654). Because such persons are in a fiduciary position,
they cannot simply ignore the power. In *Re Hay's Settlement Trusts*
[1982] 1 WLR 202, it was held that the donee of a fiduciary power
must consider the exercise of the power and survey the potential
beneficiaries from time to time. The court may intervene if the trustee
exercises the power improperly.

However, even where there is a fiduciary power the donee is not
required to exercise it. In *Re Gestetner's Settlement* **[1953] Ch
672**, a power given to trustees to distribute amongst a huge and
fluctuating class consisting of employees of a number of companies,
was considered valid, even though it was impossible to consider all
the potential objects. The test for certainty of powers, as established
in *Re Gulbenkian's Settlement* **[1970] AC 508**, is, in fact, the same
for certainty of objects in a discretionary trust. This was held to be
the appropriate test for discretionary trusts in *McPhail* v *Doulton*
[1971] AC 424. The test is that it must be possible to say with certainty whether any given individual is or is not a member of the class.

A bare power does not impose on the donee any fiduciary duties.
A donee of a bare power may exercise the power at will. If the power
is not exercised, the court cannot compel the donee to exercise it or
even to consider its exercise. If the donee predeceases the testator,
then the power lapses. If no appointment is made under any power
(whether fiduciary or not), the property will pass to the person entitled in default of its exercise, so that, if the donor of the power has
not specified who is to take over in this event, the property may go
back to the settlor or to the testator's estate under a resulting trust.

Position of Beneficiaries under a Discretionary Trust

The beneficiaries under a fixed trust own the property in equity, and, if of
full age and sound mind, can call for the trust to be extinguished and the
property distributed (*Saunders* v *Vautier* **(1841) 10 LJ Ch 354**). Under
a discretionary trust, no individual beneficiary owns a particular part of
the trust property until an appointment has been made (*Gartside* v *IRC*
[1968] AC 553). However, as a group, all the potential beneficiaries own
the trust property and, as in a fixed trust, if adult and of sound mind, they
can collectively call for the trust to be brought to an end.

Position of Objects of a Power

The objects of a power have no interest in the property. They cannot
call for a distribution to be made. They only acquire an interest once

a distribution is made in their favour. They have no right to seek the intervention of the court if no appointment is made. If no appointment is made, therefore, unless there is a gift over, the property will revert on resulting trust to the settlor or the settlor's estate. The only occasion on which the objects of a bare power can apply to court is to restrain the exercise of a power which is outside the terms of the instrument granting it, as this would be tantamount to a fraud on the power. Objects of a fiduciary power may additionally prevent or have set aside an appointment which is made capriciously, or where improper considerations are taken into account (***Klug v Klug* [1918] 2 Ch 67**).

In some cases concerning pension funds, however, the courts have taken the view that, as the beneficiaries are not volunteers, a fiduciary obligation attaches to the power and the courts do have a *locus standi* to act, even in the case of a fiduciary power, where there is nobody else to act because, for example, the company with the power has gone into liquidation (***Mettoy Pension Trustees Ltd v Evans* [1990] 1 WLR 1587**). Moreover, it was said in *Imperial Group Pension Trust v Imperial Tobacco* **[1991] 1 WLR 589** that if the company with a power to appoint under a pension fund does so, then it must do so bona fide and not in breach of its fiduciary duties to its employees.

Construction of Document to Distinguish between Power and Discretionary Trust

As indicated in the question, it may be extremely difficult to decide whether a power or a discretionary trust has been created. The language of the gift in a well-drafted document should make it clear. Failing this, the court must decide whether the intention of the instrument is to impose an obligation to benefit the objects, or merely to enable them to be benefited.

An obligation cannot be deduced where the settlor provides a gift over in default of appointment. This implicitly acknowledges that no selection might be made and there is no power to force a selection. A power, therefore, has been created and not a discretionary trust (***Re Gestetner***). The reverse does not, unfortunately, always hold true. In ***Re Weekes' Settlement* [1897] 1 Ch 289**, it was held that there was no intention to create a trust for the objects of the power, even though there was no gift over, as the disposition did not impose any obligation. In ***Burrough v Philcox*,**[4] property was left by the testator to his two children for their lives. The survivor was given a power to leave the property in her will 'amongst my nephews and nieces or their children, either all to one of them, or to as many of them as my surviving child should think proper'. The court decided that this was effective to create a trust. As no selection was made, the court would intervene and make the gift in equal shares amongst the beneficiaries. Had the

[4] It is worth setting out the facts here as they help to illustrate the point clearly.

conclusion been that the gift was a mere power, then the court would have been powerless to intervene and the property would have resulted back to the settlor's estate. Lord Cottenham in **Burrough v Philcox** said that where there is a general intention in favour of a class with a particular intention to select particular individuals from that class then, if the selection fails, the class will benefit as a whole. The significant factor is an intention to benefit the objects of the gift if no selection is made.

[5] Usually an essay merits a concluding paragraph—as here.

So, the distinction is often hard to deduce in cases where the instrument is not clear. The distinction, nevertheless, is important in terms of the differing rights and duties of the trustees and donees and the potential objects of the trust or power.[5]

LOOKING FOR EXTRA MARKS?

■ Discussing what the judge said in the case (e.g. Lord Cottenham in **Burrough v Philcox**) will gain some extra marks. Reference to the arguments in the academic literature such as Gardner (1991) (see 'Taking Things Further') would also earn more marks.

TAKING THINGS FURTHER

■ Emery, C., 'The most hallowed principle—certainty of beneficiaries of trusts and powers of appointment' (1982) 98 LQR 551.
  This article breaks down the certainty of objects requirement into four different constituent parts.
■ Gardner, S., 'Fiduciary powers in toytown' (1991) 107 LQR 214.
  This article considers the distinction between discretionary trusts and powers.

Online Resources   www.oup.com/uk/qanda/

For extra essay and problem questions on this topic, as well as advice on revision and exam technique, please visit the online resources.

Charitable Trusts

6

 KEY DEBATES

Debate: should public benefit ever be assumed in a charity?

The **Charities Act 2006** (now 2011) changed the old law in stating that public benefit can never be assumed. This led to some litigation around the charitable status of public schools and the guidance given by the Charity Commission.

Debate: should 'poor-relation' charities be allowed?

This permitted connection in poverty cases is an exception to the rule that there must be a public benefit so no connection between the recipients of charity is allowed. There is some rationale in a number of the cases for this anomaly although not all the cases deal with it.

Geoffrey, who died earlier this year, left a will directing his executors and trustees to constitute his residuary estate a trust fund and to hold one-third thereof upon trust for each of the following purposes:

a To provide snooker tables and prizes for snooker tournaments for university students.

b To assist the vicar and churchwardens of St Peter's, Faversham, in parish work.

c To encourage the preservation of the world's rainforests.

Consider whether these dispositions are of a charitable nature.

CAUTION!

- Remember that you will need to know the previous law as well in order to understand how it has been affected by the changes introduced to public benefit by the **Charities Act 2006** (now **Charities Act 2011**).

- You are asked to advise as to the *charitable nature* of each disposition which means it is unnecessary to consider whether any of them might be otherwise valid (e.g. as a trust of imperfect obligation). This is a good example of the importance of reading the question. A different question might have demanded that you 'advise as to the validity' of the dispositions, in which case a discussion of other means of upholding them would have been appropriate.

- Do not waste time dealing with points which do not cause problems. There is no need, for instance, in part (b) of the present question, to write at length about whether the advancement of various esoteric beliefs might nevertheless be charitable.

- If you are permitted to take statutes into the examination, you will not gain many marks for merely reciting what they contain. Reference to recreational charities within the **Charities Act 2011** should refer to the relevant section and paragraphs, but quotations should be limited to the key words: e.g. in the answer to part (a) of the present question, to the issue of 'need'.

- The answer does not conclude definitely whether any of the dispositions are charitable—that is a mixed question of law and fact. As a law student you are expected to know the law; but you cannot be decisive about matters of construction. For this reason, it is best merely to indicate what you consider the more likely construction and state the law relevant to it. You might, however, go on to consider the consequences which would flow from any other reasonable constructions.

DIAGRAM ANSWER PLAN

Identify the issues	▦ Charity law
Relevant law	▦ **Charities Act 2011** and old law
Apply the law	▦ Part (a) • Advancement of amateur sport? • Means of furthering a charitable purpose? • Advancement of education? • Recreational charity? ▦ Part (b) • Advancement of religion? • Gift to office-holder, but super-added words • Wholly and exclusively charitable? ▦ Part (c) • Advancement of environmental protection? • But political purpose? • Political element merely ancillary?
Conclude	▦ Discuss whether gifts charitable

A SUGGESTED ANSWER

[1] This short introduction sets the scene.

To be charitable, each of the dispositions must promote a charitable purpose, it must contain a public benefit, and the purpose must be wholly and exclusively charitable. It is necessary to consider each disposition separately.[1]

Part (a)

[2] Each sub-section is self-contained and sets out the issue, the rule, and the conclusion.

Under the **Charities Act 2011**, to be charitable a purpose must both fall within the list of purposes that are set out, and also be for the public benefit: **s. 2(1)**.[2]

The list of purposes in **s. 3(1)** includes the advancement of amateur sport (para. (g)), thereby reversing the pre-Act decision in *Re Nottage* **[1895] 2 Ch 649, CA**.[3] The provision of equipment for sport can be regarded as promoting sport. However, the Act states that 'sport' means sports or games that promote health by involving

[3] An 'extra marks' point showing knowledge of previous law and effect of changes brought about by the **Charities Acts 2006** and **2011**.

physical or mental skill or exertion: **s. 2(3)(d)**. Snooker is a game, but whilst the playing of it involves both physical and mental skills, it is less clear that snooker promotes health. However, in *Hitchin Bridge Club* **(28 Feb 2011)**[4] the Charity Commission held the club charitable for the promotion of amateur sport because it was satisfied that bridge is a game involving high mental skill and there was evidence that playing bridge reduced dementia and mental illness in later life. Snooker might therefore qualify if similar evidence of health-giving effects can be adduced.

Alternatively, it might be argued that the purpose can be regarded as a means of furthering the education of the university students, the advancement of education being itself a purpose within the statutory list (**para. (b)**). In *Re Mariette* **[1915] 2 Ch 284**, for instance, the judge regarded the playing of sport as an integral part of the boys' education, and so held charitable a gift to provide squash courts and prizes for sport in the particular school. It is clear that this principle is not limited to sports but can extend to games. In *Re Dupree's Deed Trusts* **[1945] Ch 16**, a trust for an annual chess tournament in Portsmouth for boys and young men up to the age of 21 was held charitable, the court accepting expert evidence that chess was educational. In each of these cases it seems that the court was willing to treat the purpose of the trust as the advancement of education because it was limited to young persons. In *IRC v McMullen* **[1981] AC 1**, the House of Lords held that a trust to provide facilities for pupils at schools and universities to play football was charitable for the advancement of education, even though some university students are well above school age: the fact that the majority are young persons was apparently sufficient. It is, however, a matter of construction in each case whether the expressed purpose can be treated as a means of furthering a charitable purpose: *IRC v City of Glasgow Police Athletic Association* **[1953] AC 380**. In the *McMullen* case, the trust deed expressly stated that the facilities were a means of improving the students' minds. Since no such words are expressed here, the provision of snooker tables can fall within **para. (b)** only if the court is satisfied that the playing of snooker is a means of advancing the university students' education. This is not certain: snooker is not as intellectual a game as chess, and (unlike football or squash) it does not involve significant physical exercise.

To be charitable a purpose must also be for the public benefit: **Charities Act 2011, s. 2(1)(b)**, and it is not presumed that a purpose of a particular description is for the public benefit: **s. 4(2)**. Public benefit under the 2011 Act has the same meaning as it had in the law of charities before April 2008: **s. 4(3)**. University students are therefore a sufficient section of the community to benefit for the purposes of **paras (b)** and **(g)** within the list of statutory purposes.

[4] Decisions of the Charity Commission are useful to include (unless there is higher authority) and can be found on the webpages of the Commission.

This is not, however, the end of the matter. Under the **Charities Act 2011, s. 5** it is charitable to provide facilities for recreation or other leisure time occupation in the interests of social welfare. The requirement of social welfare is satisfied if the facilities are provided to improve the conditions of life for the persons for whom they are primarily intended, and either the persons have need of such facilities (for the reasons there specified, including youth) or the facilities are to be available to members of the public at large, or male, or female, members of the public at large. As university students are clearly not the public at large, the element of 'need' would have to be satisfied. Although the majority of the Court of Appeal in *IRC* v *McMullen* **[1979] 1 WLR 130** took the view that 'need' imported some element of deprivation, the House of Lords in *Guild* v *IRC* **[1992] 2 AC 310** held that this is not so, and that 'need' merely indicates that the facilities themselves are needed, as would be the case if there were evidence that they were in short supply. Assuming, therefore, that there is evidence of a need for snooker tables at universities, the specified purpose is likely to fall within **s. 5**. To be charitable under **s. 5**, the trust must also be for the public benefit (**s. 5(5)**), and (as has been discussed)[5] this requirement would be satisfied.

[5] No need to repeat the discussion—just refer back to it.

Part (b)

[6] Key issue and rule for this part.

[7] Now start applying it to the problem.

As office-holders, the vicar and churchwardens promote a charitable purpose, regarding the advancement of religion, which is a purpose listed in **s. 3(1) of the Charities Act 2011 (para. (c))**.[6] Therefore[7] a gift to these persons described as such, without more, would be regarded as a good charitable gift for the advancement of religion. The problem here, however, is that a purpose is specified: namely, parish work. This means that the persons specified hold the property for such a purpose, and the charitable status of the gift depends upon whether a trust for parish work is wholly and exclusively charitable. In *Re Simson* **[1946] Ch 299**, a gift to a vicar 'for his work in the parish' was held charitable; whereas in *Farley* v *Westminster Bank Ltd* **[1939] AC 430, HL**, a gift to a vicar 'for parish work' was not. The difference was that in *Farley* the parish work was not limited to work which fell within the charitable scope of the vicar's office. It could, for example, include a civic reception for a footballer. In *Derby Teaching Hospitals NHS Foundation Trust & Ors* v *Derby City Council & Ors* **[2019] EWHC 3436 (Ch)** similarly NHS Trusts were held not to be exclusively charitable. It is, in each case, a matter of construction; but, unless the court can put a different construction on the present gift from that of the House of Lords in *Farley*, it will fail as not being wholly and exclusively charitable.[8]

[8] This is a small caveat to show that each case is determined on fact and law (see note in 'Caution!').

Part (c)

The advancement of environmental protection or improvement is a purpose listed in **s. 3(1) of the Charities Act 2011 (para. (i))**. The public benefit means a benefit to the public in the United Kingdom; but scientific evidence has revealed the importance of the rainforests to the world's climate, and suggests that they contain as yet undiscovered species of plants which may assist in the development of cures for human diseases. The preservation of the animals in the forests may also tend to moral improvement of the human race: *Re Wedgwood* **[1915] 1 Ch 113.** Thus, subject to the possible qualification which follows, even though no rainforests are in the United Kingdom, this trust would appear to satisfy the public-benefit requirement of **s. 4 of the Charities Act 2011**, and, therefore, to be charitable.[9]

The qualification is that a trust will be denied charitable status if its purpose is considered to be political.[10] Although the High Court of Australia has held that in Australia political objects are not excluded from charitable purposes (*Aid/Watch Inc.* v *Commissioner of Taxation* **[2010] HCA 42**), such prohibition is well established in English law.[11] A trust which aims to change the law is political because the court has no means of judging whether a proposed change in the law is or is not for the benefit of the public in the United Kingdom: *McGovern* v *A-G* **[1982] Ch 321**; *Hanchett-Stamford* v *AG* **[2008] EWHC 330 (Ch)**. It is therefore impossible for the public-benefit test in **s. 4** to be satisfied by such a trust. In the *McGovern* case it was thought that there was a risk that the aims of the trust established by Amnesty International might prejudice this country's relations with countries overseas. An additional reason for the denial of charitable status to political trusts is that the Attorney General might be required to enforce trusts whose purposes are against the interests of the state: *Bowman* v *Secular Society Ltd* **[1917] AC 406**; *National Anti-Vivisection Society* v *IRC* **[1948] AC 31, HL**. It might therefore be argued that the purpose specified in the problem could be carried out by seeking to change the law of the United Kingdom or of other countries, and this would make it a political purpose and so vitiate charitable status. It is, perhaps, the word 'encourage' which causes anxiety on this point.

Nevertheless, given the scientific evidence mentioned, the court might well consider that any potential political element is merely ancillary to the charitable purpose: *IRC* v *Temperance Council* **(1926) 136 LT 27**. If this is the case, the trust will still be wholly and exclusively charitable. Charities are, after all, permitted a limited amount of political activity, provided there is a reasonable expectation that such activity will further their stated purposes. Since the late 1990s, the Charity Commission has taken an increasingly

[9] This is how you deal with the first part of the argument, i.e. the public-benefit discussion.

[10] This then takes up the next point: political purposes.

[11] An 'extra marks' point. If you know of the position in another jurisdiction then it is well worthwhile adding it in even though it may not be binding precedent.

relaxed attitude to the extent to which charities may engage in political activity: see its guidance, CC9 (March 2008). The borderline, indeed, between education and propaganda is sometimes narrow (see *Re Koeppler Will Trusts* **[1986] Ch 423**) and the courts will deny charitable status to political propaganda disguised as education (*Southwood* v *A-G* **[2000] 3 ITELR 94, CA**). The court might save the gift for charity if it can construe the encouragement as limited to means that are not political.

LOOKING FOR EXTRA MARKS?

- Don't hesitate to cite an authority from another jurisdiction where it is relevant even if not binding (see earlier comment).

QUESTION | 2

Gina, who died last year, by her will bequeathed:

a £100,000 in trust for such of her poor relations as her trustees should select; and

b £200,000 in trust to publish her (Gina's) typescript entitled 'Pagan Plenty'.

Expert evidence has indicated that Gina's typescript has no literary merit, that it is solely about advancing Pagan beliefs, and that it encourages Pagans to live separately, so far as practicable, from non-Pagans.

Advise Gina's executors whether these dispositions are in law charitable.

CAUTION!

- Although the first part of the question involves the relief of poverty and the second the advancement of religion, a common theme in both parts is the controversial impact of the public-benefit provisions introduced in the **Charities Act 2006** (and now contained in the **Charities Act 2011**). In order to answer each part, therefore, it is necessary to describe what the law was before these provisions took effect.

DIAGRAM ANSWER PLAN

Identify the issues	■ Charitable gifts
Relevant law	■ **Charities Act 2011** and old law

Apply the law	■ Part (a)
	  • Charitable status of poor-relations cases before **Charities Act 2006**; public-benefit requirement under **Charities Act 2006** (now **Charities Act 2011**); impact on poor-relations cases; conclusion (charitable)
	■ Part (b)
	  • Advancement of education: unlikely, since merits assessed; Advancement of religion: meaning of 'religion'; public benefit; Conclusion (Need more evidence of what Gina's writings propose)

Conclude	■ Advise Gina's executors

(A) SUGGESTED ANSWER

Part (a)

[1] A brief resumé of the origins of charity law works well to kick it all off.

[2] An early application of the law to the problem is excellent. It shows focus and understanding of the issues in the problem question.

The relief of poverty has long been recognised as a charitable purpose; it was mentioned in the **Preamble to the Statute of Elizabeth 1601**, and was the third of the four heads of charity described by Lord Macnaghen in **Pemsel's Case [1891] AC 531**.[1] Even a restriction (as in Gina's will)[2] in favour of a testator's poor relations as the trustees may select may be charitable. The charitable status of the 'poor-relations' cases has long been recognised (**Isaac v de Friez (1754) Amb 595**). The restriction of the persons to benefit to such a group looks like a restriction to a private class of persons—not normally recognised as a sufficient section of the community in charity law. The charitable status of the 'poor-relations' cases was particularly put in doubt when it was held in **Re Compton [1945] Ch 123, CA** and **Oppenheim v Tobacco Securities Trust Ltd [1951] AC 297, HL**, both concerning the advancement of education, that a group of persons, however numerous, can never be a section of the community in the law of charities if they are defined by reference to a personal relationship or nexus.

In *Re Compton* and *Oppenheim* (and *Re Scarisbrick* [1951] Ch 622) various explanations were offered for their exceptional status:[3] that such cases are anomalous and exceptions to the public-benefit requirement (in the sense of the section of the community to benefit), or that it is always for the public benefit to relieve the poor. In *Dingle v Turner* [1972] AC 601, a poor-employee case, it held that they remained charitable despite *Oppenheim*. However, the majority of their Lordships dissociated themselves from Lord Cross's view[4] in that case that tax consequences should be taken into account in determining charitable status, and it is not clear from *Dingle v Turner*[5] what the explanation for the exceptional status of the poor-relations cases is.

The **Charities Act 2011** states that a charitable purpose must satisfy two requirements (**s. 2(1)(a)** and **(b)**): first, it has to fall within a specified statutory list of 'descriptions of purposes' (which includes the relief of poverty: **s. 3(1)(a)**); and, secondly, it has to be for the public benefit. It appeared that, if the charitable status of the 'poor-relations' cases was based on their being an exception to the public-benefit requirement, such status would be lost; whereas if it was based on their providing an indirect benefit to the community, such status would be retained.

Following a reference by the Attorney General, the charitable status of the poor-relations cases, as well as those relating to poor employees and poor members of a club, was considered in *A-G v Charity Commission* (2012) 15 ITELR 521 (UT) (TCC). The Upper Tribunal considered these lines of cases to be anomalous, but nevertheless upheld their status as charities on the basis that they satisfied the requirement of 'public benefit' in the sense of the purpose itself being for the public benefit.

This is consistent with the earlier decision in *R (ISC) v Charity Commission* [2012] Ch 214, where public benefit in the first sense (the purpose itself) was distinguished from public benefit in the second sense (the community to benefit).

These decisions can be criticised on the ground that the 'descriptions of purposes' specified in the **Charities Act 2011, s. 3(1)**, are necessarily for the public benefit in the first sense, so that the additional requirement of public benefit in **s. 2(1)(b)** refers only to the class to benefit (Jeffrey Hackney, 'Charities and public benefit' (2008) 124 LQR 347; Mary Synge, 'Poverty: an essential element in charity after all?' (2011) 70 CLJ 649).[6] Even if this criticism of the Upper Tribunal in *A-G v Charity Commission* is sound, however, the poor-relations cases might still be charitable as being for the 'indirect benefit' of the public, as earlier cases have suggested. It might therefore be that the Upper Tribunal arrived at the correct result but for the wrong reason.

[3] Don't just state that they are exceptional—give some rationale as to why they are exceptions to the general rule.

[4] An 'extra marks' point—it shows you have read and understood the case including the dissenting opinion. You are showing the skills of a lawyer.

[5] If it is not clear then say so.

[6] Public benefit is a key topic so investing time in some in-depth reading for the exam can be profitable.

[7] Your conclusion appears correctly here at the end of part (a) rather than at the end of the whole answer.

It can be concluded that Gina's trust for her poor relations is charitable.[7]

Part (b)

As Gina's typescript has no literary merit, it is unlikely to be charitable for the advancement of education under the **Charities Act 2011, s. 3(1)(b)**, because under this category of charity the court will assess the merits of what is proposed: *Re Pinion* **[1965] Ch 85, CA**. It might, however, be argued that the purpose is for the advancement of religion under **s. 3(1)(c)**. Publication of religious writings can be for the advancement of religion: *Thornton v Howe* **(1862) 31 Beav 14** and *Re Watson* **[1973] 1 WLR 1472**.

In charity law, a religion can involve belief in one god (*Re South Place Ethical Society* **[1980] 1 WLR 1565**), in more than one god, or in no god at all: **Charities Act 2011, s. 3(2)(a)**. It must, however, still rank as a 'religion', which seems to involve more than a philosophical or ethical belief system and to require a belief in something transcendental. There are varieties of Pagan beliefs, so it would be necessary for Gina's typescript to be read to determine what beliefs it promotes. The Commission has also said that religion requires, as under the previous law (*Re South Place Ethical Society*), an element of 'worship'; so again this would need to be sought in the Pagan beliefs that Gina's typescript promotes. The purpose must not be immoral or adverse to the foundation of religion (*Thornton v Howe*) and must advance religion: *Re Hetherington* **[1990] Ch 1**.

The public-benefit requirement under the **Charities Act 2011, s. 4**, would also have to be satisfied. This means that the persons to benefit must be a sufficient section of the community. Gina's bequest might not satisfy this, as her typescript advocates that Pagans should live apart, where practicable, from non-Pagans. In *Gilmour v Coats* **[1949] AC 426**, a gift for the benefit of Carmelite nuns was held not charitable, because, as the nuns did not leave the convent, there was no public benefit. The House of Lords considered that the benefits to the public that the Catholic Church claimed—the value of intercessory prayer and spiritual edification —were not susceptible to judicial proof. But the public-benefit requirement is satisfied if masses for the soul of a deceased can be said in public (*Re Hetherington*), and even if the religious services are open only to members of the particular religion, the court recognises the indirect benefit to the public where the members mix with their fellow citizens in the world (*Neville Estates v Madden* **[1962] Ch 832** at p. 853).

Apart from this, there could be a problem with Gina's bequest because the Charity Commission does not accept, merely because a purpose satisfies the criterion of being for 'the advancement of religion', that it is itself necessarily for the public benefit. Pointing to the **Charities Act 2011, s. 4(2)**, the Commission claims that the subsection has reversed a previous presumption that the purposes listed in the first three heads of **Pemsel's Case**, including the advancement of religion, were for the public benefit. The Commission considers that the statute has thereby reversed the effect of **Thornton v Howe**, so that the Commission now requires evidence that the purpose will be carried out for the public benefit even if it falls within one of the 'descriptions of purposes' in **s. 3(1)**. Thus, the Charity Commission has said that, to be a religion for charity law, there has to be 'an identifiable positive beneficial, moral or ethical framework', and this was a reason for its declining to register the Gnostic Centre as a charity (**Gnostic Centre (2009)**, Charity Commission, paras 43–48); whereas it was satisfied that the Druid Network met this criterion: **Druid Network (2010)** (Charity Commission, paras 49–53). There is, however, no clear authority for the Commission's statement.

Nevertheless, the Upper Tribunal in **A-G v Charity Commission (2012) 15 ITELR 521**, considering the charitable status of poor-employee cases and the like, stated that there is no longer any presumption that any religion, even an established religion such as the Church of England, is for the public benefit. These dicta, which were made in a case which did not itself involve religion, could undermine equity's traditionally tolerant attitude to religion (**Thornton v Howe**), and seem open to challenge. It is also possible[8] that an attempt to assess the public benefit of different religions in order to determine charitable status could breach various articles of the **European Convention on Human Rights**, including **article 9** (freedom of religion).

More therefore needs to be known of Gina's writings to determine if they are charitable.

[8] This last point in the answer is an 'extra marks' point. It adds to the word length of this exam answer but has been included to give you a practical demonstration of what an examiner would reward with a very high mark indeed.

 LOOKING FOR EXTRA MARKS?

- This answer in its discussion on public benefit and the public school litigation achieves a very high mark—knowledge of the debate on this issue gets you there.

- The inclusion of a possible yet untested challenge (i.e. the reference in the last part to the **European Convention on Human Rights**) is an example of 'extra marks'. You would be doing fine without that section (it adds over 100 words to what would be a standard answer) but its inclusion in this context would guarantee you a first class mark for this answer.

a Consider how the cy-près doctrine has been extended by statute.

AND

b By his will made in 1975, Tommy gave his entire estate to his executors and trustees upon trust to use the same to build a hostel for the working people of Walkley. Tommy died last year. The value of his estate is insufficient to enable the hostel to be built. Tommy's next-of-kin are claiming his estate.

Discuss.

CAUTION!

- Note that part (a) asks you to consider, not to describe. If you have the statutes in the examination room with you, there should be no problem with mere description, and clearly some description of the scope of the provisions is needed. The examiners, however, will be looking for more than a recitation of the statutory provisions. Avoid copying out the statutory provisions—that will not achieve many marks and is not to be recommended.

- Part (b) demands that you consider the charitable status of the gift before going on to consider a possible application cy-près. Take each part in turn.

DIAGRAM ANSWER PLAN

Part (a)

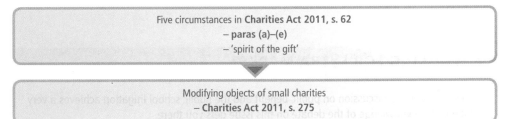

Five circumstances in **Charities Act 2011, s. 62**
– paras (a)–(e)
– 'spirit of the gift'

Modifying objects of small charities
– **Charities Act 2011, s. 275**

Part (b)

Identify the issues	■ Charitable gifts
Relevant law	■ **Charities Act 2011, s. 62**
Apply the law	■ Charitable purpose?—relief of poverty? Failure of purpose; cy-près scheme: **Charities Act 2011, s. 62**; failure *ab initio*: general charitable intention?
Conclude	Conclusion: will cy-près be applied?

SUGGESTED ANSWER

Part (a)

Section 62 of the Charities Act 2011 re-enacts a provision originally contained in the **Charities Act 1960** which extended the scope of the cy-près doctrine beyond cases of failure and surplus. The section specifies five circumstances in which the original purposes of a charitable gift can be altered. **Paragraphs 1(a)** and **(b)**[1] apply where the purposes have been fulfilled, or cannot be carried out, or where they provide a use for part only of the gift. **Paragraphs (e)(i)** and **(ii)** apply where the purposes have, since being laid down, been adequately provided for by other means, or have ceased to be charitable in law. This last provision might, for instance, be applicable if the courts were to hold the purposes of gun clubs (which can be charities under the principle in *Re Stephens* **(1892) 8 TLR 792**) no longer charitable. Essentially, however, these paragraphs merely put pre-existing cy-près circumstances onto a statutory basis.

Paragraph (c), however, was an important extension of the doctrine. It enables property to be applied cy-près where it, and other property applicable for similar purposes, can be more effectively used in conjunction and made applicable to common purposes. Before the **Charities Act 1960,**[2] in the absence of failure or a surplus, neither the court nor the Charity Commissioners had power to alter the purposes

[1] Avoid copying out the statute beyond what is necessary to explain and consider it.

[2] An 'extra marks' point showing your knowledge of how the statutes changed the old law.

of charities. Thus, whilst a scheme might facilitate the administration of several trusts for broadly similar charitable purposes, such scheme could not make any alteration to the specific purposes of each charitable trust: *Re Faraker* **[1912] 2 Ch 488**. This would now be possible.

Under **para. (d)**, cy-près is permissible where the original purposes were laid down by reference to an area which has since ceased to be a unit for some other purposes, or by reference to a class of persons or to an area which has since ceased to be suitable or practical. *Peggs* **v** *Lamb* **[1994] Ch 172** concerned a charitable trust for the freemen of Huntingdon, whose numbers had seriously declined. The court applied **para. (d)** in order to extend the class of persons who could benefit to everyone living in that borough.

Paragraph (e)(iii) applies where the original purposes have ceased 'in any other way' to provide a suitable and effective method of using the property. It was used in *Varsani* **v** *Jesani* **[1999] 2 Ch 219, CA**, where there was a split over doctrinal matters amongst adherents of a charitable trust which had been set up to promote the faith of a particular Hindu sect. The Court of Appeal directed that the property be applied cy-près between the majority and minority groups.

All the paragraphs except **(b)** require reference to 'the spirit of the gift'. In *Re Lepton's Charity* **[1972] Ch 276** it was stated that this means the basic intention underlying the gift. In that case the court used **paras (a)(ii)** and **(e)(iii)** to authorise an increase, to allow for inflation, in the stipend payable to a minister out of the income of an eighteenth-century charitable trust. **Paragraphs (c)**, **(d)**, and **(e) (iii)** also require consideration to be given to the social and economic circumstance at the time of the proposed alteration: **Charities Act 2011, s. 62(2)(b)** (originally inserted by the **Charities Act 2006**).[3] It should also be noted that **s. 62(3)** apparently preserves the need for a general charitable intention where that was required before the Act, i.e. in cases of initial failure only. A general charitable intention is not therefore needed in any other cy-près circumstances in **s. 62**.

Powers of trustees of small charities to modify their objects were first introduced in the Charities Act 1985 (since repealed) and were re-enacted and simplified in later Charities Acts.[4] **Section 275 of the Charities Act 2011** applies to an unincorporated charity if its gross income does not exceed £10,000, and if it does not hold any land held on trusts that state that it is to be used for the purposes of the charity: **s. 275(1)**. The trustees of such a charity may resolve to modify the trusts by replacing all or any of the charity's purposes with other charitable purposes: **s. 275(2)**, **(3)**. The trustees can do this only if it is expedient in the interests of the charity, and only, so far as reasonably practical, if the new purposes are similar to those

[3] Again an 'extra marks' point—as above.

[4] More extra marks. This is detailed knowledge. Don't worry if you think you wouldn't have included it. You will still score well without it.

replaced: **s. 275(4)**. The resolution must have at least a two-thirds majority, and the trustees must notify the Charity Commission, which can require public notice to be given and can request additional information or explanations: **s. 275(5)**, **(6)** and **s. 276**. Unless public notice is required or the Commission objects, the resolution takes effect after 60 days: **s. 277**.

Part (b)

The specified purpose, a hostel for the working people,[5] may be a charitable purpose within category **(a)** of the statutory list in **s. 3(1) of the Charities Act 2011**, namely the prevention or relief of poverty. Poverty is not confined to destitution but includes simply going short. The trust may still be charitable for the relief of poverty if a poverty requirement can be inferred from the instrument—as occurred in *Re Cottam* **[1955] 1 WLR 1299**—but not from extrinsic evidence alone: *Re Drummond* **[1914] 2 Ch 90**. In *Re Sanders' Will Trusts* **[1954] Ch 265**, a trust to provide dwellings for the working classes in Pembroke Dock was held not to be charitable: the judge did not consider the working classes were necessarily poor. By contrast, in *Re Niyazi's Will Trusts* **[1978] 1 WLR 910**, Megarry V-C held that a trust to build a working men's hostel in Cyprus was charitable: the case was near the borderline, but the two expressions together contained just enough indication that the purpose was to relieve poverty. On this basis, the present trust is likely to be held charitable.

If the trust is held to be charitable, the next issue is the insufficiency of the estate.[6] This ranks as a failure of the purpose, which is a cy-près circumstance within the **Charities Act 1993, s. 13**. Since the trust fails *ab initio*, however, the court must be satisfied that the testator had a general charitable intention, i.e. an intention to benefit a wider purpose than that specified: *Biscoe* v *Jackson* **(1887) 35 ChD 460**. The issue is whether the testator intended the avowed purpose to be merely a means of effecting a wider purpose: see *Re Wilson* **[1913] 1 Ch 314** and *Re Lysaght* **[1966] 1 Ch 191**. Whether a general charitable intention is present is ascertained by construing the words used in the context of the instrument as a whole and in the light of admissible extrinsic evidence: *Re Woodhams* **[1981] 1 WLR 493**. Generally, the more detailed the specified purpose, the more difficult it becomes to find the requisite intention: *Re Good's Will Trusts* **[1950] 2 All ER 653**. On the other hand, the fact that a gift is one of residue (or of the testator's entire estate) may indicate a general charitable intention, since no specified amount is provided: cf. *Re Goldschmidt* **[1957] 1 WLR 524**.

[5] Go straight into the application to the problem. You have only a small number of words (and time) to play with after the longish discussion in part (a).

[6] And here I start the second part of (b). You could use a sub-heading, e.g. 'the failure of purpose' or 'the application of cy-près'.

If a general charitable intention is found, the property will be applied cy-près; if not, it will pass to Tommy's next-of-kin.

LOOKING FOR EXTRA MARKS?

▪ Detailed knowledge of the Act gets you extra marks (as demonstrated in the suggested answer to part (a)).

QUESTION | 4

a By his will made in 1990, Boris, who died last month, gave one-third of his residuary estate to each of the following institutions: the Rotherham Rabbit Sanctuary; the Dronfield Donkey Home; and the Broomhill Animal Hospital.

The Rotherham Rabbit Sanctuary was an incorporated charity, which closed last week. In accordance with a provision in its constitution, its members have decided to apply its assets to another charity, the South Yorkshire Rabbit Fund. The Dronfield Donkey Home was an unincorporated charitable association which ceased to exist a year before Boris's death because of lack of funds. No institution called the Broomhill Animal Hospital has ever existed.

Advise Boris's executors how they should deal with Boris's residuary estate.

AND

b Earlier this year, the residents of the village of Eastwick decided to raise funds to build a cottage hospital. Money was raised for this purpose by means of street collections and the sale of raffle tickets. The appeal fund trustees also received a large number of cheques for various amounts. Unfortunately, the total sums raised proved insufficient to enable the hospital to be built.

Advise the trustees how they should deal with the funds raised.

CAUTION!

▪ Note that in part (a), you are told that the first two named institutions were charities. So, don't waste time discussing whether these institutions are charitable—there will be no marks for that.

DIAGRAM ANSWER PLAN

Identify the issues	■ Cy-près schemes

Relevant law	■ **Charities Act 2011, s 63** and relevant case law

Apply the law	(a) RRS: beneficial gift that vested at Boris's death DDH: trust for purposes of home: can purposes be carried out (scheme)? (b) failure *ab initio*? (general charitable intention?) (c) BAH: mere misdescription or failure? (d) if failure, cy-près only if: (e) charitable institution intended (f) general charitable, intention (since *ab initio*)

Conclude	■ Advise trustees

SUGGESTED ANSWER

Part (a)

Rotherham Rabbit Sanctuary[1]

[1] Separate the gifts to each institution either by sub-headings or clearly spaced paragraphs.

A gift to an incorporated charity, such as the Rotherham Rabbit Sanctuary, will be construed as a gift to the particular institution beneficially, unless (which does not appear to be the case here) the words of the will indicate otherwise:[2] *Re Vernon's Will Trusts* **[1972] Ch 300n**, applied *Re ARMS (Multiple Sclerosis Research) Ltd* **[1997] 1 WLR 877**. Therefore, as the Sanctuary was in existence at Boris's death, the gift to it would have vested on his death, and will be applied in the same way as its existing assets: *Re Slevin* **[1891] 2 Ch 230**. In *Re Slevin* itself, the court held that the legacy passed, with the charity's other assets, to the Crown, but this might be explained on the basis that the members of the charity had not made provision for the application of its assets to another similar charitable institution before its dissolution. In the problem, therefore, this share of Boris's residuary estate will pass to the Rotherham Rabbit Sanctuary.[3]

[2] This is an 'extra marks' point. Although it doesn't apply, it neatly combines a statement of law with an application to the problem thus showing knowledge and ability.

[3] Say where it will go.

Dronfield Donkey Home

As the Dronfield Donkey Home ceased to exist before Boris's death, it might appear that the gift would lapse, in the same way that a gift by will to an individual generally lapses if the legatee predeceases the testator. The Home was, however, an unincorporated charitable association, and it has been held that a gift to such an institution is treated as being made upon trust for its purposes: *Re Vernon's Will Trusts*. If, therefore, those purposes are still capable of being carried out, the gift will be applied to them. The failure of the particular institution, the Home, is regarded as a mere failure of the particular machinery by which those purposes were to be carried into effect, not a failure of the purposes themselves. A scheme will therefore be needed; but as the purposes are the same, this is not a cy-près scheme, so no general charitable intention need be sought.

If the purposes of the Dronfield Donkey Home can no longer be carried out after its closure, however, there will be a failure of the purposes of the gift. As the institution closed before Boris's death, the failure will be failure *ab initio*. This share of residue can therefore be applied cy-près only if a general charitable intention can be found on Boris's part. A general charitable intention means an intention to benefit charity in a broader way than merely benefiting the particular named institution: *Re Finger's Will Trusts* **[1972] Ch 286**. Where (as here) a specific institution has been named, the finding of a general charitable intention might be difficult (*Re Rymer* **[1895] 1 Ch 19**; *Re Spence* **[1979] Ch 483**); but it is not impossible (*Re Finger's Will Trusts*). It is a matter of construction of Boris's will whether a general charitable intention can be found. The fact that the gift is one of residue is slight evidence that a general charitable intention might be present: *Re Goldschmidt* **[1957] 1 WLR 524**; but contrast *Kings* v *Bultitude* **[2010] 13 ITELR 391**. The fact that a gift is one of several to charity in the same will might also suggest a general charitable intention (*Re Satterthwaite's Will Trusts* **[1966] 1 WLR 277**); but whether this principle can be applied here depends upon whether the gift to the Broomhill Animal Hospital is charitable. If no general charitable intention can be found, this second share of residue will go (in the absence of any gift over) on resulting trust for Boris's next-of-kin.[4]

Broomhill Animal Hospital

As no such institution by the name of the Broomhill Animal Hospital has ever existed, the court will first need to determine if Boris has merely misdescribed an existing institution which does exist: *Bunting* v *Marriott* **(1854) 19 Beav 163**. If he has, that share of residue will simply pass to that institution (regardless of whether it is a charity or not). In the absence of mere misdescription, the gift will fail *ab* *initio* unless it can be applied cy-près. The cy-près doctrine is, however, available only to charitable gifts, and it is unclear whether Boris had a charitable institution in mind, or a non-charitable institution, such as an anti-vivisection society. In **Re Jenkins's Will Trust [1966] Ch 249**, it was held that a gift to a non-existent anti-vivisection society was clearly not a charitable gift and so not applicable cy-près.

In the problem, however, the name of the legatee does not necessarily suggest a non-charitable body, and is consistent with a charitable institution. In **Re Satterthwaite's Will Trusts**, the court considered that the fact that the gift to a non-existent animal hospital was one of several made to charity in the will, indicated both that a charitable institution was intended and that the testator had a general charitable intention. In that case, therefore, the court applied the gift to the non-existent institution cy-près. If the court were able to take the same approach to the gift to the Broomhill Animal Hospital, it too would be applicable cy-près. It has also been pointed out that if a gift is made to a non-existent charitable institution, it is easier to find a general charitable intention than if the gift is made to an institution which formerly existed but has closed down: **Re Harwood [1936] Ch 285**. If the gift is found not to be to a charitable institution, or not to be made with a general charitable intention, this share of residue will pass (in the absence of a gift over) to Boris's next-of-kin.

Part (b)

The provision of a cottage hospital[5] is clearly a charitable purpose under **para. (d) of s. 3(1) of the Charities Act 2011**, namely the advancement of health.

The insufficiency of the funds raised means that the charitable purpose has failed *ab initio*.[6] In such circumstances, equity itself does not permit an application cy-près unless the donors had a general charitable intention. Donors putting money in collecting boxes, however, might be presumed to be giving for a specific purpose and not with a general charitable intention. Thus, in **Re Gillingham Bus Disaster Fund [1959] Ch 62** anonymous contributions to a non-charitable fund were ordered to be held for such contributors on a resulting trust.

To avoid a similar outcome with failed charitable collections, the **Charities Act 2011, s. 63** (which re-enacts with amendments provisions originally contained in the Charities Act 1960) provides that, in certain circumstances, funds given to charity are applicable cy-près, i.e. to other charitable purposes similar to those for which the funds were raised. **Section 63** can apply only where (*inter alia*) the property belongs to donors who gave for specific charitable purposes which fail. It has been argued that the section has little impact on anonymous contributions, since these never belong to the donors: Wilson

[1983] Conv 40. First, anonymous contributions may be treated as abandoned and so pass as *bona vacantia* to the Crown, which results in an application cy-près: see dicta in *Re Ulverston* **[1956] Ch 622**. Secondly, they may be treated as having been given out and out: see dicta of Denning LJ in *Re Hillier* **[1954] 1 WLR 700**. Out-and-out gifts might be considered to be made with the widest possible general charitable intention: see Sheridan and Delany, *The Cy-près Doctrine*, Sweet & Maxwell, 1959.[7]

[7] An erudite reference! But then, there aren't many texts just on cy-près.

If, however, **s. 63** applies, some donations made by cheque may be applicable cy-près under **s. 63(1)**: first, where, after prescribed advertisements and inquiries, a donor cannot be identified or found; and, secondly, where a donor has executed a disclaimer in the prescribed form: **s. 63(1)**. Some of the remaining donors by cheque may have given such small amounts that it would be unreasonable to incur expense in returning their money. This is dealt with by **s. 64(2)**, which enables the court or the Charity Commission to treat property as belonging to unidentifiable donors where it would be unreasonable either:

(i) having regard to the amounts likely to be returned to the donors, to incur the expense of returning it; or

(ii) having regard to the nature, circumstances, and amount of the gifts, and the lapse of time since they were made, for the donors to expect them to be returned.

A donor who cannot be identified, but whose donation is applied cy-près other than by virtue of **s. 64**, must claim within six months of the making of the scheme, and the charity trustees are permitted to deduct properly incurred expenses from any repayment: **s. 63(4), (5)**. This might enable the trustees to deal, for instance, with a large donation made by a donor who cannot be identified or found.

Under **s. 65**, special provision is made for the situation where a solicitation for funds was accompanied by a statement that the property given would, in the event of failure of purposes, be applicable cy-près as if given for charitable purposes generally, unless the donor made a declaration that he wished to be given the opportunity to request its return. If the donor made such a declaration at the time of making the gift, then, in the event of failure, the trustees must notify him and inquire whether he wishes it to be returned; and they must return it to him if he so requests within the prescribed period. If the trustees cannot find him, or if he does not request the return of the property, or if he did not make a declaration at the time he made the gift, then the property is applicable cy-près as if it belonged to a donor who had executed a disclaimer within **s. 64(1)**.

The street collections and the money raised by raffles will be dealt with by **s. 64(1)**. Thus the proceeds of cash collections made by means of collecting boxes and (*inter alia*) of any lottery (after allowing for prizes) are deemed (without advertisement or inquiry) to belong to unidentifiable donors. Such money will therefore be applicable cy-près.

LOOKING FOR EXTRA MARKS?

* You could consider including an analysis of the statutory predecessor to the **Charities Act 2011, s. 63**. A good source for this would be the valuable article by Wilson [1983] Conv 40. There is also a general discussion of the impact of the section in Luxton, *The Law of Charities*, Oxford University Press, 2001, at pp. 583–594. Note that other sources of fundraising which a question such as this might require you to deal with are membership subscriptions and deeds of covenant.

TAKING THINGS FURTHER

* Hackney, J., 'Charities and public benefit' (2008) 124 LQR 347.
  *An article that gives a broad discussion of the public-benefit agenda post **Charities Act 2006**.*

* Luxton, P. and Evans, N., 'Cogent and cohesive? Two Charity Commission decisions on the advancement of religion' [2011] Conv 144.
  This article discusses two key cases decided by the Charity Commission on the controversial area of charities for religious purposes.

* Luxton, P., 'Opening Pandora's box' (2012) 15 Charity Law & Practice Review 27 (comment on **ISC v Charity Commission (2011)**).
  A comment on the Independent Schools Case.

Online Resources

www.oup.com/uk/qanda/

For extra essay and problem questions on this topic, as well as advice on revision and exam technique, please visit the online resources.

cally to deny validity to them where they do not satisfy the requirements of charity law is harsh.

The debate is twofold:

a should the exceptions to the rule which have always been recognised continue and, indeed, be extended?

b and, is it right that the courts should continue to interpret purpose trusts more generously where possible to recognise 'indirect' objects and so validate them?

Cases such as *Re Lipinski* and *Re Recher* develop this point and Baughen (2010) and Luxton (2007) argue aspects of this debate. There is also the question of whether a statutory code could provide some resolution to this area of law. For this argument, see Pawloski (2019). (For both references see 'Taking Things Further'.)

Q   QUESTION | 1

Daniel, who died last month, made the following dispositions in his will which was executed on 1 January 2018:

a   £50,000 to the Seaview District Council for the erection and maintenance of a statue on the promenade in memory of my late wife.

b   £5,000 for the care of my cat Tortoiseshell and any kittens she may have.

c   £20,000 for the fostering of cordial relations and understanding between countries.

d   The residue of my estate to the Cranford Cricket Club for the purpose of building a new pavilion and changing rooms.

The Cranford Cricket Club is a non-charitable unincorporated association.

Advise Daniel's executors as to the validity of these dispositions.

!   CAUTION!

■   This is a typical problem question on this area of the law, where the examiner chooses from the cases examples of trusts which may or may not fail for certainty of objects or perpetuity. Although it is a fairly compact area of law, you need to know the cases on it and the reasoning applied in them to answer the question well.

■   Notice that you are asked to comment 'on the validity of each disposition'. So, you need to consider this broadly.

■   It is possible that such a question might also include a charitable disposition. For example, in part (a), if the disposition had been for the erection and maintenance of a shelter on the promenade, it might have been valid as a charitable disposition under the fourth head of charity (trusts for other purposes beneficial to the community). As you are asked to consider the validity of the disposition you have to consider this too.

○ **DIAGRAM ANSWER PLAN**

Identify the issues	◾ Non-charitable purpose trusts
Relevant law	◾ *Morice v Bishop of Durham, Re Endacott, Re Koeppler's Will Trusts, Re Lipinski's Will Trusts, Re Denley's Trust Deed* and related case law
Apply the law	◾ (a) This is a non-charitable purpose trust and therefore risks failing for certainty of objects and perpetuity. By virtue of **s. 18 of the Perpetuities and Accumulations Act 2009** does not apply to non-charitable purpose trusts ◾ (b) A trust for the care of individual animals is not charitable but is an anomalous exception to the rule as to certainty of objects ◾ It has not been limited to the perpetuity period however and so would be void. As kittens are included, it may not fall within such cases as *Re Haines* and *Re Dean*, where the judges appear to have taken judicial notice that the animal could not live for longer than 21 years ◾ (c) Unlikely to be charitable; no ascertainable objects and not limited to perpetuity period. Therefore fails as a non-charitable purpose trust (similar to *Re Astor*) ◾ (d) Although expressed as a purpose trust, it is possible to say that the members of the club are the indirect beneficiaries. It will not infringe the perpetuity rule if it can be construed as a gift to the members beneficially, which is how such a gift was construed in *Re Lipinski* ◾ But in *Re Barlow*, this type of disposition was construed as a series of conditional individual gifts to persons able to prove that they were old friends, and so was valid
Conclude	◾ Advise Daniel's executors

Ⓐ **SUGGESTED ANSWER**

(a) Statue

[1] Statement of the law with case to follow.

To be valid, a trust must comply with the requirement for certainty of objects, that is, there must be ascertainable persons able to enforce the trust.[1] In *Morice v Bishop of Durham* (1804) 9 Ves 399, 32 ER 656 a trust for 'such objects of benevolence and liberality as the Bishop of Durham in his own discretion shall most approve of' was held to be void. Grant MR said that such 'an uncontrollable power of disposition would be ownership and not trust'.

To be valid a trust must also comply with the rule against per-petual trusts, unless it is a charitable trust. This rule is not affected by the **Perpetuities and Accumulations Act 2009**. In any event, this Act does not apply to wills executed before the date (6 April 2010) on which the Act came into force (**s. 16(5A)(a), Perpetuities and Accumulations Act 1964**).

[2] Here comes the application of the law to the problem.

The gift in this clause is essentially a trust for a purpose[2] and there are no particular objects that are able to enforce it. It cannot be brought within any of the four heads of charity in *Pemsel's Case* **[1891] AC 531** and is therefore a non-charitable purpose trust. It is not dissimilar to the disposition in *Re Endacott* **[1960] Ch 232**, where a testator left his residuary estate to the North Tawton parish council 'for the purpose of providing some useful memorial to myself'. The gift could not take effect as an outright gift to the parish council as the purpose attached to it created a trust. It was not charitable, and was too wide and uncertain to fall within the anomalous cases 'when Homer has nodded' (per Harman LJ), namely, the maintenance of tombs. A valid trust within this category should probably have some funerary association and should not be excessive in amount (*Re Endacott*). £50,000 might well be regarded as excessive.

The courts have made a concession for such trusts for the main-tenance of tombs and monuments and of individual animals (such trusts having been described by Roxburgh J in *Re Astor's Settlement Trusts* **[1952] Ch 534** at p. 547 as 'concessions to human weakness or sentiment'), but only as regards lack of objects and not perpetuity, so that a trust for the erection and maintenance of a monument lim-ited to 21 years might be valid. The gift here is for the maintenance of the statue as well as its erection, and therefore will be void addition-ally as infringing the perpetuity rule.

[3] Your conclusion.

If the statue could be regarded as a monument[3] then a donation for its erection, but not its maintenance, might be valid under this exception to the general rule (*Mussett* v *Bingle* **(1876) WN 171**).

(b) Tortoiseshell and Kittens

[4] Identification of the issue and the statement of the law start here.

Although a trust for the care of animals generally (*Re Wedgwood* **[1915] 1 Ch 113**) and the care of cats in particular (*Re Moss* **[1949] 1 All ER 495**) can be a charitable trust, a trust for the care of indi-vidual animals is not.[4] Nevertheless, a trust for the care of individual animals can be valid as a private trust, this being another anomalous exception to the rule requiring certainty of objects. Again, however, any such trust must not infringe the rule against perpetuities.

Although there are cases such as *Re Haines*, *The Times*, **7 November 1952** and *Re Dean* **(1889) 41 ChD 552**, where the judges appear to have taken judicial notice of the fact that the particular animals concerned would be unlikely to live beyond the perpetuity period (a cat in *Re Haines* and horses and hounds in *Re Dean*), it would seem that such judicial indulgence is misguided. The rule against perpetual trusts,[5] which was expressly preserved by the **Perpetuities and Accumulations Act 1964, s. 15(4)** (and which is not affected by the **Perpetuities and Accumulations Act 2009**), must be applied at the time the trust is created and it must be possible to say at that time that the trust will not continue for longer than the perpetuity period, which in the present case is 21 years. Moreover, the rule against perpetuities has never recognised animal lives as lives in being for the purposes of calculating the perpetuity period (*Re Kelly* [1932] IR 255).

[5] In most courses nowadays the rule against perpetuities is mostly dealt with in the briefest detail—except when it comes to trusts of imperfect obligation as here. Then you find a testing question with a reference to future kittens and find yourself having to deal with it.

One must therefore conclude[6] that the disposition to Tortoiseshell and her kittens is void, although had it been limited to 21 years or 'for so long as the law allows' then it could have been valid for 21 years. It could also have been limited to the life or lives in being of a person or persons living plus 21 years as in *Re Howard*, *The Times*, **30 October 1908**, where the lifetime of the survivor of two specified servants was used from which to measure the perpetuity period for the maintenance of a parrot.

[6] Application and conclusion in this paragraph.

(c) Cordial Relations

This disposition would again be a purpose trust[7] without objects able to enforce it and would therefore fail unless it could be brought under one of the heads of charitable trusts. However, a disposition with laudable objects is not necessarily charitable and it is unlikely that this one would be. Although similar objects were held to be charitable within the head of education in *Re Koeppler's Will Trusts* [1986] Ch 423, the disposition there was to 'Wilton Hall', a recognised series of lectures which the testator had organised during his lifetime. This is much more vague however in its application.

[7] Here you can go quickly into the application as the broad statements of the law have already been made so they are implicit here.

In *Re Astor's Settlement Trusts*, a trust for (*inter alia*) the maintenance of good understanding between nations and the preservation of the independence and integrity of the newspapers was considered too vague and uncertain as to its application for the court to administer and was void.[8]

[8] There is really nothing more to be said in this part—so deal with it concisely.

(d) Cranford Cricket Club

A gift to a non-charitable unincorporated association may also fail for lack of certainty of objects and for perpetuity (note as at (a) that the rule against perpetual trusts is not affected by the **Perpetuities and Accumulations Act 2009**).[9]

[9] If you have already discussed the point then refer back to your discussion as here.

There have been cases where the courts have interpreted gifts to associations as being gifts to the current members beneficially as in *Re Clarke* **[1901] 2 Ch 110**, where a gift to the 'Corps. of Commissionaires' was held to be a valid gift to the members beneficially for the time being.

In *Re Lipinski's Will Trusts* **[1976] Ch 235** however, Oliver J followed the principle of *Re Denley's Trust Deed* **[1968] 1 Ch 373** by finding that although a trust for the erection of buildings for the Hull Judeans (Maccabi) Association was expressed as a purpose trust, it was in fact for the benefit of ascertainable individuals, namely, the members of the club, and he therefore held the trust to be valid. It was argued that because the testator had made the gift in memory of his late wife, this tended to a perpetuity and precluded the association members for the time being from enjoying the gift beneficially: this argument was rejected by Oliver J. Applying the principle of *Re Lipinski's Will Trusts* to this disposition therefore, it might well not fail for certainty of objects.

The further requirement of compliance with the rule against perpetuities must also be satisfied as regards a disposition to an unincorporated association. Gifts to members of an unincorporated association were considered in detail by Cross J in *Neville Estates Ltd* v *Madden* **[1962] Ch 832**. He identified two categories of gifts to unincorporated associations which would not infringe the perpetuity rule, namely, where the gift is to the members themselves as joint tenants beneficially, or to the members as members of the association, but there is nothing in the rules of the association to preclude the members from deciding, if they so choose, to divide the gift up between themselves. In both these cases the possibility of immediate division of the gift makes it inoffensive to the rule against perpetuities. Cross J's third category, however, is where there is some factor, such as the rules of the association (see *Re Grant's Will Trusts* **[1980] 1 WLR 360**), or the nature of the gift (see *Leahy* v *A-G (NSW)* **[1959] AC 457**), which precludes any immediate division of it between the members of the association for the time being. Such gifts will be void. This analysis by Cross J was adopted by Brightman J in *Re Recher* **[1972] 1 Ch 526** where he was prepared to accept as valid a gift to the members of an association on a contractual basis according to the terms of the association's rules, which did not preclude the members from dividing up the gift between themselves if they so decided. The decision in *Hanchett-Stamford* v *A-G* **[2008] EWHC 30 (Ch)** supports this approach.

Assuming that there is nothing in the rules of the Cranford Cricket Club which would preclude the members for the time being from dividing the gift between themselves if they decided to do so, the gift would not fail for perpetuity and could therefore be a valid trust.[10]

---

[10] This short paragraph contains your final conclusion on this part.

LOOKING FOR EXTRA MARKS?

■ To obtain good marks on such a question, you would have to demonstrate not merely a knowledge of any authorities which may be relevant to the precise terms of the gifts, but also a broader understanding of the underlying principles, for example a knowledge of the cases on monuments in part (a) and of Cross J's analysis of gifts to unincorporated associations in part (d).

QUESTION | 2

There can be no trust over the exercise of which this court will not assume control ... (Grant MR in *Morice* v *Bishop of Durham* (1804) **9 Ves 399, 32 ER 656**.) Keeton and Sheridan, *The Law of Trusts*, 10th edn, Professional Books Ltd, 1974, wrote: Modern cases regard (Grant MR) as saying that a trust must have definite human or corporate objects or be charitable. Construing his judgment in this sense has impeded the development of purpose trusts.

Critically examine the rationale for Grant MR's dictum and discuss the solutions which the courts have found to some of the problems raised by the rule.

CAUTION!

■ This is a fairly typical essay question on trusts of imperfect obligation which requires you to demonstrate an understanding of the rationale for such a rule. You should also be aware of the criticisms of the rule and the ways in which the courts have mitigated the harshness of it in some of the more recent cases.

DIAGRAM ANSWER PLAN

Every trust must have objects as otherwise there would be nobody able to enforce the trust obligation and the trust property would be left unfettered in the hands of the trustees

⬇

The courts must be able to control a trust and to administer it if necessary, but it would be impossible to do this if the objects were too wide or uncertain

⬇

Purpose trusts may also infringe the perpetuity rule unless they are expressly limited to the perpetuity period. The rule against perpetual trusts is not affected by the **Perpetuities and Accumulations Act 2009 (s. 18)**

⬇

Gifts to unincorporated associations present problems as to certainty of objects (the members are a fluctuating body which will also include future members) and perpetuity (no limited time for their existence)

▼

Gifts to unincorporated associations will be valid if they can be construed as gifts—beneficially to the members for the time being, or there is nothing in the rules of the association to prevent the members from deciding to treat them as such, or if the gift can be construed as one to be held by the members under a contract (*Re Recher*)

(A) SUGGESTED ANSWER

[1] The question asks for a critical examination so present a critical perspective. This version adopts a negative criticism. You could do the reverse but whatever your view is assert it and then explain it.

The effect of this dictum was to prevent the development of purpose trusts where they fell foul of the rules for certainty of objects or charity law.[1] This policy decision is not necessarily justifiable as there may be good reasons for permitting funds to be allocated for a purpose which may not be charitable. This dictum has caused considerable difficulties in creating trusts for groups of individuals formed loosely together in unincorporated associations where there is no good reason why their activities should not benefit from the munificence of a donor.

[2] Now set out the basic principle.

One of the three requirements for certainty for a trust is certainty of objects.[2] The reason expressed for this by Grant MR was that there must be a person or persons able to enforce the obligations of the trust against the trustees, as otherwise property would be left in their hands entirely without obligation attaching to it. This would abnegate the essential nature of a trust of division of legal and equitable ownership and would be equivalent to unfettered ownership.

[3] Then explain charities as exceptions.

[4] That naturally leads you to this next point.

Trusts for charitable purposes[3] are enforced by the Attorney General so that this problem does not arise. However, trusts for non-charitable purposes clearly do present a problem in this respect.[4]

A further objection to enforcing a non-charitable purpose trust is the difficulty of interpreting and applying the purpose. This was illustrated in *Re Astor's Settlement Trusts* [1952] Ch 534. The court must be able to control and administer a trust itself if necessary. Any uncertainty or ambiguity as to the purpose to be carried out will make this impossible and is a further reason for the invalidity of such trusts.

[5] Each paragraph takes a new point.

A further problem[5] with non-charitable purpose trusts is the unlimited scope of purposes which the courts might be called upon to recognise as valid. Although many non-charitable purpose trusts might be useful and beneficial to some persons, other such purported trusts may benefit nobody. The case of *Brown v Burdett* (1882) 21 ChD 667, where a house was left in trust to be shut up for 20 years, illustrates the undesirable purposes for which eccentric testators might create trusts. Such capricious trusts will not be recognised. However, any decision on the desirability or otherwise of any particular purpose necessarily involves a difficult value judgement. From a practical point of view, Roxburgh J said in *Re Astor's Settlement Trusts* 'it is not possible to contemplate with equanimity the creation of large funds devoted to non-charitable purposes which no court and no department of State can control, or in the case of maladministration, reform'.

Non-charitable purpose trusts must also comply with the perpetuity rule.[6] An application of this rule invalidates any non-charitable purpose trust which might subsist for more than a life or lives in being plus 21 years, or if no lives are specified, then for more than 21 years. This rule is not affected by the **Perpetuities and Accumulations Act 2009** which establishes a new perpetuity period for other trusts (other than those which are for charitable purposes). Purpose trusts infringe this rule if they provide for the tying up of capital for more than the permitted period. If all the capital can be spent at once, this problem does not arise: *Re Lipinski's Will Trusts* [1976] Ch 235.

Nevertheless,[7] it must be conceded that many purpose trusts may be valuable and for the law automatically to deny validity to them is harsh. There are certain exceptions to the rule therefore which have always been recognised, and more recently the courts have been prepared to interpret purpose trusts more generously where possible to recognise 'indirect' objects and so validate them.

The clearly recognised anomalous exceptions are trusts for the maintenance of tombs and monuments and of individual animals. All such trusts must, however, comply with the perpetuity rule.[8]

A gift to an unincorporated association may necessarily involve problems as to both certainty of objects and perpetuity, as the association is a fluctuating body of people which may include future members, and may have purposes which are perpetual. This problem was addressed by Cross J in *Neville Estates Ltd* v *Madden* [1962] Ch 832, who was able to find that a disposition to the members for the time being beneficially (either as joint tenants or tenants in common) is unobjectionable. They themselves are the object of the gift and so they may, if they wish, divide the gift between themselves at any time. Such a disposition is also unobjectionable as regards perpetuity.

A second possibility is that the gift is one to the members as members of the association, in which case they take beneficially, but subject to the contractual rules of the association. Provided that there is nothing in the rules to prevent the members from agreeing to change them if necessary in order to take the gift beneficially, then the gift will again be unobjectionable on grounds of certainty of objects or perpetuity. If, however, there is something in the nature or terms of the gift, or the rules of the association, which precludes the members from taking beneficially, then the gift will be for the purposes of the association and will offend the certainty of objects rule and possibly

[6] This paragraph deals with the perpetuity point.

[7] Nice word to start a paragraph which is setting out a counterpoising point to the previous one.

[8] Good to repeat this important point.

also the perpetuity rule. In *Re Grant's Will Trusts* **[1980] 1 WLR 260**[9] the rules of the local Chertsey and Walton Constituency Labour Party were subject to the rules of the National Labour Party and could not be altered by the local party. The members could not alter the rules to make the gift one which they had control over and it therefore failed.

In *Re Recher's Will Trusts* **[1972] Ch 526**, Brightman J found that a gift to an anti-vivisection society would have been valid as within Cross J's second category, although it might have surprised the testatrix to know that this was the legal position! (In this case, a gift to an amalgamated association which was incorporated after the testatrix's death was void, as it contemplated a different contractual situation from that subsisting at death.)

In *Re Denley's Trust Deed* **[1968] 1 Ch 373**, land was left on trust for use as a recreation ground for the employees of a company. Goff J upheld the trust as he was able to find that the employees were the *de facto* beneficiaries, even though the trust was expressed as a purpose trust, and so had *locus standi* to enforce the trust. This was followed in *Re Lipinski's Will Trusts* where a trust 'solely' for the erection and improvement of new buildings for the Hull Judeans (Maccabi) Association was held to be valid on two separate grounds, one of them being that the members of the association could be treated as the *de facto* objects of the trust. The other ground was on the contract-holding construction described in *Re Recher's Will Trusts*. Oliver J held in *Re Lipinski* that the expressed purpose of the gift being 'in memory of my late wife' did not imply an intention to create a permanent endowment but was merely a tribute to the testator's wife and therefore did not necessarily tend to a perpetuity. The decision in *Hanchett-Stamford* v *A-G* **[2008] EWHC 30 (Ch)** supports this approach.

[10] Give a view in this concluding paragraph to show that you have thought about these issues and are not just describing them.

Clearly legal recognition afforded only to trusts with objects able to enforce them is open to criticism on the grounds of harshness and inflexibility and creates difficulties with endowments for unincorporated associations. Whilst any general abrogation of the rule would be undesirable, the modifications made by the courts where there are discernible 'indirect' objects are to be welcomed.[10]

LOOKING FOR EXTRA MARKS?

- Some development of a critique going further than the resumé in the conclusion in the suggested answer would earn you more marks. For example, you could include discussion of Mark Pawlowski's (2019) proposal for a statutory code (see 'Taking Things Further') as well as reference to the other literature listed there.

TAKING THINGS FURTHER

- Baughen, S., 'Performing animals and the dissolution of unincorporated associations: the "contract-holding" theory vindicated' [2010] Conv 216.

- Brown, J., 'What are we to do with testamentary trusts of imperfect obligation?' [2007] Conv 148.

  This is a good article to get across this topic.

- Luxton, P., 'Gifts to clubs: contract-holding is trumps' [2007] Conv 274.

  These two articles cover the contract-holding theory for gifts for incorporated associations.

- Pawlowski, M., 'Private purpose trusts—a statutory scheme for validation' (2019) 25(4) Trusts & Trustees 391–396.

  This article discusses whether the UK should introduce legislation to validate non-charitable purpose trusts, as some offshore jurisdictions have already done.

Online Resources

www.oup.com/uk/qanda/

For extra essay and problem questions on this topic, as well as advice on revision and exam technique, please visit the online resources.

Implied and Resulting Trusts

8

ARE YOU READY?

In order to attempt the questions in this chapter you will need to have covered the following topics:

● Implied trusts
● Presumed and automatic resulting trusts
● Resulting trusts and the distinction with constructive trusts

 ## KEY DEBATES

Debate: the theoretical basis for resulting and implied trusts crops up frequently in case law as well as in academic journal articles.

There is a view that resulting trusts do not arise on the basis of unjust enrichment but instead reflect the presumed intention of the person transferring the property that they should have a beneficial interest in the property. But the debate in respect of an unjust enrichment basis for resulting trusts was developed by Professor Birks in his book, *An Introduction to the Law of Restitution*, and still is controversial. The US approach reflects this basis. Question 1 covers this debate.

Debate: the theoretical basis for the *Quistclose* trust is fatally flawed.

This debate continues to be fashionable and there is a wealth of academic articles on the subject. The issue is whether the resulting trust which protected unsecured creditors who had loaned money for a particular purpose which failed (in *Quistclose* to bail out a company by providing for a payment to cover the dividends on shares) fails to follow established principle. You might take the view that that is the point of equity—it does depart from time to time from established principle—but the topic does provide an opportunity for you to criticise academic writers on this. Question 2 provides on argument on this point. The reading material in 'Taking Things Further' underpins this debate and the question.

Distinguish a resulting trust from an implied trust and a constructive trust.

CAUTION!

■ This question reflects the academic discussion of the theoretical basis for resulting and implied trusts and compares them with constructive trusts so you will need to have knowledge of that debate. It is a highly theoretical area so it's great if you like getting your teeth into such debates. You do need to have thought hard about this debate before tackling it in an exam though.

DIAGRAM ANSWER PLAN

■ Resulting and implied trusts compared
- ambiguity in phrase 'resulting trust'
- distinction from implied trust
- automatic and presumed resulting trusts

▼

■ Comparing each with constructive trusts
- basis for imposition
- substantive institution or remedy
- common intention constructive trust

SUGGESTED ANSWER

[1] This is one way of introducing the question. It is helpful as in setting out the statutory reference it shows a linkage between the concepts. You could start though with the last phrase: 'Resulting, implied and constructive trusts are drawn from different methods of classification etc.'.

[2] This is a very academic debate so early reference to one of the leading thinkers is imperative.

[3] Here the two senses are set out making a good clear start to the discussion.

The Law of Property Act 1925, s. 53(2) excludes from the scope of **s. 53(1)** the creation or operation of 'resulting, implied or constructive trusts'. This might suggest that these are different examples within a single classification; but this is not so. These are, in fact, examples drawn from different methods of classification, and the terms are not therefore necessarily mutually exclusive.[1]

The term 'resulting trust', is ambiguous. As Professor Birks has indicated,[2] it appears to be used in two distinct senses: Birks, *An Introduction to the Law of Restitution*, pp. 57–64. First,[3] it is used merely descriptively, i.e. to denote a trust under which a transferor or settlor retains a beneficial interest. Birks calls such a trust 'resulting in pattern'. In this sense, a beneficial interest, retained by a settlor under even an express trust, can be described as resulting: e.g. where S transfers property to T in trust for B for life, remainder for S himself.

Secondly, the term is used to denote, additionally, that the settlor's interest under such a trust arises only by implication—which therefore makes it a particular species of implied (or presumed) trust. Birks calls such a trust 'resulting in origin'.

An implied trust[4] is a trust which arises from the presumed intention of the transferor. Thus if A transfers property into the name of B, who is in law a stranger, there is an equitable presumption (except in the case of land) that B holds the legal title in trust for A: *Re Vinogradoff* **[1935] WN 68**. The presumption (which can easily be rebutted by evidence of a contrary intention) is therefore one of resulting trust. Where an implied trust leaves the beneficial interest with the settlor, it is also (in both senses) a resulting trust.

Because of this closeness of identity, resulting trusts have sometimes been treated as synonymous with implied trusts. This, however, disregards the fact that some trusts classifiable as implied (e.g. those arising under mutual wills) are not resulting. It is equally wrong to treat resulting trusts solely as a sub-species of implied trust because, as Megarry J lucidly explained at first instance in *Re Vandervell's Trusts (No. 2)* **[1974] Ch 269**, not all resulting trusts are implied. Megarry J there distinguished between 'presumed resulting trusts', which arise from the implied intention of the transferor, and 'automatic resulting trusts',[5] which do not depend upon intentions or presumptions, but are an automatic consequence of the transferor's failure to dispose of what is vested in him. An automatic resulting trust therefore arises where, for instance, S transfers property to T upon trust for B for life, but does not state what is to happen to the property on B's death. In this instance, the resulting trust arises, not from S's implied intention, but merely from S's failure to dispose of the entire beneficial interest in the property transferred to T.

[5] Here comes the Megarry classification.

The distinction between the two types of resulting trust emerged in the litigation involving the Vandervell family. In *Vandervell v IRC* **[1967] 2 AC 291**, the House of Lords held that Mr Vandervell was liable to pay tax on dividends declared on shares which he had transferred to a charity. One reason was that he had failed to dispose of his interest under a resulting trust of an option to repurchase the shares. The retention of an interest under a resulting trust was probably the last thing Mr Vandervell intended, since it deprived the scheme of the very tax advantages which it was designed to secure. As Megarry J pointed out in *Re Vandervell's Trusts (No. 2)*, however, Mr Vandervell's interest under a resulting trust was automatic, and not based upon his presumed intention.

[6] This paragraph contains the differing views and sets out the cases accordingly.

A different view was taken in *Davis v Richards & Wallington Industries Ltd* **[1990] 1 WLR 1551**,[6] where Scott J inferred from the circumstances that the members of a pension scheme should not be taken to have intended to retain any interest in a surplus by way of resulting trust. Similarly, in *Westdeutsche Landesbank Girocentrale v Islington LBC* **[1996] AC 669**, at p. 708, Lord Browne-Wilkinson doubted that there was such a thing as an automatic resulting trust; in his view, all resulting trusts are based on intention. More recently, however, Lord Millett, giving the advice of the Privy Council in *Air Jamaica Ltd v Charlton* **[1999] 1 WLR 1399**, at p. 1412, whilst expressing the view that a resulting trust gives effect to intention, said that a resulting trust can arise even when the transferor positively wishes to part with the beneficial interest, and he expressed the view that, on this point, *Davis v Richards & Wallington Industries Ltd* was wrongly decided. Lord Millett's observations effectively support the automatic resulting trust, since, in the light of his comments, it is difficult to see how evidence of intention could ever rebut a resulting trust of this sort: see Harpum [2000] Conv 170, at p. 178. Rickett and Grantham[7] suggest that the resulting trust is a default mechanism which deals with the situation where there is uncertainty about the location of the beneficial interest. The Supreme Court decision in *Prest v Petrodel* **[2013] UKSC 34** deals with the question of the deduction of intention through inference.

It has been said that both resulting and constructive trusts arise by operation of law, although only the former give effect to intention: *Air Jamaica Ltd v Charlton*, at p. 1412 (Lord Millett). Indeed, a constructive trust frequently arises regardless of intention. In English law, a constructive trust is not founded on a single principle, but it might be broadly stated that it is a trust imposed by equity in specific circumstances to promote justice and good conscience. In some circumstances, these objectives might involve the imposition of a constructive trust in order to ensure that effect is given to the intention of a settlor (as under the rule in *Re Rose* **[1952] Ch 499**) or of parties to an agreement. Examples within the latter category are the trusts which arise under mutual wills, or the common intention constructive trust in relation to a family home (as illustrated in *Grant v Edwards* **[1986] Ch 638**). Since these sorts of constructive trust are based upon the intention of the parties, they might also be classified as implied trusts. Such constructive trusts are also closely akin to the doctrine of proprietary estoppel: *Yaxley v Gotts* **[2000] Ch 162, CA**.

A resulting trust is always a substantive trust, and therefore arises from the moment the defendant has the property in his hands. A constructive trust, by contrast, although generally treated as a substantive institution, does sometimes have remedial overtones[8] (as in the case

[7] See 'Looking for Extra Marks?' for the references to these writers. There is a doctrinal debate as to whether a resulting trust arises when there is an *absence* of intention to gift the beneficiary.

[8] This raises the issue of the constructive trust as a remedial (rather than a substantive) trust.

of the trust which arises under mutual wills). In the **Westdeutsche Landesbank** case, Lord Browne-Wilkinson opined that there might be merit in developing the concept of a remedial constructive trust in English law as part of the broader development of the law of restitution. The advantage of a remedial constructive trust (which is recognised in the USA) would be that it would arise only when imposed by the court instead of when the property was acquired by the defendant, and so would not interfere unjustly with the property rights of third parties.

An area in which the distinction between a resulting and a constructive trust has not always been made clear is in the determination of beneficial interests in a family home[9] where the parties have failed to specify what their interests should be. The original source of the confusion is to be found in dicta of Lord Diplock in **Gissing v Gissing [1971] AC 886, HL**. In various cases in the Court of Appeal, Lord Denning MR attempted to develop the concept of a new model constructive trust of a remedial nature. This approach was subsequently rejected in **Burns v Burns [1984] Ch 317, CA**, and in **Lloyds Bank plc v Rosset [1991] AC 107, HL**.

Some recent cases have, however, renewed the confusion between resulting and constructive trusts in relation to the family home. Under a resulting trust the size of the claimant's share is determined by the amount of his or her contribution: **Re Densham [1975] 1 WLR 1519**. By contrast, under a common intention constructive trust the size of the share depends upon the agreement of the parties. In **Midland Bank plc v Cooke [1995] 4 All ER 562**, however, the Court of Appeal held that a wife who had contributed less than 7 per cent of the purchase price was nevertheless entitled to a half share in the matrimonial home. The fact that she had contributed financially indicated that she was to have a beneficial interest; and the court inferred from the circumstances that the parties intended her to have an interest, even though there was no evidence that they had ever discussed this matter. Furthermore, in calculating the size of that interest, the court considered that it could have regard to the parties' overall conduct, whether such conduct related to the acquisition of a beneficial interest or not. The decision seems to revive the confusion between resulting and constructive trusts which it was thought that **Lloyds Bank plc v Rosset** had finally expunged. Similar criticisms can also be made of **Drake v Whipp [1996] 1 FLR 826, CA**.

[9] This is a big issue and very practical in terms of the case law. You could spend longer on this section and go into a deeper analysis of the cases. But be careful about that—is it how your lecturer taught this topic?

(+) LOOKING FOR EXTRA MARKS?

- There is a doctrinal debate as to whether a resulting trust arises when there is an *absence* of intention to gift the beneficiary (rather than a positive, albeit imputed, intention to create a trust). While this makes little practical difference, it entertains some academics so for extra marks read and discuss: C. E. F. Rickett and R. Grantham, 'Resulting trusts—the true nature of the failing trust cases' (2000) 116 LQR 15. M. Hsiao, 'A shift in the objective deduction of secondary fact in presumption' [2017] Conv 101 is a useful discussion of *Prest v Petrodel* and W. Swadling, 'Explaining resulting trust' (2008) 124 LQR 72–104, gives a comprehensive analysis of the resulting trust. There is some support for this view of resulting trusts to be found in the High Court decision of *McKenzie v McKenzie* [2003] **EWHC 601 (Ch)**. Otherwise, reference to P. Birks, *An Introduction to the Law of Restitution*, Oxford University Press, 1989, which places many different areas of law, including the law of trusts and the rules relating to tracing in a restitutionary framework, may be fruitful if your lecturer is keen on the restitution debate, as well as R. Chambers, *Resulting Trusts*, Oxford University Press, 1997. Check your lecturer's reading list for which particular parts of these works would be especially useful.

(Q) QUESTION | 2

Critically discuss the concept of a *Quistclose* trust.

(!) CAUTION!

- This question reflects the controversy over the *Quistclose* trust. You need to have read not only the cases carefully but also the academic literature (see 'Taking Things Further'). Many worthy academics have made their careers on the basis of this controversy and any critical reflection on the case needs to demonstrate knowledge and understanding of their arguments. So, the question requires a critical reflection of this literature. This suggested answer takes one view but you are fully entitled to take a different position. For instance, you may consider that the dual trust theory is correct or you may consider that *Quistclose* offends against the principles of insolvency law. If so, then you will gain a first class answer if you argue your case critically based on the literature. This question may well appear as coursework so suggestions are made in the commentary as to how you could develop it for that purpose.

DIAGRAM ANSWER PLAN

> Consider whether the *Quistclose* trust is so flawed that it cannot exist as a trust

> Discuss whether the *Quistclose* trust can exist as either a resulting or constructive trust.

> Argue that the basis of the *Quistclose* trust should be a constructive trust on the basis of unconscionability of unjust enrichment

A SUGGESTED ANSWER

[1] For coursework you could expand this introduction to discuss the extent to which this may be regarded as the most controversial development in trust law this century.

[2] In an exam it is vital to marshal your arguments carefully. Decide your headings in your plan and stick to them. They will help you structure your work. Headings are just as useful in coursework where a longer piece of work is required.

[3] This suggested answer takes one critical approach. There is no reason why you shouldn't consider that it is perfectly acceptable to deduce intention from the action. After all, several judges have said so and they (not the academics) make the law.

Barclays Bank **v** *Quistclose Investments Ltd* **[1970] AC 567** decided that money advanced as a loan for a specific purpose could be held on trust if that purpose was not fulfilled. The decision was revisited in *Twinsectra* **v** *Yardley* **[2002] 2 AC 164**.[1]

Is the *Quistclose* trust fatally flawed?[2]

In *Quistclose*, money had been loaned into a separate bank account for a specific purpose and it was held that the money would initially be held on a primary trust. A secondary trust would arise for the lender if the purpose of the loan had not been fulfilled before the insolvency. This 'dual trust' is the controversial element of this decision and presents considerable difficulties in terms of trust principles. Academic writers have sought to analyse this dual trust by assuming that the primary trust would take the form of a private express trust as, if it fails, then it results back to the lender under an automatic resulting trust.

One academic critic of this decision, Swadling, argues that the fundamental principle of certainty of intention is breached and that it is not correct to assume such an intention in relation to what is a loan arrangement. To do so, he argues, would be economically outrageous. This flaw is difficult to support and even proponents of the *Quistclose* trust, such as Chan, question it. On the other hand, further to the decision in *Re Kayford Ltd* approved by Scarman LJ in *Paul* **v** *Constance* **[1977] 1 WLR 527**, Megarry J deduces an intention to hold the money separately from the act of opening a separate bank account. Nevertheless, justifying this inference of intention is problematic and weakens the fundamental and well-established principles required to create a trust.[3]

More problematic is the failure of the *Quistclose* trust to comply with the requirement of certainty of objects. As Swadling argues, the beneficiary principle is essential to the law of private trusts. Deviation from the principle is only permitted in public charitable trusts (or those few aberrant private trusts which the judges maintain will never be extended). Hudson criticises *Quistclose* on the basis that there is a time gap between the collapse of the primary trust and the operation of the secondary trust during which the beneficial interest goes missing. As McCormack argues, the location of the beneficial interest must be identified at all times and Stevens argues that during this 'beneficial vacuum' the liquidator would have taken the loan money into the company assets as part of normal insolvency procedure. On the other hand, Deepa Parmar cites the 'Denley exception' as evidence that 'purpose trusts can be upheld as long as the purpose confers an indirect benefit on a class of human beneficiaries' and, interestingly, Lord Sumption in *Angove's Property Ltd* v *Bailey* **[2016]** **UKSC 47** described *Quistclose* trusts as 'special purpose trusts' (at paras 21 and 29).

By contrast, Millett and Smolyansky have offered other, albeit conflicting, interpretations justifying *Quistclose* trusts.[4] Millett, in his dissenting judgment in *Twinsectra* v *Yardley* **[2002] 2 AC 164**, adopts a single resulting trust theory arguing that the beneficial interest of the property is held throughout by the lender under a resulting trust. The money is subject to a power as to how it is to be used and, once used for the specified purpose, the trust is extinguished. Chambers argues in sympathy with this interpretation that a resulting trust takes effect at the start where the lender does not intend to benefit the recipient and Birks describes this as a presumed absence of intention. This analysis of the single resulting trust backed up by contractual rights for repayment where the purpose is carried out is endorsed in *Bellis* v *Callinor* **[2015] EWCA Civ 59**. Unfortunately, this approach was misused in *Re EVTR* **[1987] BCLC 646** where the purpose was carried out to buy equipment with the money. But then, when the company went into receivership, the supplier of the equipment retook it and repaid the money. The lender was allowed under the *Quistclose* approach to take the *supplier's* money back. *Re EVTR* is definitely a bridge too far in the application of the resulting trust.

Penner, however, opposes this interpretation emphasising the lack of beneficiary and criticising Millett's view that the use of the money is a mere power not amounting to a purpose trust[5] although Chan suggests that Millett's argument can be aligned with the argument for certainty of objects in discretionary trusts in *McPhail* v *Doulton* where the test for certainty of objects in powers was adopted. But Glister argues that Millett's classification of the *Quistclose* trust as a resulting trust does not conform with Megarry J's analysis of resulting trusts in *Re Vandervell's Trusts (No. 2)* **[1974] Ch 269** (as refined in *Westdeutsche Landesbank* v *Islington* **[1996] AC 669**). It cannot be a presumed resulting trust as the money is transferred as a loan

[4] Now introduce some other arguments which support the trust.

[5] If you examine Millett's dissenting judgment in *Twinsectra* you will see some contradictions in his description at one point of the power giving rise to fiduciary duties.

not a trust and it cannot be an automatic resulting trust as there is a lack of intention to create the trust. However, as Chan observes, there is room for development in the law relating to resulting trusts and no good reason why *Quistclose* trusts could not be added to Megarry's classification. But this is not the case as the law stands at the moment.

By contrast, Smolyansky argues for a constructive trust interpretation making the case that such a trust does not rest upon the intentions of the parties. He argues that it would be unconscionable for the loan money to go to unsecured creditors where the purpose failed. Chan, however, supported by Rickett, condemns this approach as taking too wide a view of the meaning and application of unconscionability and suggests that the development of this principle through case law would be unacceptable as creating confusion in the commercial world.

But this seems to be contrary to the whole development not just of constructive trusts but to trust law in general. It has been a gradual development and accretion of principle through the slow process of judicial authority. Why stop now? Not only does the *Quistclose* trust provide protection for lenders but it adds a useful commercial practice which can support companies in financial difficulties. If lenders were not so protected then they might be less willing to risk assets on a company in difficulty. *Romalpa* clauses[6] have been well understood by the commercial world for decades and it is not unreasonable to suppose that commerce will grasp the development of principle with the *Quistclose* trusts. Historically, equity has intervened to prevent unconscionable behaviour and it is argued that the court of equity should reflect the intention of the lenders in seeking to make a loan for a specified purpose through the medium of a constructive trust. There are too many breaches of fundamental principle in the use of the dual trust theory and its reliance on resulting trusts. The beneficiary principle and the requirement of certainty of intention to create a trust require a step too far in the interpretation of the *Quistclose* trust. But the same cannot be said for the constructive trusts. The *Quistclose* trust allows lenders to advance money on loan for a specific purpose which is to provide some succour for a company whether in straitened circumstances or otherwise. This is a straightforward commercial transaction which, as Chan argues, does not involve the complexity of finding security for that arrangement. If the purpose is made clear then no commercial uncertainty arises and no breach of the rules of insolvency arises.

[6] These are contractual and come from the decision in *Aluminium Industrie Vaassen BV v Romalpa Aluminium Ltd* [1976] 1 WLR 686.

Conclusion[7]

[7] A conclusion is useful at the end of an essay. Unlike a problem question where the advice is wrapped up in the discussion, an essay needs tying up at the end especially when there has been a whole lot of he says this but he says that . . .

The *Quistclose* trust is a classic example of the evolution of equity which is still producing offspring. What is lacking is a clear and arguable basis for its formulation which should be a constructive trust given the unconscionable nature of the outcome if the clearly stated nature of the commercial transaction is not recognised. In the absence of any reform, such as that advocated by the Law Commission in its 2003 consultation paper *Registration of Security Interests: Company Charges and Property other than Land*, unsecured creditors should not be able to receive an undeserved enrichment from what would amount to a windfall.

LOOKING FOR EXTRA MARKS?

■ Some further analysis of the Law Commission consultation paper *Registration of Security Interests: Company Charges and Property other than Land* (2003) would be useful. To tackle this question (especially if coursework) you need to have read *all* the literature listed in 'Taking Things Further'.

QUESTION | 3

Five years ago, Rook bought shares which he transferred into the name of his nephew, Pawn, then aged 17. Pawn, however, delivered the share certificate to Rook, and always paid the dividends he received in respect of the shares into Rook's own bank account.

Two years ago, Rook voluntarily, and without any expression of intention, conveyed his freehold land known as 'Castle' into Pawn's name.

Last year Rook handed Pawn a cheque in the sum of £5,000 which he had made out in Pawn's favour. At the same time Rook declared: 'This is to enable you to pay your creditors'. In fact Pawn's debts at the time amounted to only £3,000. Having paid off his creditors, Pawn gave the balance of £2,000 to his girlfriend, Queenie.

Rook died last month. In his will he gave all his property to Knight.

Advise Knight whether he has any claim to the shares, to 'Castle', or to the money received by Queenie.

CAUTION!

■ This question is clearly in three parts, each dealing with a different item of property, so you need to deal with each part in turn using separate headings. All three parts involve a discussion of resulting trusts, although the last part (involving the cheque to enable Pawn to pay his creditors) also requires a more wide-ranging discussion of other concepts. As all the issues turn on matters of construction and evidence, it is not possible to reach any definite conclusion upon the facts.

■ At the time of writing, s. 199 of the **Equality Act 2010**, which will abolish the presumption of advancement, had not been implemented but check before your exam.

DIAGRAM ANSWER PLAN

Identify the issues	▓ Resulting trusts

Relevant law	▓ Shares: presumption of resulting trust or advancement?
	▓ 'Castle': **LPA 1925, s. 60(3)**
	▓ Money received by Queenie: case law

Apply the law	▓ Shares: significance of Pawn's acts after the transfer
	▓ 'Castle': possible interpretations of **LPA 1925, s. 60(3)** and attitude of courts
	▓ Money received by Queenie: Trust for creditors? *Quistclose* resulting trust? Gift subject to equitable charge? Contract?
	▓ Conditional gift?

Conclude	▓ Advise Knight

A SUGGESTED ANSWER

[1] Very brief introduction to show what the key issue is.

[2] Use sub-headings even though the question is not set out in that way. It makes for clarity in your answer and shows clear thinking (a mark earner).

[3] The law.

[4] Note 'Caution!' point on future effect of the **Equality Act 2010**.

Introduction[1]

As the sole beneficiary under Rook's will, Knight will have a claim to these items of property if he can establish that Rook retained a beneficial interest in them by way of a resulting trust. I will deal with each item in turn.

The Shares[2]

In certain cases, where a person puts his property into the name of another, it is presumed (in the absence of evidence to the contrary) that he intended the legal title to carry with it the beneficial interest.[3] This is known as the presumption of advancement. It arises in three instances: transfers from husband to wife; transfers from a father to his legitimate child;[4] and transfers from a person *in loco parentis* to his quasi-child. Transfers which do not fall within these three categories are known as transfers to strangers. Here the presumption is reversed, i.e. there is a presumption of resulting trust. It is presumed that the transferor did not intend the legal title to carry with it the beneficial interest. These presumptions are weak and are easily rebutted by evidence of the transferor's intention. Even evidence of a close relationship between the parties may be sufficient: *Fowkes v Pascoe* **(1875) LR 10 Ch App 343**; contrast *Re Vinogradoff* **[1935] WN 68**.

There is nothing in the question[5] to indicate that, at the time he transferred the shares into the name of his nephew, Pawn, Rook stood *in loco parentis* to Pawn. In the absence of contrary evidence,[6] therefore, the presumption is that Pawn holds the shares on a resulting trust for Rook. It is necessary to consider the impact upon this presumption of Pawn's acts subsequent to the transfer. The payment of the dividends to Rook is somewhat equivocal: it could indicate that Pawn considers himself merely a trustee for Rook, who (under a resulting trust) would have the entire equitable interest under the trust and thus (*inter alia*) a right to the dividends received. On the other hand, the payment to Rook of the dividends could be characterised as merely a series of independent gifts to Rook, of property which is now Pawn's both at law and in equity: see the judgment of Lord Denning MR in *Re Vandervell's Trusts (No. 2)* **[1974] Ch 269, CA**.

Pawn's delivery of the share certificate to Rook per se is evidence of a resulting trust, since it effectively puts it out of Pawn's power to deal with the shares. Unless this can be explained on some other basis—that the certificate was returned, for instance, to Rook for safe-keeping[7]—it points away from Pawn having the beneficial interest in the shares. However, were Rook found to be *in loco parentis* to Pawn in 1993, the mere delivery to Rook of the share certificate might not be sufficient to rebut the presumption of advancement: see *Scawin v Scawin* **(1841) 1 Y & CCC 65**. Some additional evidence may be needed: in *Warren v Gurney* **[1944] 2 All ER 472, CA**, this was supplied by a contemporaneous declaration by the father that no gift was intended. In the present case, the additional factor may be the gift of the dividends. Such evidence is not as cogent, however, as that in *Re Gooch* **(1890) 62 LT 384**. There, a father bought shares in a company in the name of his son, but the latter always paid the dividends to his father and even handed him the share certificate. Additionally, it was shown that the shares were transferred to the son in order that he could qualify as a director of the company. The presumption of advancement was rebutted.

'Castle'

Although the normal presumption upon a transfer to a stranger is one of resulting trust, it was for many years uncertain whether this presumption applied to a voluntary transfer of land.[8] The uncertainty arose because the **Law of Property Act 1925, s. 60(3)**, states: 'In a voluntary conveyance a resulting trust for the grantor shall not be implied merely by reason that the property is not expressed to be conveyed for the use or benefit of the grantee.' **Section 60(3)** could be

---

[5] Application of law to problem.

[6] You have to say that because although there may well be such evidence in a real case, in the context of your exam question you are not going to have much information to go on.

[7] Again—you will have only a few facts on the question to play with so you could offer a possible alternative. But don't speculate too much about other possibilities. Stick with the facts as given.

[8] Statement of the law here.

interpreted to mean that in a voluntary conveyance of land there is always a presumption that the equitable interest passes to the grantee even if the conveyance does not state that it is for his use or benefit. Another interpretation, however, is that **s. 60(3)** is merely intended to ensure that, with the repeal of the Statute of Uses 1535, a beneficial interest can pass post-1925 if intended to pass even where the words 'use or benefit' are not contained in the conveyance. In *Hodgson* v *Marks* [1971] **Ch 892**, the court found evidence of the transferor's intention and therefore found it unnecessary to consider the effect of **s. 60(3)**, which Russell LJ considered to be debatable, as did Lord Browne-Wilkinson in *Tinsley* v *Milligan* [1994] **1 AC 340**.

The former interpretation was preferred at first instance in *Lohia* v *Lohia* [2001] **WTLR 101** (left open on appeal at [2001] **EWCA Civ 1691, CA**), and has since been accepted as the correct interpretation by the Court of Appeal: *Ali* v *Khan* (2002) **5 ITELR 232**. In neither of those cases, however, did the result ultimately depend on the interpretation of **s. 60(3)**. In *Lohia* v *Lohia*, any statutory presumption of resulting trust would in any event have been rebutted by evidence that the transferor intended to pass his beneficial interest. In *Ali* v *Khan*, where a father had transferred a house into the names of his daughters, it was held that there was a resulting trust. This decision was, however, based on evidence of the father's intention to retain his interest, such evidence being sufficient to rebut the presumption of advancement. *Prest* v *Petrodel Resources Ltd* [2013] **UKSC 34**, a case centred in matrimonial legislation (and subsequently followed in *M* v *M* [2013] **EWHC 2534 (Fam)**), is a decision where the Supreme Court decided that a resulting trust arose on the basis of the conduct of the parties from which they inferred evidence of intention and failed to refer to **s. 60(3)** at all. The dispute involved the application of the **Matrimonial Causes Act 1973** and the determination of what interests the husband had in various items of property and is possibly coloured by the testy nature of the divorce proceedings where the husband was described as 'obstructive'. But the apparent failure to deal with **s. 60(3)** is not helpful in clarifying the interpretation of the sub-section.

In the light of these decisions, therefore, it appears that a resulting trust is not presumed *merely* because the conveyance is voluntary. This interpretation of **s. 60(3)** does not, however, rule out the possibility that a resulting trust might be inferred from *other* circumstances as is evidenced by the Supreme Court decision in *Prest* v *Petrodel*. A relevant circumstance might be the relationship between the parties, so that, where the voluntary transferee is in law a stranger to the transferor, that fact alone might be sufficient for the court to infer a resulting trust: see Chambers, *Resulting Trusts*, Oxford University

[9] This conclusion sums up the options as you cannot come to a firm view because of lack of information in the question (which is perfectly normal).

Press, 1997, at pp. 18–19. On this basis, in the absence of direct evidence of Rook's intention, the court might infer a resulting trust if Pawn was a stranger to him, but infer an intention that the beneficial interest should pass if Rook was *in loco parentis* to Pawn (i.e. the presumption of advancement).[9]

Money Received by Queenie

In order to determine whether Knight has a claim to the surplus, it is necessary to construe Rook's intention when he handed Pawn the cheque.

[10] There is going to follow a listing of points. You could even number them if you prefer. But it helps you tick off the points (and helps your examiner see clearly that you have them all).

First,[10] if certainty of intention can be found,[11] his words might be interpreted as creating a trust in favour of Pawn's creditors, so that the creditors became beneficiaries (and thereby acquired proprietary rights in equity) from the outset. If this is so, the normal principle is that once the trust has been performed, the surplus is held on a resulting trust for the settlor—in this case, Rook. Other outcomes are, however, possible, depending upon a construction of Rook's intention. Thus, it might be found that he intended that, once the trust had been performed, any surplus should belong to the trustee (Pawn) beneficially: *Re Foord* **[1922] 2 Ch 519**. This might be presumed if Rook stands *in loco parentis* to Pawn. Yet again, it might be found, as in *Smith* v *Cooke* **[1891] AC 297**, that Rook intended that the beneficiaries (in this case the creditors) should take any surplus.

[11] A cross-over here from certainties—be ready for this and don't assume that, if this is not a 'certainty' question, you may not have to deal with them.

[12] Another point of law here followed by several more which are all numbered.

Secondly,[12] the transaction might be treated as giving rise to what has become known as a '*Quistclose* trust': *Barclays Bank Ltd* v *Quistclose Investments Ltd* **[1970] AC 567**. Applying the analysis of such a trust suggested by Lord Millett in *Twinsectra Ltd* v *Yardley* **[2002] 2 AC 164**, the beneficial interest in the £5,000 would have remained with Rook under a resulting trust, subject to Pawn's having a mandate to apply it in payment of his creditors. Such payment would have reduced Rook's beneficial interest under the resulting trust to an interest in the remaining £2,000.

Thirdly, Rook's words could be held to indicate a gift of the money subject to an equitable charge in favour of the creditors. Upon this construction, it is presumed that the recipient of the fund (in this case Pawn) takes the beneficial interest in it subject only to the payment of the creditors.

Fourthly, the matter could be construed as a contract, whereby Rook pays Pawn £5,000 in consideration for Pawn paying off his own creditors. On this basis, Pawn has performed his part of the agreement. Strictly, there is no surplus because no debts are charged upon the £5,000, but, in effect, the remaining £2,000 is Pawn's own.

Fifthly, it might be possible to treat Rook as making Pawn a conditional gift of £5,000, i.e. a gift subject to a condition that Pawn pays his own creditors.

[13] Notice that in each of the above points the application of the law to the problem incorporates the conclusion. So don't try to put one in here.

In each of these last three constructions, neither Rook nor Knight, as the beneficiary under Rook's will, has any claim to the money paid to Queenie. Knight will therefore have a claim to trace the money into the hands of Queenie only if the first or second construction is adopted, with a resulting trust of the surplus.[13]

LOOKING FOR EXTRA MARKS?

- You will see that there is reference to obiter dicta in some of the cases—this gets you extra marks. Critical discussion of the rationale for presumed resulting trusts and reference to Hsiao [2017] Conv 101 and Swadling 'Explaining resulting trust' (2008) 124 LQR 72–104 would be another extra mark point—although time and space in a problem question limits the opportunity for exploring their views in greater detail than a passing reference.

QUESTION | 4

Three years ago, a bowling club was set up in Plymouth as an unincorporated non-charitable association. Under the rules of the club, members were required to pay an annual subscription of £20, which entitled them to play bowls at the club throughout the year, to use its tea room and other facilities, and to be considered for inclusion in the team for matches with other clubs. Non-members could also play bowls at the club, subject to the payment of £2 per game. Additional funds to support the club were raised through street collections in Plymouth.

The opening of a massive new sports complex in Plymouth has caused interest in the bowling club to decline, and the club's committee has now decided to disband the club. At present, some £20,000 remains in the club's 'Common Fund', into which all payments and donations had been placed.

Advise the club's committee how they should deal with this fund.

CAUTION!

- This is the sort of question frequently found in examinations. Sometimes it will involve a members' club, sometimes more outward-looking types of association. Make sure you deal with the allocation of each part of the fund. Note that the question-setters have been kind, and have expressly told you that the club is a non-charitable unincorporated association. Do not look this gift horse in the mouth.

DIAGRAM ANSWER PLAN

Identify the issues	■ The legal issues are: resulting trust and the approach to the surplus funds
Relevant law	■ Case law such as *Re Hobourn Air Raid Distress Fund*, *Clayton's Case*, *Cunnack v Edwards*, *Re West Sussex Constabulary's Widows, Children and Benevolent (1930) Fund Trusts*, *Re Recher's Will Trusts*
Apply the law	■ Resulting trust for identifiable contributors? not appropriate for unidentifiable donors ■ *Bona vacantia*? (members' subscriptions and non-member payments) ■ Contrast contract-holding approach (everything belongs to present members) ■ Contrast out-and-out gift
Conclude	■ Advise the club's committee

A   SUGGESTED ANSWER

[1] Brief introduction to establish the key issue.

[2] You could give a heading as in the diagram answer plan but this paragraph opener also does the trick of establishing the first key point.

A number of different legal approaches have been applied to resolve the issue of entitlement to the surplus funds of an unincorporated association upon its dissolution.[1]

One approach is to treat the contributors to the fund as entitled to the surplus by way of a resulting trust.[2] Such a trust arises because the court will presume, in the absence of an expression of intention on the part of the contributors, that they did not intend to part with their contributions out and out. This principle was applied in *Re Hobourn Air Raid Distress Fund* **[1946] Ch 194**, where factory employees raised a fund to provide for those amongst them who suffered in air raids. The Court of Appeal held that the surplus was held on a resulting trust for the contributors in proportion to the amount each had paid in.

This approach can cause administrative problems, however, where there are many contributors and where the fund has existed for a long time. In such circumstances, two alternative outcomes are possible without abandoning the concept of the resulting trust.

First, it might be presumed that each contributor initially retained an interest in his contribution under a resulting trust until his contribution is spent. On this basis, withdrawals from the fund could be treated as being made according to the rule in *Clayton's Case* (1816) **1 Mer 572**, i.e. first in, first out. This would clearly favour later contributors over earlier ones. No reported decision, however, has applied *Clayton's Case* in this context.

Secondly, in *Re Printers* [1899] **2 Ch 184**, upon dissolution of a trade union, the surplus of the funds (which had been raised by weekly contributions from members) was held by way of resulting trust for existing members only, rateably according to their contributions. As was pointed out in *Re St Andrews Allotment Association* [1969] **1 WLR 229**, however, it is difficult to see how the existing members could take by way of resulting trust a surplus partly derived from the contributions of past members.

An alternative approach[3] is to treat the matter, not as one of trust, but as one of contract. Thus in *Cunnack v Edwards* [1896] **2 Ch 679**, a surplus remained in a friendly society's funds after the death of the last widow annuitant. The Court of Appeal held that the members had contributed on the basis of contract, i.e. each payment was made in consideration for the payment of an annuity to the subscriber's widow. Each member had therefore enjoyed their full contractual entitlement from the fund. Thus the surplus went *bona vacantia* to the Crown. This contractual approach was also used in *Re West Sussex Constabulary's Widows, Children and Benevolent* (1930) **Fund Trusts** [1971] **Ch 1**, to deal with parts of the surplus remaining on the dissolution of a police benevolent fund. Goff J held that members' contributions, together with funds raised by way of entertainments and raffles, had all been given on a contractual basis, and should therefore go *bona vacantia* to the Crown. There, in contrast to *Re Gillingham Bus Disaster Fund* [1958] **Ch 300**, the judge said that anonymous contributors must be taken to have given out and out, so that this part of the surplus also went to the Crown. That part which represented the contributions of identifiable donors, however, was held for such donors on a resulting trust. However, this principle regarding the disposition of surplus in *Re West Sussex* was rejected in *Hanchett-Stamford v AG* [2008] **EWHC 330 (Ch)** where it was held that where there was one remaining member of the unincorporated association the contract inevitably came to an end and the property was then held absolutely by that survivor.

A different line of reasoning,[4] however, emerges from a more recent line of authorities. Thus in *Re Recher's Will Trusts* [1972] **Ch 526**, Brightman J considered that the property of an unincorporated association was held for the members beneficially for the time being subject to the contract which exists between them, i.e. the association's rules. On this basis, unless the rules provide otherwise, the

[3] Here is the second analytical approach to the problem (see 'Diagram Answer Plan').

[4] Here is the third approach.

assets are held for the members at the date of dissolution equally, not on any principle of resulting trust, but simply because it is their property.

[5] There are problems so here is where you set them out.

Problems with the contract-holding approach[5] remain to be addressed: how, for instance, interests can be acquired and lost by new and old members respectively without written assignments complying with the **Law of Property Act 1925, s. 53(1)(c)**. Nevertheless, for the time being at least, this approach has found favour with the courts, e.g. in *Re Sick and Funeral Society of St John's Sunday School, Golcar* [1973] Ch 51, *Re GKN Bolts Nuts Ltd (Automotive Division) Birmingham Works Sports and Social Club* [1982] 1 WLR 774, *Re Horley Town Football Club* [2006] EWHC 2386 (Ch), and it could also explain *Re St Andrews Allotment Association*. The contract-holding approach was applied to a friendly society in *Re Bucks Constabulary Friendly Society (No. 2)* [1979] 1 WLR 936. Walton J considered that the judge in *Re West Sussex* was wrong to rely on *Cunnack v Edwards*. In Walton J's view, *Cunnack v Edwards* turned on the friendly society statutes then in force which forbade distribution of surplus to the members. *Hanchett-Stamford v AG* [2008] EWHC 330 (Ch) confirms this point and it seems clear now that a surplus under the contract-holding approach will go to the members.

In the context of outward-looking associations and those which benefit members' widows and orphans, the authorities remain in some disarray. Furthermore, pension funds may be a special case, where contractual principles are not necessarily incompatible with a resulting trust: *Davis v Richards & Wallington Industries Ltd* [1990] 1 WLR 1511. In the context of members' clubs, however, such as the bowling club in the problem, where the benefits are confined to the members alone, there is now a fair body of opinion favouring the contract-holding approach of *Re Recher*. Thus, subject to a contrary indication in the bowling club's rules, that part of the surplus representing members' subscriptions belongs to the members at the date of dissolution.

The members' club cases, however, have not substantially had to deal with outside contributions. Assuming the criticisms of *Re West Sussex* made in *Re Bucks* and confirmed in *Hanchett-Stamford v AG* are sound, the receipts from non-members for use of the green are paid under a contract and therefore form part of the general assets of the club. The contributions from street collections will probably be treated as absolute gifts, whether or not for the reasons stated in *Re West Sussex*. Greater difficulties might arise in the case of donations from identifiable donors. Dicta in *Re Bucks* suggest that even these would belong to the present members.

[6] This is as strong a conclusion as you can get really.

In conclusion then, in the absence of anything to the contrary in the club's rules, it is probable that the whole 'Common Fund' belongs equally to those who were members at the date of dissolution.[6]

LOOKING FOR EXTRA MARKS?

- For extra marks (or additional discussion in essays), you will find valuable analyses by Rickett (1980) 39 CLJ 88, and by Green (1980) 43 MLR 626 which could usefully be incorporated.

TAKING THINGS FURTHER

- Birks, P., 'Restitution, resulting trusts in equity: contemporary legal developments', Hebrew University of Jerusalem, 1992.

  This article provides an analysis of the unjust enrichment theory.

- Chambers, R., 'Is There a Presumption of Resulting Trust?', in *Constructive and Resulting Trusts* (Mitchell, ed.), Hart Publishing, 2010.

  This chapter gives a broad discussion of the way in which resulting trusts are presumed.

  This list of references comprises essential reading for the thorny area of **Quistclose** *trusts:*

- Chambers, R., *Resulting Trusts*, Clarendon Press, 1997.
- Chan, B. D., 'The enigma of the *Quistclose* trust' (2013) 2 UCL Journal of Law and Jurisprudence 1.
- Glister, J., 'Review of "The *Quistclose* Trust: Critical Essays" by William Swadling' (2004) 67 MLR 1032.
- McCormack, G., 'Conditional payments and insolvency—the *Quistclose* trust' (1994) 9 Denning Law Journal 93.
- Parmar, D., 'The uncertainty surrounding the *Quistclose* trust—Part One' (2012) 9(2) International Corporate Rescue.
- Penner, J., 'Lord Millett's Analysis', in *Quistclose Trust: Critical Essays* (W. Swadling, ed.), Oxford University Press, 2004.
- Rickett, C., 'Unconscionability and commercial law' (2005) 24(1) University of Queensland Law Journal 73.
- Smolyansky, M., 'Reining in the *Quistclose* trust: a response to *Twinsectra* v *Yardley*' (2010) 16(7) Trusts & Trustees 558.
- Stevens, R., 'Insolvency' in *Quistclose Trust: Critical Essays* (W. Swadling, ed.), Oxford University Press, 2004.
- Swadling, W, 'Orthodoxy' in *Quistclose Trust: Critical Essays* (W. Swadling, ed.), Oxford University Press, 2004.

Online Resources   www.oup.com/uk/qanda/

For extra essay and problem questions on this topic, as well as advice on revision and exam technique, please visit the online resources.

Constructive Trusts

9

ARE YOU READY?

In order to attempt the questions in this chapter you will need to have covered the following topics:

- Definition of constructive trust
- Substantive and remedial constructive trusts
- Accessory and recipient liability
- Fully-secret and half-secret trusts
- Mutual wills

KEY DEBATES

Debate: liability of agents and other third parties who assist in a breach of trust or who receive trust property in breach of trust.

The issue of dishonesty in cases of 'knowing' or 'dishonest' assistance in a breach of trust keeps cropping up and case after case keeps trying to resolve the matter. *Twinsectra Ltd* v *Yardley* [2002] 2 AC 164, *FHR European Ventures LLP* v *Cedar Capital Partners LLC* [2014] UKSC 45, *Ivey* v *Genting Casinos UK Ltd (t/a Crockfords Club)* [2017] UKSC 67, and now *Group Seven Ltd* v *Notable Services LLP* [2019] EWCA Civ 614 have all tackled this vexed question. For an interesting short piece on whether this does conclude the argument, see Dixon (2019) ('Taking Things Further').

Q QUESTION 1

English law provides no clear and all embracing definition of a constructive trust. Its boundaries have been left perhaps deliberately vague ...

(Edmund Davies LJ in *Carl Zeiss Stiftung v Herbert Smith & Co. (a firm) (No. 2)* [1969] 2 Ch 276)

Discuss with reference to decided cases.

! CAUTION!

- This is a general essay question on the nature of constructive trusts—the sort of question for which you might achieve a pass if you had not actually revised constructive trusts too specifically but had a general overall knowledge of the subject. However, to do well on it, you would need to have a good knowledge of the cases and of recent developments.

- Remember, however, that no matter how similar two essay questions may be, you should always slant your answer to the particular question asked. The material in this essay answer might well be adapted to similar essays on constructive trusts, such as a discussion of Lord Denning's statement in *Hussey v Palmer* [1972] 1 WLR 1286, CA, that 'a constructive trust is one imposed by equity whenever justice and good conscience require it' but then you would need to get the angle right for the particular essay topic.

O DIAGRAM ANSWER PLAN

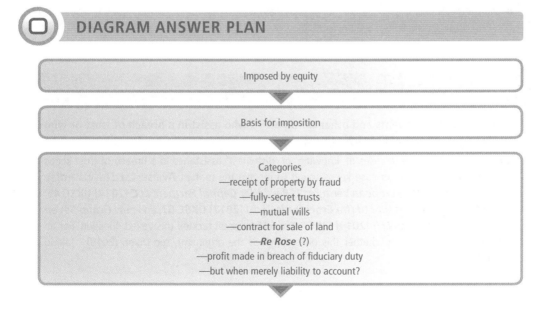

Imposed by equity

Basis for imposition

Categories
—receipt of property by fraud
—fully-secret trusts
—mutual wills
—contract for sale of land
—*Re Rose* (?)
—profit made in breach of fiduciary duty
—but when merely liability to account?

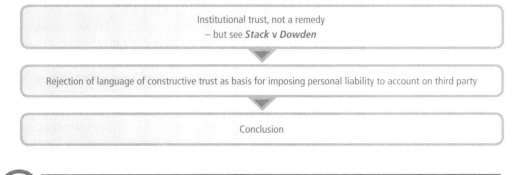

Institutional trust, not a remedy
– but see *Stack* v *Dowden*

Rejection of language of constructive trust as basis for imposing personal liability to account on third party

Conclusion

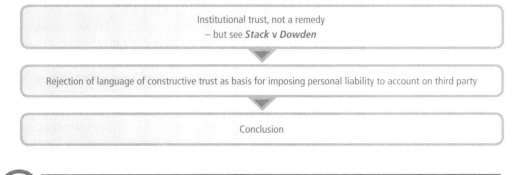

SUGGESTED ANSWER

[1] First paragraph sets the scene by outlining the basics, i.e. imposed by equity and basis in equity.

A constructive trust is one imposed by equity on a person in whom the legal title to property is vested.[1] It has the effect of divesting such person of the whole, or part, of the equitable beneficial interest which they then hold as trustee for someone else. The underlying rationale for the imposition of most constructive trusts is the unjust enrichment of the legal owner that would result if he were allowed to retain the whole of the beneficial interest, and a constructive trust usually involves some fraudulent behaviour on the part of the legal owner. This is the application of a very general equitable principle and it is hardly surprising that the circumstances in which the courts have been prepared to impose a constructive trust are wide and varied. Moreover, it is an ever-evolving area of equity where the courts are constantly redefining and reviewing the principles on which a constructive trust will be imposed in new cases, often applying the maxims of equity to do so.

[2] Now introduce the categories of CTs.

There are several well-established categories of constructive trusts.[2] These include where the defendant has obtained property by fraud, and where a third party receives and holds property in breach of a trust or fiduciary obligation with notice of the breach. Other, less certain, classifications are fully-secret trusts (whereas half-secret trusts appear to be express trusts: *Re Baillie* (1886) 2 TLR 660) and mutual wills (if not treated as implied trusts). A specifically enforceable contract for sale (such as a contract for the sale of land) is also considered to give rise to a constructive trust: *Lysaght* v *Edwards* (1876) 2 Ch D 499. The trust that arises under the doctrine of *Re Rose* [1952] Ch 499, CA has sometimes been treated as constructive (e.g. in *Pennington* v *Waine* [2002] 1 WLR 2075 at p. 2091 (Arden LJ)), but, as such a trust is intended to give effect to the donor's intention, it might be better classified as implied.

A constructive trust will also arise where a fiduciary has made an unauthorised profit from his position as fiduciary. In *FHR European Ventures LLP* v *Cedar Capital Partners LLC* **[2014] UKSC 45**, the Supreme Court held that the fiduciary held all unauthorised benefits including bribes and secret profits received from a third party on a constructive trust.

In *Hussey* v *Palmer* **[1972] 1 WLR 1286, CA**, Lord Denning MR treated a constructive trust as a remedy 'imposed by law whenever justice and good conscience require it'. However, whilst in the USA a constructive trust is a remedy based on unjust enrichment,[3] the approach of the English courts has generally been to treat the constructive trust as a substantive institution that arises at the date the defendant receives the property, so that the court, in holding there to be a constructive trust is not imposing the trust, but merely declaring that a trust already exists. The English courts have also been generally wary of treating such a vague concept as 'good conscience' as a basis for a constructive trust. Thus in *Cowcher* v *Cowcher* **[1972] 1 WLR 425** at p. 429, Bagnall J stated that rights of property are not to be determined according to what is 'reasonable and fair or just in all the circumstances', but (at p. 430) on 'sure and settled principles', as otherwise 'no lawyer could safely advise on his client's title and every quarrel would lead to a law suit'. Lord Millett was of a similar opinion in *Foskett* v *McKeown* **[2001] 1 AC 102** at p. 127.

Some individual judges have been prepared to recognise the introduction of the remedial constructive trust,[4] notably Lord Browne-Wilkinson in *Westdeutsche Landesbank Girocentrale* v *Islington LBC* **[1996] AC 669**, at p. 716, and Lord Scott in *Thorner* v *Major* **[2009] 1 WLR 776**. Indeed, in *Re Basham* **[1986] 1 WLR 1498**, a case on proprietary estoppel, the judge satisfied the equity by awarding a constructive trust as a remedy. This is, however, a minority view. English courts are generally concerned that a remedial constructive trust could affect third parties or a bankrupt defendant's creditors, and have repeatedly stated explicitly that English law does not recognise the remedial constructive trust: *Halifax Building Society* v *Thomas* **[1996] Ch 217, CA**; *Re Polly Peck International plc* **[1998] 3 All ER 812, CA**.

Some decisions, however, can be more easily explained through the remedial constructive trust. Thus, where the parties have made mutual wills, the imposition of the trust on the death of the first to die seems generally to be treated as remedial in nature, since the court is usually dealing only with whatever property the survivor retains at his own death, as in *Olins* v *Walters* **[2009] Ch 212, CA**. The 'suspensory trust' mentioned in *Ottaway* v *Norman* **[1972] 1 Ch 698**

[3] This shows knowledge of the 'unjust enrichment' debate and the differing national approaches.

[4] This develops the unjust enrichment debate.

at p. 713, looks like an attempt to fit into an institutional framework that which might be better explained as a remedial constructive trust. Etherton J, writing extrajudicially, considered that the decision of the House of Lords in *Stack* v *Dowden* **[2007] 2 AC 432**, although not expressed to be based on a remedial constructive trust, looks very much like it: [2009] Conv 104. The House of Lords in *Stack* indicated that, in a domestic consumer context, where the legal title to the family home is in joint names but without any declaration of the beneficial interests, there is a strong presumption that the legal owners are also joint tenants in equity. Lady Hale noted, however, a variety of factors that might indicate what the parties intended other than an equitable joint tenancy. The House of Lords in that case seems, as the dissenting judge, Lord Neuberger, indicated, to be moving away from property law into the area of judicial reallocation of property rights—which would be incompatible with the House of Lords' earlier decisions in *Pettitt* v *Pettitt* **[1970] AC 777** and *Gissing* v *Gissing* **[1971] AC 886**. The majority in *Stack* sought to avoid such heresy by placing reliance on the parties' intentions, but, unconvincingly, they blurred the distinction between an 'inferred' and an 'imputed' intention. In the Supreme Court in *Jones* v *Kernott* **[2012] 1 AC 776**, Lady Hale and Lord Walker, who had been in the majority in *Stack*, not surprisingly adhered to their earlier views. The notion that the size of the beneficial interests might vary after acquisition (as they clearly had in *Kernott*) might nevertheless still be squared with the notion of an institutional constructive trust if the trust could have been treated as 'ambulatory' in character, the size of the parties' respective beneficial shares varying from the moment that the equitable joint tenant was severed until the date of judgment: *Stack* v *Dowden*, at para. 62; *Jones* v *Kernott*, at para. 14.

In the past, the language of constructive trust was often used when imposing personal liability on a third party who either assisted in a breach of trust, or who received trust property in breach of trust. Where equity imposed liability upon such persons, it usually did so by holding them 'liable to account as constructive trustees', as for instance in *Barnes* v *Addy* **(1874) LR 9 Ch App 244**. The problem with this terminology, however, was that it suggested that the defendant was holding property on trust, whereas a defendant who merely assisted in a breach of trust might never have received any trust property at any stage, and even a defendant who had received trust property might have meanwhile disposed of it. In *Paragon Finance plc* v *D. B. Thakerar & Co.* **[1999] 1 All ER 400**, at pp. 408–409, Millett LJ pointed out the different situations involved when using the expressions 'constructive trust' and 'constructive trustee'.

It seems that equity might have attached the appellation 'constructive trustee' to a defendant who had never received trust property both because the language of trust came naturally to the Court of Chancery and because of some uncertainty whether a personal action would lie in equity against someone other than a trustee. There was, however, no underlying trust, and the expression was 'nothing more than a formula for equitable relief' (*Selangor United Rubber Estates Ltd v Cradock (No. 3)* [1968] 1 WLR 1555, at p. 1582, per Ungoed-Thomas J).[5]

[5] For extra marks you could include here some of the secondary literature—see the 'Looking for Extra Marks?' section for details.

In *Dubai Aluminium Co. Ltd v Salaam* [2003] 2 AC 366 at para. 142, Lord Millett said that the reference to the constructive trust in such cases creates a trap; he suggested that the courts should now discard the words 'accountable as a constructive trustee' in this context and substitute the words 'accountable in equity'.

Persons who purport to act as trustees without having been appointed have traditionally been called trustees *de son tort*. Such persons can appropriately be considered to be holding the property on trust, and whilst they have sometimes been called constructive trustees (e.g. in *Mara v Browne* [1896] 1 Ch 199), their liability to the beneficiaries is the same as if they were express trustees. In the *Dubai Aluminium* case, at para. 138, Lord Millett said that it might now be preferable to term such persons *de facto* trustees.

It is clear from the widely differing situations in which a constructive trust has been applied that it is a versatile and flexible weapon of equity, capable of apparently unlimited adaptability to changing social and commercial circumstances. It justifies the statement by Lord Denning MR in *Eves v Eves* [1975] 1 WLR 1338 that 'Equity is not past the age of childbearing'. However, its adaptability necessarily requires that its boundaries should not be too rigidly defined.[6]

[6] A summarising conclusion referring directly back to the quotation in the question. Make sure you get this link back to show you haven't lost sight of the question in all the discussion.

⊕ LOOKING FOR EXTRA MARKS?

- There is widespread academic literature on the issue of knowing or dishonest receipt and assistance and you could include here for extra marks an analysis of the arguments presented by R. Chambers, 'The end of knowing receipt' (2016) 2(1) Canadian Journal of Comparative and Contemporary Law 1. This article is wide-ranging and deals with a number of the arguments around this contemporary debate considering whether the situation amounts to a breach of trust, a constructive trust, or unjust enrichment. It introduces much of the earlier literature and would repay careful study on this particular topic. And in that vein, the decision in *Ivey v Genting Casinos* [2017] UKSC 67 might also be another fruitful avenue for inclusion in this answer (especially if coursework).

- You could also deal with the national differences in their judicial approach to the remedial constructive approach, i.e. the difference between the USA's approach and that in the UK as outlined in the answer above.

Alf is a trustee of the Beta Trust which has a 30 per cent shareholding in Gamma Ltd, a pharmaceutical company developing a new drug to stimulate memory, primarily for students taking examinations. In his position as trustee, Alf learned that tests on the drug were indicative of a successful outcome, and he therefore purchased a 25 per cent shareholding in the company himself. He was subsequently elected as a director of the company and has received considerable sums in director's fees.

Shortly after Alf became a director, the company's lease on its factory premises expired and its landlord wanted to sell the reversion for £100,000. The company could not afford this, so Alf and the company's solicitor, Delta, put up £50,000 each and purchased the reversion themselves jointly. They then granted a new lease to the company at a lower rent than under the previous lease.

The company were also interested in a new drug for improving concentration which had been patented. It was agreed between Alf and Delta that Alf would negotiate to buy the patent and, if successful, would receive for his efforts 1 per cent of the purchase price. He negotiated a purchase for £20,000.

Alf began to have doubts about the company's future and decided to sell his shareholding and retire from the directorship. Having retired as a trustee from the Beta Trust six months previously, he sold his shares in Gamma Ltd to the trust for £5,000 below the market value.

The new drugs which the company were developing have recently failed pharmaceutical tests and the company's shares are now almost worthless.

Alf and Delta have received an offer of £150,000 for the freehold of the factory premises and would like to sell it.

Discuss Alf's liability as a fiduciary in the various circumstances.

! **CAUTION!**

- This is a long question involving different fiduciary relationships and different breaches of fiduciary duties. It is the type of question which you should therefore spend some time thinking through, jotting down different points and any relevant cases before embarking on the answer. The risk is, if you do not do this, that you will get to the end and find that there are some points or cases which you have omitted.

- The question is wide in its scope and requires a fair knowledge of the subject to produce a reasonable answer.

DIAGRAM ANSWER PLAN

Identify the issues

- The legal issue is the duty of a fiduciary

Relevant law

- Case law—the rule that a fiduciary must not profit from his or her position has been very strictly applied, even where the fiduciary's acts benefit his or her principal as well as himself and there is no real possibility of conflict of interests

- A trustee who uses his or her position to obtain his or her appointment as a director is accountable for any profit, such as his or her director's fees, unless the appointment is authorised by the trust deed or the dictum of Harman J in *Re Gee* applies

Apply the law

- Alf's role as director and fiduciary
- Can Delta authorise the payment of commission to Alf?
- Does Alf's knowledge of the good prospects for Gamma Ltd derive from his trusteeship?
- The sale by Alf to the trust is a breach of the self-dealing rule, which can apply even when he is no longer a trustee, and the transaction will be voidable by the trust

Conclude

- Alf's liability as a fiduciary

SUGGESTED ANSWER

[1] Introduction to the position of fiduciaries and the relevant law.

Equity has consistently demonstrated a harsh attitude to the rule that a fiduciary may not benefit from his position.[1] The rule has been applied even where there is no conflict of interest between the fiduciary and the principal and no evidence of an actual consequent injury to the principal. Indeed, in the House of Lords' case of *Boardman* v *Phipps* **[1967] 2 AC 46**, the trust, as well as the fiduciary, benefited from the fiduciary's activities, but the strict accountability rule was nevertheless applied. Even in these circumstances, a fiduciary will still be accountable for a profit derived from his fiduciary relationship. The only modification of this strict approach is the Privy Council case of *Queensland Mines Ltd* v *Hudson* **(1978) 18 ALR 1**, which appears to be a decision on the particular merits of the case.

Moreover, a fiduciary relationship is broadly defined and is not restricted to trustee and beneficiary. A director is in a fiduciary position to his company, an agent to his principal, and an employee may also be in a fiduciary relationship to his employer (*Agip (Africa) Ltd* v *Jackson* [1991] Ch 547, CA) although this depends on the nature of the work and the terms of the employment contract (*Nottingham University* v *Fischel* [2000] IRLR 471). In *Reading* v *A-G* [1951] AC 507, it was held that an army officer was in a fiduciary position to the Crown.

A trustee who uses his position to appoint himself as a director of a company is prima facie accountable to the trust for any remuneration he receives as a director: *Re Macadam* [1946] Ch 73. In order to be able to keep his director's fees, Alf would have to show[2] that his appointment as a director would have been made even if the votes attaching to the trust's shares had been used against him (per Harman J in *Re Gee* [1948] Ch 284). So if Alf can show that he would still have been elected as a director, notwithstanding that the voting rights of the Beta Trust's shares had been used to vote against him, then he will be able to keep his director's fees. Otherwise, he will be prima facie accountable to the Trust for them. He would also be able to retain his director's fees if authorised in the trust instrument: *Re Llewellin* [1949] Ch 225.

If the trust property includes a lease, a trustee to whom the lease is renewed (*Keech* v *Sandford* (1726) Sel Cas Ch 61), or who purchases a reversion on the lease (*Protheroe* v *Protheroe* [1968] 1 WLR 519, CA), will become a constructive trustee of the lease or reversion for the beneficiaries. In *Protheroe*, a husband and wife were co-owners of a leasehold interest in their matrimonial home. They separated and the husband subsequently purchased the reversion on the lease. It was held that this became trust property in which his wife also had an interest. As a director of Gamma Ltd, Alf is in a fiduciary position to the company and would therefore hold one-half of the reversion on the lease as a constructive trustee for the company. He would similarly be accountable for one-half of any profit made on its sale. It is irrelevant that the company itself could not have purchased the reversion, or that the company itself benefited from the transaction. In *Regal (Hastings) Ltd* v *Gulliver* [1942] 1 All ER 378, HL, directors purchased shares, which the company could not afford to purchase, in order to enable the company to take a lease of a cinema and subsequently to sell it with other property owned by the company at a profit. They were nevertheless held accountable for their profits as they had acquired their shares through their fiduciary position. Delta, as the company's solicitor, would also be in a fiduciary position and similarly accountable.

[3] This exposition of the law introduces the next point of application.

[4] Application of law to problem.

[5] This opens the concluding point.

In *Guinness plc v Saunders* **[1990] 2 AC 663**, a director who received an unauthorised fee of 0.2 per cent of the value of a takeover bid was held by the House of Lords to be a constructive trustee of this for the company. Neither was he able to claim payment for his services on a *quantum meruit* as he had created a conflict of interest between himself (in whose interest it was to pay a high price) and the company.[3] Assuming that Delta was not authorised to award director's remuneration, the agreement between Delta and Alf would not be binding on the company, and any commission would be a profit derived from Alf's fiduciary position as a director.[4] He would therefore not be able to claim any such commission. As in *Guinness plc v Saunders*, any such agreement would also create a conflict of interest between Alf and the company in that Alf has an interest in purchasing for a high price and the company in purchasing for a low price. He would similarly not have any claim for work undertaken in this connection on a *quantum meruit*.

The case of *Boardman v Phipps* **[1967] 2 AC 46, HL**, indicates that a trustee or fiduciary who uses information obtained as a result of his fiduciary position to make a profit will be a constructive trustee of that profit for the trust. If Alf's knowledge were the reason for his acquisition of his 25 per cent shareholding and this resulted in profits, he might be accountable for these. If it could be shown that Alf had serious doubts about the company's future when he sold the shares to the Trust, this would amount to a breach of his fiduciary duty and he might be made liable for the subsequent loss to the Trust.

The rule in *Ex parte Lacey* **(1802) 6 Ves 625**, which is strictly applied, precludes a trustee from purchasing trust property, and this applies even after a trustee has retired: *Wright v Morgan* **[1926] AC 788**.[5] A trustee's liability does not necessarily cease on his retirement: he or his estate will remain liable for breaches of trust committed during his trusteeship. The rule in *Ex parte Lacey* applies to any dealing between the trustee in his personal capacity and in his capacity as trustee. In *Bentley v Craven* **(1853) 18 Beav 75**, it was held that an agent employed to purchase sugar for a company could not sell to the company sugar he had purchased himself, even at the market price, unless his interest was declared and accepted by the company. In that case, Romilly MR said (obiter) that the same principle would apply to other fiduciary relationships, including a dealing by a trustee with a trust. The transaction necessarily puts the agent in a position of conflict with his principal as to price. Unless there is a full disclosure as to the agent's interest, which is accepted by the principal, the principal may either repudiate the transaction or claim any profit which the agent makes on it. It is quite possible here, therefore, that the Trust could repudiate the sale to them and claim back the purchase price. It is irrelevant that it was an advantageous sale to the Trust at the time when it was made.

LOOKING FOR EXTRA MARKS?

▤ Take a look at M. Bryan, '*Boardman v Phipps*: Doing Equity Inequitably', in *Landmark Cases in Equity* (C. Mitchell and P. Mitchell, eds), Hart Publishing, 2012, p. 581. This analysis of the case law could be explored for further discussion in the answer for extra marks.

QUESTION | 3

A year ago, Grab plc (Grab) appointed Edward its agent for the purpose of acquiring land that could be developed and sold at a profit. The following month, Edward agreed on behalf of Grab the purchase of land from Victoria for £910,000. Victoria secured the sale by agreeing to transfer 1,000 of her shares in Tiger Ltd to Edward upon receipt of the sale proceeds from Grab. On completion of the sale of the land to Grab, Victoria transferred the shares to Edward. At that time the shares were worth £10,000; they have since trebled in value. Edward, who did not disclose to Grab either the agreement he had with Victoria or the share transfer, recently became bankrupt.

Advise Grab.

CAUTION!

▤ Some problems involve many different issues, but this one deals essentially with only one: whether an agent who makes a profit through a breach of fiduciary duty is merely accountable to the principal for the value of the profit or holds the profit on a constructive trust for the principal.

▤ The answer to the problem needs, first, to address the problem by identifying that issue and by explaining why, on the facts of the problem, a constructive trust has considerable advantages for the claimant.

▤ Secondly, there should be a discussion of the relevant principal case law. This is where, if you have read and understood the authorities and the extent to which (under our system of judicial precedent) they are binding, you will have a chance to showcase your knowledge. You should analyse the reasoning in the cases, criticising where appropriate, and should explain whether apparently conflicting cases can (or cannot) be reconciled.

▤ Thirdly, the case law must be applied to the particular facts of the problem. Many students do not give enough attention to this aspect of answering a problem question, yet examiners generally set great store by it. This part of the answer cannot be simply learned in advance, but the technique for dealing with it can be mastered by working through problem questions in tutorials and in past examination papers.

- Fourthly, there should be a conclusion. The conclusion should not repeat what has already been said, but should draw the threads together. The conclusion may be brief: in the suggested answer it is just a few words.

- Note that the suggested answer begins and ends with reference to the problem itself. This is a useful technique, particularly in a single-issue problem such as this, as it helps to ensure that the relevant authorities do not run away with themselves, but are seen to be mustered so as to answer the particular problem set. There are different ways to answer a problem and this is one of them which works in this sort of question.

DIAGRAM ANSWER PLAN

Identify the issues

- Agent—breach of fiduciary duty—remedies. The key issue is whether Grab has a proprietary interest in the shares or is restricted to a personal claim only

Relevant law

- *Lister* (bribe—personal liability)
- *Reid* (bribe—constructive trust)
- *Versailles* (fraud, but profit from own asset—personal liability) now overruled by *FHR* (undisclosed commission—constructive trust)

  Note too that in *Group Seven* it was stated that the decision also applied to a claim for dishonest assistance of a breach of fiduciary duty.

Apply the law

- Edward personally liable to account to Grab for his profit made through such breach. As Edward is bankrupt, however, a personal action against him by Grab for equitable compensation may recover very little, since Grab would have to prove in Edward's bankruptcy as an unsecured creditor. Grab's position would be transformed if it could establish an equitable proprietary interest in the shares (under a constructive trust) upon Edward's receiving them. This would enable Grab to claim them from Edward's trustee in bankruptcy (effectively as if it had priority over Edward's creditors), and Grab would benefit from the shares' increase in value.

Conclude

- Advise Grab

[1] Start with applying the law to the problem. This works here because there is a single issue in the problem so it can be simply stated at the outset.

As Grab's agent, Edward owed fiduciary duties to Grab, which he breached by taking from Victoria a commission (the shares) without disclosing to Grab either his agreement with Victoria or his receipt of the shares.[1] Edward is undoubtedly personally liable to account to Grab for his profit made through such breach, the measure being the market value of the shares at the time they were transferred to him, i.e. £10,000. As Edward is bankrupt, however, a personal action against him by Grab for equitable compensation may recover very little, since Grab would have to prove in Edward's bankruptcy as an unsecured creditor.

Grab's position would be transformed if it could establish an equitable proprietary interest in the shares (under a constructive trust) upon Edward's receiving them. This would enable Grab to claim them from Edward's trustee in bankruptcy (effectively as if it had priority over Edward's creditors), and Grab would benefit from the shares' increase in value. The key issue is therefore whether Grab has a proprietary interest in the shares or is restricted to a personal claim only.[2]

[2] Now state the key issue of law.

The legal position has been subject to much litigation with the recent Supreme Court decision in *FHR European Ventures LLP v Cedar Capital Partners LLC* [2014] UKSC 45, the latest word on the topic. The case development is lengthy and has been contentious and is set out next.

In *Lister v Stubbs* (1890) 45 ChD 1, the defendant, a purchasing agent, used a bribe he received from a purchaser to buy investments in his own name. His principal, wishing to trace into the investments, tried to stop the defendant from dealing with them. The action failed, the Court of Appeal holding that the relationship between an agent and principal is not that of trustee and beneficiary, but merely one of debtor and creditor.

[3] Continue by laying out the case law.

In *A-G for Hong Kong v Reid* [1994] 1 AC 324, however, the Privy Council declined to follow *Lister v Stubbs*.[3] Reid, a senior prosecutor in Hong Kong, had taken bribes for agreeing not to prosecute. The Attorney-General for Hong Kong sought to prevent Reid's disposing of land that he had bought with the bribe. Lord Templeman (at p. 300) referred to bribery as an evil practice that threatens civilised society. He said (at p. 331) that, in accordance with the equitable maxim that 'Equity considers as done that which ought to be done', Reid held the bribe on a constructive trust for his principal from the moment he received it. His Lordship commented (at p. 332) that to permit the fiduciary to retain the benefit of an increase in value in the land would be to permit him to profit from his breach.

The maxim to which Lord Templeman referred has usually been applied to a contract of sale of land, where the vendor 'ought' to do what it had agreed to do, i.e. transfer the legal estate to a purchaser who has provided valuable consideration and who is able and willing to pay the purchase monies. Lord Templeman's reliance on the maxim in this different context, however, is unhelpful, as what the defendant 'ought' to do depends on whether the principal has an equitable proprietary interest in the bribe or not. If the principal has no such interest, what the defendant 'ought' to do is to account personally for the value of the bribe. Only if the principal has a proprietary interest in the bribe (by means of a constructive trust) can it be said that the defendant 'ought' to transfer the bribe (or its traceable product) to the principal.

Where the agent could not have purchased the investment without using the bribe, the decision in *Reid*, which denies the agent the increase in value of the investment, might still be justified as preventing the agent's being unjustly enriched at the principal's expense. If, however, the agent is bankrupt, the result provides the principal with a windfall at the expense of the agent's general creditors. The court cannot, however, determine whether to impose a constructive trust according to the circumstances that pertain at the date of the hearing, since English law does not recognise the remedial constructive trust in order to remedy unjustified enrichment: *Re Polly Peck (No. 2)* **[1998] 3 All ER 812, CA**; *Foskett* v *McKeown* **[2001] 1 AC 102, HL**.

[4] Here follows a detailed analysis of *Versailles* which is at the heart of the discussion. Although now overruled in *FHR* the academic debate still rages on this point.

Reid was not followed by the Court of Appeal in *Sinclair Investments (UK) Ltd* v *Versailles Trade Finance Ltd* **[2012] Ch 453**,[4] where one Cushnie, the director of a company (TPL), had breached his fiduciary duty to TPL by transferring investors' monies in TPL to another company, Versailles (VTF), in which he had shares. VTF was not trading but was fraudulently paying returns out of the investors' own monies. As a result of the fraud, VTF's share price rose considerably, and Cushnie sold his VTF shares for £29 million. The scheme later collapsed and Cushnie became bankrupt. TPL claimed a proprietary right under a constructive trust to the proceeds of sale of Cushnie's shares, as only this would effectively give it priority over VTF's creditors.

The Court of Appeal in *Versailles* preferred *Lister* v *Stubbs*, which it in any event considered to be binding, to the reasoning in *Reid*. Lord Neuberger MR said that TPL had no proprietary interest in Cushnie's profit because it was derived from the increase in value of property (his VTF shares) that he had acquired before TPL took money from investors. Whilst, as Lord Neuberger admitted (at para. 51), 'there was a close commercial causal connection' between Cushnie's misapplication of the funds and his making a profit on his shares, it was difficult to see (at para. 52) how TPL's proprietary rights in the misused funds could be traced into the profit made on the sale of the shares. He criticised Lord Templeman's reasoning in **Reid** for begging the question of whether a principal has a proprietary interest in a bribe: para. 78. Lord Neuberger considered (at para. 80) that a bribe taken by a fiduciary could not possibly be said to be an asset that he was under a duty to take for the beneficiary. He also thought (para. 83) that Lord Templeman had taken insufficient account of the potentially unfair consequences of the fiduciary's other creditors.

Lord Neuberger considered that a beneficiary could have a proprietary claim only in two exceptional circumstances, namely, where 'the asset or money is or has been beneficially the property of the beneficiary or the trustee acquired the asset or money by taking advantage of an opportunity or right which was properly that of the beneficiary': para. 88. He treated **Keech v Sandford (1726) Sel Cas Ch 61**, as a case in which the trustee had taken advantage of an opportunity that 'was effectively owned by the trust' because the court at that time treated the right to renew a lease as a legal right: para. 58. As Cushnie's profit fell into neither of these exceptional categories, TPL's claim failed.

Lord Millett, the former Lord of Appeal in Ordinary, writing extrajudicially, unequivocally condemned **Versailles**, as being wrong both in law and as a matter of policy in ignoring the prophylactic nature of the no-conflict and no-profit rules, thereby enabling a fiduciary to profit from his breach: P. Millett (2012) 71 CLJ 583. His view is reflected in the rule now established by the Supreme Court in its most recent review of this area:[5] **FHR European Ventures LLP v Cedar Capital Partners LLC [2014] UKSC 45** where it overruled **Versailles**, and, preferring **Reid**, decided that the defendant fiduciary did hold his commission on a constructive trust for his principal. In this case, a company called Cedar acted for an investor group (the group) in negotiating the purchase price of a hotel that the group wished to buy from a company called Monte Carlo. Ultimately, the group acquired the hotel for €211.50 million, which sum they paid directly to Monte Carlo. Cedar had not told the group, however, that it had received a fee of €10 million from Monte Carlo under an agreement that the latter would pay it such sum within five days of receiving the purchase monies. Cedar had clearly breached its fiduciary duty in entering into such agreement and in receiving the fee without having the group's informed consent. The group ultimately wished to trace into the product of the fee, and so claimed that Cedar had held that fee on a constructive trust for them. The Supreme Court ruled

[5] See the second 'Key Debates' at the beginning of this chapter and 'Taking Things Further' at the end.

[6] Regardless of the academic debate about the correctness of the position, at least, thankfully, you can come to a clear conclusion now post the Supreme Court ruling in **FHR**.

that all unauthorised profits including bribes and secret profits received by a fiduciary are held on constructive trust.

So, following the decision in **FHR**, Edward will hold the benefit of its fee agreement with Victoria on constructive trust for Grab.[6]

LOOKING FOR EXTRA MARKS?

- As demonstrated in the answer, a clear and detailed analysis of the case law leading to the clear ruling by the Supreme Court in **FHR** earns those extra marks. But **FHR** is also not universally welcomed in the academic world. For extra marks you could introduce some of this critique by introducing some secondary material here. For suggestions, see 'Taking Things Further'.

QUESTION | 4

Wynken and Nod are the two partners in a firm of solicitors, Blynken & Co. Wynken acts for the Fishnet Trust. On the instructions of the sole trustee of the Trust, Sleepy, Wynken paid out £30,000 to Chloë, believing her to be a beneficiary under the Trust and properly entitled to be paid this sum. Had Wynken looked at the trust deed in the firm's strong-room, however, he would have realised that she was neither a beneficiary under the Trust nor a person entitled to any payment. Chloë, who was Sleepy's daughter, did not realise that the sum was paid to her in breach of trust, and she spent it all on a luxury round-the-world cruise.

a Consider the liability to the beneficiaries of the Fishnet Trust of (i) Wynken; (ii) Nod; and (iii) Chloë.

AND

b Explain whether your answers to (i) and (ii) might differ if it were found that Sleepy's appointment as trustee had not been properly effected.

CAUTION!

- The equitable requirements for imposing personal liability on an accessory to a breach of trust or a breach of fiduciary duty were laid down in **Royal Brunei Airlines Sdn Bhd v Tan [1995] 2 AC 378**, **Barlow Clowes International Ltd v Eurotrust International Ltd [2005] UKPC 37**, and (obiter) **Ivey v Genting Casinos UK Ltd [2017] UKSC 67**. These cases, however, did not involve the personal liability of a person who received property under a breach of trust. The precise requirements of recipient liability are regrettably uncertain; moreover, since liability will depend upon a detailed analysis of the facts you cannot be expected to reach any definite conclusion in this problem question. So what you need to do is to demonstrate a knowledge of the principles involved, and to suggest how they might be applied to the facts of the problem.

○ **DIAGRAM ANSWER PLAN**

Identify the issues	▓ Equitable requirements for imposing personal liability on an accessory to a breach of trust or a breach of fiduciary duty

Relevant law	▓ *Royal Brunei Airlines Sdn Bhd* v *Tan* [1995] 2 AC 378, *Barlow Clowes International Ltd v Eurotrust International Ltd* [2005] UKPC 37, and *Ivey v Genting Casinos UK Ltd* [2017] UKSC 67

Apply the law	▓ **Part (a)** (i) Liability of W: depends upon his dishonesty (*Royal Brunei Airlines*) (ii) Liability of Nod: vicariously liable for W's acts if W acting in ordinary course of business (*Dubai Aluminium*; Partnership Act 1890, s. 10) (iii) Liability of Chloë: No proprietary action to recover the money from C (since spent). Does C incur recipient liability? May depend on her constructive knowledge, on unconscionability, or on restitutionary principles ▓ **Part (b)** If W realised that S was not properly appointed: • W is acting as a trustee *de son tort* • N would not be liable (not part of a solicitor's business to act as the trustee of an express trust) • If W believed the trustee was properly appointed: W's liability turns on dishonest assistance as in part (a)(i); N's liability as a partner is as in part (a)(ii)

Conclude	▓ Liability to the beneficiaries of the Fishnet Trust of (i) Wynken; (ii) Nod; and (iii) Chloë

Ⓐ **SUGGESTED ANSWER**

Part (a)

(i) Liability of Wynken[1]

Wynken would be personally liable to the beneficiaries of the Fishnet Trust if he has dishonestly assisted in a breach of trust in accordance with the principles for accessory liability laid down in *Royal Brunei Airlines Sdn Bhd* v *Tan* [1995] 2 AC 378, and followed in *Barlow Clowes International Ltd* v *Eurotrust International Ltd* [2005]

UKPC 37, *Ivey v Genting Casinos UK Ltd* [2017] UKSC 67 (obiter), and *Group Seven Ltd v Notable Services LLP and another* [2019] EWCA Civ 614.[2] Although Sleepy might have been acting dishonestly in seeking to obtain a payment for his daughter, Wynken's liability does not require dishonesty on the part of the trustee: *Brunei*, at p. 392. It must, however, be shown that Wynken was dishonest. In *Group Seven Ltd v Notable Services LLP and another* [2019] EWCA Civ 614, the court stated that, following *Ivey v Genting*, where the discussion on this point was obiter, it is now settled law that the requirement for knowing assistance is dishonesty which is to be determined objectively and there is no room to consider the subjective opinion of the defendant as to whether he believed he was behaving dishonestly under the now discredited second limb of the *R v Ghosh* [1982] QB 1053 test. Whether Wynken is dishonest is therefore a matter of evidence—what he knew about the relevant facts is important but it is then to be determined by the standard of what ordinary decent people would think to be dishonest. Liability is triggered by the defendant's lack of probity which requires a much higher hurdle to be cleared than evidence of negligence. So, merely failing to refer to the trust instrument before making the payment, whilst perhaps amounting to negligence, does not itself indicate dishonesty so as to satisfy the high test for dishonesty required by *Royal Brunei* and *Group Seven* following *Ivey v Genting*.[3]

(ii) Nod's liability

Even if Wynken is personally liable for dishonest assistance, his partner, Nod, is not necessarily also liable.[4] If Nod knew what Wynken was doing and stood by, doing nothing to prevent Wynken from assisting in the breach of trust, the beneficiaries might seek to make Nod also liable for dishonest assistance. It could be argued, however, that merely standing by while Wynken acts does not itself amount to 'assistance'.

The beneficiaries might seek to recover from Nod on the ground that he is liable in equity for his partner's acts. In *Mara v Browne* [1896] 1 Ch 199,[5] at p. 208, Lord Herschell had stated obiter that 'it is not within the scope of the implied authority of a partner … [in a solicitor's] business that he should so act as to make himself a constructive trustee, and thereby subject his partners to the same liability'. In *Re Bell's Indenture* [1980] 1 WLR 1217, this dictum was apparently interpreted to mean that, when a partner in a firm of solicitors incurred liability for dishonestly assisting in a breach of trust, his co-partner could not as a matter of law be liable, since such an act was necessarily outside the scope of his implied authority. In *Dubai Aluminium Co. Ltd v Salaam* [2003] 2 AC 366, however, their Lordships disapproved of this interpretation and overruled *Re Bell's Indenture*. Lord Millett suggested that Lord Herschell's

---

[2] This sets out the law and applies it.

[3] Here is the conclusion to this section.

[4] Identifies issue.

[5] The relevant cases are now set out.

dictum referred only to trustees *de son tort*, these being persons who, without being appointed, nevertheless take it upon themselves to act as trustees. Lord Millett said that the expression 'constructive trustee' was best abandoned in the context of liability for dishonest assistance, and that it was more appropriate to refer to the defendant as being merely 'accountable in equity'.

[6] And now the statutory reference.

Under the **Partnership Act 1890, s. 10**,[6] the firm is liable where a person suffers loss 'by any wrongful act or omission of any partner in the ordinary course of the business of the firm'. In the *Dubai Aluminium* case, the House of Lords held that the phrase 'wrongful act or omission' was not confined to common law torts but included a fault-based equitable wrong such as liability for dishonest assistance in a breach of trust. On this interpretation, Nod's liability as a partner depends on the ordinary principles of partnership law. It is therefore a matter of evidence whether, in paying out money on the instructions of Sleepy in breach of trust, Wynken was acting in the ordinary course of the firm's business. As the act in question was performed by Wynken in his capacity as a solicitor, it would be difficult to argue that it was not also performed in the ordinary course of the firm's business.

[7] The conclusion.

Assuming this to be the case, if Wynken is liable for dishonest assistance, Nod is vicariously liable.[7]

(iii) Chloë's liability

[8] Introducing the key issue here.

As Chloë did not give consideration for the £30,000 paid to her, the beneficiaries could have traced it into her hands (or into its product in her hands) if she still retained it.[8] As Chloë has spent the money, however, the beneficiaries cannot bring any proprietary action to recover it from her. The beneficiaries will be able to bring a personal action against her to recover the equivalent value, however, if they can establish the ingredients for recipient liability. The initial requirement is met, as Chloë received the money beneficially and as a result of a breach of trust. Unfortunately, the courts have expressed different views about what else is required for recipient liability.[9]

[9] It is unfortunate as it means that the law is not clear. You just have to express that position and explain what it means.

[10] Here comes the exposition of the law.

In *Brunei*, Lord Nicholls said that recipient liability is restitution-based,[10] and his Lordship expressed a similar view in dicta in *Criterion Properties plc v Stratford UK Properties LLC* [2004] 1 WLR 1846, HL. If, therefore, the general principles of restitution were to apply to this type of liability, Chloë would be strictly liable as a beneficial recipient; but, as she has already spent the money, if she is an innocent volunteer she would have the defence of change of position. This analysis met with the approval of Lord Millett in the *Twinsectra* case, but his Lordship recognised that English law had not yet developed in that way. Where property is wrongly distributed under a will, those entitled under it may bring a personal action against the recipients, even if the latter are innocent volunteers: *Re Diplock* [1948] Ch 465, affirmed *Ministry of Health* v *Simpson* [1951] AC 251. The action *in personam* resembles what might now be termed a restitutionary claim based on the fact of receipt, and available even against an innocent volunteer. It appears, however, that the *Re Diplock* action *in personam* is limited to claims against recipients of assets wrongly distributed during the course of administration of an estate: ibid., at pp. 265–266 (Lord Simonds). If this limitation still applies today, such action cannot be brought against Chloë, who receives property wrongly distributed under an *inter vivos* trust. The beneficiaries would therefore have to content themselves with a claim based on accessory liability.

Most authorities hold that liability depends on the recipient's knowledge, but even these are in disagreement about what amounts to knowledge. Some are prepared to accept any of the five categories of knowledge set out in *Baden Delvaux* as sufficient: *Cowan de Groot Properties* v *Eagle Trust* [1992] 4 All ER 700; *Belmont Finance Corp.* v *Williams Furniture (No. 2)* [1980] 1 All ER 393, CA. Others require knowledge within the first three categories only: *Re Montagu's Settlement* [1987] Ch 264.

In *Eagle Trust* v *SBS Securities* [1993] 1 WLR 484, it was held that liability under any of the five heads sufficed where the receipt occurred (as in *Re Montagu*) in a non-commercial transaction. If *Eagle Trust* is applied, then as Chloë was not a commercial recipient, her liability would effectively depend on whether she had constructive notice of the breach of trust. More precisely, her liability would turn on whether she had knowledge within category (iv) of *Baden Delvaux* (knowledge of circumstances that would indicate the facts to an honest and reasonable person), or category (v) (knowledge of circumstances that would put an honest and reasonable person on inquiry).

Other views have, however, been expressed judicially. In *Dubai Aluminium Co. Ltd* v *Salaam* [2000] 3 WLR 910, the Court of Appeal considered the substantive ingredient for knowing receipt to be dishonesty, not knowledge. In *BCCI (Overseas) Ltd* v *Akindele* [2001] Ch 437, Nourse LJ said that the test was rather whether the recipient's state of knowledge was such as to make it unconscionable for him to retain the benefit of the receipt.

If the correct test is dishonesty or knowledge within the first three heads of *Baden Delvaux* only (all of which seem to involve some consciousness of wrongdoing), Chloë's lack of awareness of her receipt's being in breach of trust would save her from incurring recipient liability. If, however, the correct test is knowledge within any of the five heads of *Baden Delvaux*, or merely unconscionability, then the question provides insufficient facts for any determination of her liability to be made.[11]

[11] A conclusion to this part—inevitably a tentative one because of the state of the law.

Part (b)

[12] This raises some different points with accompanying cases.

If Sleepy's appointment as trustee had not been properly effected, Wynken could not have been acting as an agent.[12] In **Blythe v Fladgate** [1891] **1 Ch 327**, Smith, a partner in a firm of solicitors, continued to deal with trust funds after the death of the sole trustee. He was held liable as an inter-meddler (a trustee *de son tort*), and his co-partners were also held liable on this basis. If in the problem Wynken realised that he was effectively acting as principal, he may be liable as a trustee *de son tort*, in effect as a *de facto* trustee (which latter expression Lord Millett in the **Dubai Aluminium** case thought preferable today). If Wynken were liable as a *de facto* trustee, it would appear that Nod would not be liable, since Lord Millett thought that it was still not within the ordinary scope of a solicitor's practice to act as a trustee of an express trust. These would be the precise circumstances in which Lord Herschell's dictum in **Mara v Browne** would apply.

If, however, Wynken believed that the trustee had been properly appointed, so that he did not realise that he was himself acting as a principal, it would be difficult to characterise him as a *de facto* trus-

[13] A conclusion to this part.

tee, since he would not be purporting to act as a trustee. In these circumstances, his liability would depend upon his having dishonestly assisted Sleepy in the breach of trust as considered in (i), and the liability of Nod would be the same as previously considered in (ii).[13]

LOOKING FOR EXTRA MARKS?

- You could go much further in discussing the different judicial positions on recipient liability. For an example of how to tackle that, look at the previous answer to question 3. Given the recent flow of case law on the issue of dishonesty, you could include some discussion of these articles: S. Panesar, 'Test of dishonesty revisited' (2019) 210 (Oct) Trusts and Estates Law & Tax Journal 14–16 which considers the decision in **Group Seven Ltd v Notable Services LLP**, **CA**, where the criteria of dishonesty for knowing assistance in breach of trust is discussed, if the alleged accessory had suspicions but they did not amount to blind-eye knowledge; and M. Dixon's editorial, 'Dishonest strangers' [2019] Conv 195–198 which also discusses the **Group Seven** decision.

TAKING THINGS FURTHER

- Bryan, M., '*Boardman v Phipps*: Doing Equity Inequitably', in *Landmark Cases in Equity* (C. Mitchell and P. Mitchell, eds), Hart Publishing, 2012, p. 581.
  See this chapter for a discussion of breach of fiduciary duty.

- Chambers, R., 'The end of knowing receipt' (2016) 2(1) Canadian Journal of Comparative and Contemporary Law 1.
  This article discusses the circumstances surrounding knowing receipt and knowing assistance.

- Dixon, M., 'Dishonest strangers' [2019] Conv 195–198 (Editorial).

  The test for honesty and the relevant case law is considered in this article.

- Etherton, T., 'Constructive trusts: a new model for equity and unjust enrichment' (2008) 67 CLJ 265.

  This article covers the issue of whether constructive trusts are remedial or substantive.

- Panesar, S., 'Test of dishonesty revisited' (2019) 210 (Oct) Trusts and Estates Law & Tax Journal 14–16.

  *This article discusses **Group Seven Ltd v Notable Services LLP, CA**, on the criteria of dishonesty for knowing assistance in breach of trust, if the alleged accessory had suspicions but they did not amount to blind-eye knowledge.*

- Salmons, D., 'Claims against third-party recipients of trust property' (2017) 76 CLJ 399–429.

  This article considers the unjust enrichment argument.

Online Resources

www.oup.com/uk/qanda/

For extra essay and problem questions on this topic, as well as advice on revision and exam technique, please visit the online resources.

Trusts of the Family Home

ARE YOU READY?

In order to attempt the questions in this chapter you will need to have covered the following topics:

- Common intention constructive trusts
- Presumption of resulting trusts

KEY DEBATES

Debate: constructive trusts cover some of the 'high growth' areas such as family property.
For example, the 'new model constructive trust' of property owned by cohabitees was developed
by Lord Denning MR in the 1960s and 1970s. Although the post-Denning Court of Appeal rejected
his new model, a crucial idea underpinning it—that a constructive trust might be treated as a
remedy—was approved by Lord Browne-Wilkinson in *Westdeutsche Landesbank Girozentrale
v Islington LBC* **[1996] AC 669**, and so could be the subject of future development. Further development occurred in the House of Lords' decision in *Stack v Dowden* **[2007] UKHL 17, [2007]
2 WLR 831**, which also considered the Law Commission papers on the principles relating to the
property rights of cohabitees in a shared home. (See *Cohabitation: the Financial Consequences of
Relationship Breakdown—A Consultation Paper* (Law Com Consultation Paper No. 179, Part 2,
2006) and *Sharing Homes: A Discussion Paper* (Law Com No. 278, 2002).) A further report followed:
Cohabitation: The Financial Consequences of Relationship Breakdown (Law Com No. 307, 2007)
which proposed a statutory scheme for cohabitees provided they satisfy certain eligibility criteria.)
Further decisions include the Privy Council decision in *Abbott v Abbott* **[2008] 1 FLR 1451**, and
the Supreme Court decision in *Jones v Kernott* but it remains to be seen whether Parliament will
see fit to adopt this scheme which represents a radical approach to the determination of property
issues between cohabitees in the light of similar developments in other jurisdictions.

Angela was the council tenant of a house when Bertram, a married man, went to live with her there ten years ago. A year later, the council offered to sell the house to Angela at a discounted price, being 40 per cent less than the market price of £50,000, and Angela discussed this with Bertram. They agreed that the house should be conveyed into Angela's name alone as she was the tenant with the right to buy and Bertram was involved in divorce proceedings and property claims from his wife. Of the £30,000 discounted price, £5,000 was contributed by Bertram and the remaining £25,000 was raised by means of a loan to Angela from the Quicklend Bank plc, which it secured by a legal mortgage; Bertram acted as Angela's guarantor.

Angela and Bertram contributed equally to the mortgage repayments until Angela had a baby about a year later, after which they were paid by Bertram alone. Angela and Bertram decided to modernise the kitchen, and Bertram, being a qualified carpenter, made all the fitments and did most of the work. Six months ago Bertram left Angela and is now claiming half the beneficial interest in the house.

Advise Angela.

CAUTION!

- There has been much litigation surrounding this area of constructive trusts, of which *Stack* v *Dowden* [2007] 2 AC 432, in the House of Lords, and *Jones* v *Kernott* [2012] 1 AC 776, in the Supreme Court, are the most important. But bear in mind there are different routes to resolving this problem, namely—the acquisition of an equitable interest by proprietary estoppel.

DIAGRAM ANSWER PLAN

Identify the issues	■ Constructive trusts. Where does legal title lie? Who might have equitable title?
Relevant law	■ *Stack* v *Dowden*; *Jones* v *Kernott*

Apply the law	■ 'Domestic consumer context' but legal title in Angela's name only—so consider whether resulting trust still applicable despite *Stack* and *Marr* v *Collie*: Angela 90 per cent (includes discount); Bertram 10 per cent
	
	■ Constructive trust
	  • Express agreement—excuse for not putting Bertram's name on title—detrimental reliance
	  • Common intention—inferred from paying deposit, contributing to mortgage payments, and improvements—detrimental reliance from such payments
	
	■ Size of shares
	  • what parties intended in light of conduct (*Stack* v *Dowden*)
	  • later agreement to vary the shares (*Jones* v *Kernott*)

Conclude	■ Advise Angela

SUGGESTED ANSWER

[1] Establishes the key issue.

For Bertram to succeed, he would have to show that he had acquired a beneficial interest in the house by one of the ways recognised by law, under either a resulting or a constructive trust.[1]

[2] Some students miss this point and discuss the case as though it was a decision where the legal title was in one name only.

Although the majority of the House of Lords in **Stack v Dowden** **[2007] 2 AC 432**, said that the resulting trust has no role in the domestic consumer context, **Stack** itself was a case where the property had been put into joint names.[2] The majority view was that, in such circumstances, there was a strong presumption, based on the maxim that equity follows the law, that the parties also hold the equitable interest as joint tenants. Where property is vested in a single name, as it is in the problem, the application of such maxim would result in there being a strong presumption that he or she is solely beneficially entitled. This would mean that, in a single name case, it would make it more difficult for a non-legal owner, such as Bertram, to establish a beneficial interest, and it is unlikely that this is what the House of Lords intended. As their Lordships did not express that they were departing from the House's earlier (sole-name) decisions in *Pettitt* v *Pettitt* **[1970] AC 777** and *Gissing* v *Gissing* **[1971] AC 886, HL**, those cases remain binding where, as in the problem, the property is transferred into the name of one party only. Those decisions recognised that, in the absence of an express declaration of trust evidenced in writing and signed as required by the **Law of Property Act 1925, s. 53(1)(b)**, where the non-legal owner has made a financial contribution to the purchase price, the starting point is the presumptions of advancement and of resulting trust.

[3] Start with the resulting trust scenario.

There being no evidence of any express declaration of trust in the problem,[3] and as Angela is not Bertram's wife (where the presumption of advancement would apply), the starting point is that Angela and Bertram acquired, upon purchase, beneficial interests under a resulting trust in proportion to the size of their contributions. In *Springette* v *Defoe* **(1993) 65 P & CR 1, CA**, the discount on the market price on a sale to a council tenant was credited to the tenant statutorily entitled to buy, and this was followed in *Oxley* v *Hiscock* **[2004] 2 FLR 669**; so Angela is treated as having made a contribution of £20,000 by means of the discount. Angela also acquires a beneficial interest through the £25,000 advanced by the first mortgagee, as Angela was the borrower, and the loan would have been paid to the purchaser on her behalf. At the time the house was acquired, therefore, the beneficial interests under a resulting trust would have been: Angela 90 per cent (based on her total contributions of £45,000), and Bertram 10 per cent (based on his initial contribution of £5,000). Neither Bertram's acting as a guarantor nor his making contributions to the mortgage payments acquires for him a beneficial interest under a resulting trust, although these factors may be relevant in determining the size of his share under a constructive trust.

[4] Continue with the constructive trust scenario.

Bertram may also acquire an equitable interest in property under a constructive trust[4] if he satisfies the requirements set out in *Gissing* v *Gissing* **[1971] AC 886, HL**, and the constructive trust effectively supplants the resulting trust. For a constructive trust, there must be evidence of an (informal) agreement (express or inferred) or a common intention (as in *Drake* v *Whipp* **[1996] 1 FLR 826**) that he was to have a beneficial interest in the property at the time of its acquisition, and he must have acted on this understanding to his detriment. In *Lloyds Bank Ltd* v *Rosset* **[1991] AC 107, HL**, Lord Bridge said that, in the case of an express (informal) agreement, the detriment could be some material alteration in a party's position, but that, in the case of an inferred agreement, some direct contributions to the purchase price of the property, either initially or by way of contribution to the mortgage instalments, were necessary. Baroness Hale in *Stack* v *Dowden* suggested obiter that Lord Bridge's approach may have been too narrow. In any event, as Bertram contributed to the initial purchase price, he has surmounted this first hurdle.

[5]Deal here with the detrimental conduct cases.

It is also possible to acquire a beneficial interest under a constructive trust if there is evidence of an informal express agreement and the non-legal owner acts to his detriment in reliance on it.[5] Excuses for not putting a woman's name on the title jointly with the man's were held to evidence an express agreement in *Eves* v *Eves* [1975] 1 WLR 1338, CA (the excuse being that she was too young to be a legal owner), and in *Grant* v *Edwards* [1986] Ch 638 (the excuse being that her divorce settlement would be prejudiced). In both cases, the reasons given for omitting the woman's name indicated that her name would otherwise have been included on the legal title, from which it could be concluded that she was intended to have a share of the beneficial interest in the property. *Curran* v *Collins* [2015] EWCA Civ 404 makes clear though that the converse is not true. That is, where there is a denial of an interest at the outset with an explanation then that signifies the express absence of a common intention to share in the beneficial interest. Something like a 'but for' test, the point is that if Angela says to Bertram that he would have had an interest but for his divorce proceedings then the court will imply an intention. If she says that he is not getting an interest because of his court proceedings then that operates as a denial of an intention for him to have an interest. So, the basis on which the decision to vest the legal title in Angela's name alone will be critical.

[6]Deal here with the common intention cases.

The parties' reasons for not making Bertram a joint legal owner might similarly be evidence of a common intention that he should have a share of the beneficial interest.[6] His initial contribution of £5,000 and his guarantee of the mortgage (as in *Falconer* v *Falconer* [1970] 1 WLR 1333, CA) would be conduct from which a common intention could be inferred. The Court of Appeal in *Midland Bank* v *Cooke* [1995] 4 All ER 562, adopted a more liberal approach than Lord Bridge in *Rosset* as to circumstances which might give rise to an inference of common intention, and indicated that the court may consider all the dealings between the parties with regard to the property.

Assuming there is sufficient evidence of a common intention, Bertram would then have to show that he subsequently acted to his detriment in reliance upon this. He paid a deposit, contributed substantially to the mortgage repayments, and modernised the kitchen. These might all be regarded as sufficient conduct to his detriment to enable him to acquire an interest under a constructive trust. Once the existence of a beneficial interest under a constructive trust has been established, it is necessary to determine the size of the interest so acquired. It was said by the Court of Appeal in *Oxley v Hiscock* [2004] **3 WLR 715**, that the court should have regard to the whole course of dealing between the parties in relation to the property in deciding their respective shares. This view was largely confirmed by the House of Lords in *Stack v Dowden*, although Baroness Hale emphasised (at para. 61) that 'the search is still for the result which reflects what the parties must, in the light of their conduct, be taken to have intended' and 'that did not enable the court to abandon that search in favour of the result which the court itself considers fair'. Conduct may, of course, include financial contributions as well as discussions between the parties. Baroness Hale (at para. 69), in emphasising that 'context is everything', set out a non-exhaustive list of other factors which may lead to evidence of intention such as: the nature of the parties' relationship; the responsibility for children; the arrangement of finances; the discharge of outgoings and household expenses. The intention of the parties may also be deduced from their individual characters and personalities.

Thus, at the outset, a relevant factor in determining the respective shares under a constructive trust would include the fact that Angela and Bertram contributed equally to the mortgage repayments at first. The parties' intentions might, however, change, and with it the respective size of their beneficial interests: *Jones v Kernott* [2012] **1 AC 776**. It might be argued that the birth of the baby one year after the purchase of the property together with the change in their financial arrangements, whereby Bertram assumes responsibility for the mortgage payments, could affect the relative shares. Bertram's modernisation of the kitchen, if substantial, might also be an indicator of their intentions.

There being so many factors to take in account under *Stack v Dowden* in determining the size of the parties' respective shares, it is difficult to advise Angela what beneficial interest Bertram might have.[7] As in *Marr v Collie* where the determination of these issues was remitted back to the court of first instance this will be an inquiry of fact.

[7] Not defeatist—just realistic!

⊕ LOOKING FOR EXTRA MARKS?

- Further reference to Law Commission reports and secondary material could be made for extra points. Incorporating some of the academic debate into your answer is usually an excellent way to gain extra marks. Take a look, for example, at the discussion of the decision in ***Lloyds Bank* v *Rosset*** in Mills (2018) (see 'Taking Things Further').

ⓠ QUESTION | 2

Context here is set by the parties' common intention—or by the lack of it. If it is the unambiguous mutual wish of the parties, contributing in unequal shares to the purchase of property, that the joint beneficial ownership should reflect their joint legal ownership, then effect should be given to that wish. If, on the other hand, that is not their wish, or if they have not formed any intention as to beneficial ownership but had, for instance, accepted advice that the property be acquired in joint names, without considering or being aware of the possible consequences of that, the resulting trust solution may provide the answer.

(Lord Kerr in ***Marr* v *Collie*** [2017] UKPC 17)

Discuss.

⚠ CAUTION!

- The expectation with many tutors now is that you need to focus on secondary sources to do well. So, if your tutor falls into this camp, then only tackle this question if you are familiar with the commentary on the case.

▢ DIAGRAM ANSWER PLAN

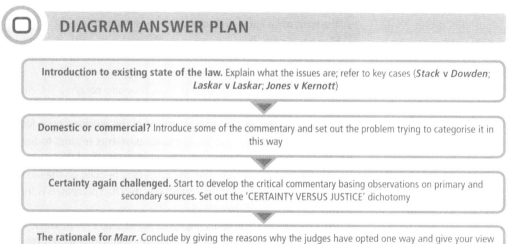

Introduction to existing state of the law. Explain what the issues are; refer to key cases (*Stack* v *Dowden*; *Laskar* v *Laskar*; *Jones* v *Kernott*)

⬇

Domestic or commercial? Introduce some of the commentary and set out the problem trying to categorise it in this way

⬇

Certainty again challenged. Start to develop the critical commentary basing observations on primary and secondary sources. Set out the 'CERTAINTY VERSUS JUSTICE' dichotomy

⬇

The rationale for *Marr*. Conclude by giving the reasons why the judges have opted one way and give your view with reasons

Introduction to existing state of the law

[1] This starting sentence shows you have spotted the underlying issue of law.

The problem of deciding ownership on relationship breakdown where unmarried parties have acquired co-owned property during the course of their relationship continues to produce much judicial activity.[1] Unsurprisingly, in such a situation the parties may well find themselves to be at odds over who owns what and in what shares. The possibility presented by the courts in recent cases opens up the chance to increase respective shares and potential litigants in such febrile circumstances may be willing to risk all (or a great deal) on fighting for what they consider is their right where their relationship has broken down. But after *Stack* v *Dowden* [2007] UKHL 17, *Laskar* v *Laskar* [2008] EWCA Civ 347, and *Jones* v *Kernott* [2011] UKSC 53,[2] there did at least seem to be some clarity in that a distinction had been drawn between property bought as a family home, on the one hand, and investment properties, on the other. In relation to family homes, it seemed that a 'holistic' common intention constructive trust approach applied whereas in relation to investment properties, a resulting trust analysis focused on financial contributions applied. This was the case even where the co-owners were in a relationship or simply members of the same family. But the Privy Council's decision[3] in *Marr* v *Collie* suggests that that blue line is not as clearly drawn as previously supposed.

[2] Bring in the leading cases.

[3] The status of Privy Council decisions in English law's system of precedent was clarified by the Supreme Court in *Willers* v *Joyce (No. 2)* [2016] UKSC 44.

[4] Give a succinct analysis of *Marr*.

The Privy Council in *Marr* v *Collie*[4] has decided that the correct basis for determining the beneficial ownership of a jointly-held asset, even one acquired as an investment, rather than as a home for the legal co-owners, is that established in *Stack* v *Dowden* rather than on the basis of an initial presumption of a resulting trust.

[5] The following paragraph sets out all the facts you need to set the scene.

Marr and Collie[5] began a personal relationship in 1991 and over the following years before their relationship broke down in 2008, acquired in their joint names, 11 investment properties. These were not subject to any express declaration of trust. They also bought a vehicle and a motor boat in their joint names and other various items including art. Marr contributed the cash element of the purchase price for these items and most, if not all, mortgage payments relating to the investment properties. Collie, who was a builder, claimed that it was intended that he would renovate the properties or build on the land and that all the items including the property they had purchased were intended to be equally owned.

The case brought into focus the approach of Lady Hale in *Stack* v *Dowden* [2007] 2 AC 432, that a conveyance into joint names creates a presumption of equal beneficial ownership, and, in contrast

[6] You could make much more of this point about the dissenting reason of Lord Neuberger in *Stack* if you have time in the exam (see 'Looking for Extra Marks?').

to that of Lord Neuberger[6] in *Laskar* v *Laskar* [2008] EWCA Civ 347 that the *Stack* principle was confined to domestic cases: i.e. trusts of the family home. Thus, where the cohabitees purchased a commercial property by way of investment then the traditional presumption of resulting trust applied, such presumption being capable of being rebutted by contrary evidence.

The case came to the Privy Council where Lord Kerr, giving the lead opinion, decided that the *Stack* approach was not to be confined to purely domestic cases and that where the parties are involved only in a personal relationship then, when they jointly acquire commercial property, their intention is a significant factor. It is noteworthy that the decision relates to all assets (not just land). Lord Kerr set out the principles to be considered when such circumstances arise. First, the 'context' should be considered. This approach reflects Lady Hale's approach in *Stack* which looked at all the circumstances of the relationship. So, context implies that an inquiry is made as to whether it is intended to be a purely commercial transaction—that then falls outside *Stack* and is subject to the traditional resulting trust approach. If context tells us it is not purely commercial then, again following *Stack*, joint legal ownership suggests equal beneficial ownership (equity follows the law). If any evidence of contrary intention is found at any point from the date of the purchase throughout the whole course of dealings between the parties, then that may rebut the presumption of equal beneficial ownership. Again that follows Lady Hale's list of factors relevant to determining the respective shares in the family home which she set out in *Stack* (para. 69). In the absence of any such intention, then the court may fall back on the presumption of the resulting trust.

Domestic or commercial?

So, when is a case domestic or commercial? Some cases are clearly domestic only as in *Stack*. But others may involve family members and yet concern property bought as an investment as in *Laskar*. Others, like the decision in *Marr*, can be a mixture of family home and commercial investments. The difficulty is clear when it involves those individuals as in *Marr* who are in a personal relationship and then together embark on a business investment. Is that a new adventure in their joint lives or the continuation of their relationship with its unwritten and probably even unexpressed sentiments about ownership as part of their joint future? Piska[7] (writing before the decision in *Marr*) suggested that it would be problematic for a court, in those circumstances, having to fit the case into the appropriate rule for domestic or commercial situations when the same factors are relevant to the determination of a common intention or a resulting trust. Indeed,

[7] N. Piska, 'Two recent reflections on the resulting trust' [2008] Conv 441 at p. 446.

[8]M. Yip and J. Lee, 'The commercialisation of equity' (2017) 37 LS 647.

the question of whether it is at all desirable to apply trust law to commercial contexts has been queried by Yip and Lee.[8] Similar problems have arisen in **Erlam v Rahman [2016] EWHC 111 (Ch)** (which is clearly now in conflict with **Marr**) and **Wodzicki v Wodzicki [2017] EWCA Civ 95** where commercial property was involved or the family members who were parties to the case were at arm's length. The possibility of mixed purposes was indeed recognised in **Stack** and it is clear now, post-**Marr**, that the **Laskar** attempt to confine **Stack** to the domestic context is wrong.

Certainty again challenged

The problem with this decision is that it yet again challenges that lawyer's hoped-for degree of certainty in resolving disputes in a post-breakup relationship. As George and Sloan point out:[9] presumptions give a degree of certainty in the uncertain and litigious world of relationship breakdowns. A resulting trust presumption gives a degree of certainty—where money is contributed then a resulting trust is presumed to arise in relation to that contributory money and was a starting point for Lord Bridge in **Lloyds Bank plc v Rosset [1991] 1 AC 107**. Inserting as a mechanism to dispute resolution an approach which requires a trot through all the circumstances of the relationship over the years leads to uncertainty and the likelihood of increased litigation which, in Dickensian terms, is likely to lead to more anxiety and financial gloom. What is worse is that **Marr** extends the uncertainty introduced by **Stack**, affirmed in **Laskar v Laskar** and **Jones v Kernott** to *all jointly acquired assets*. Further, as George and Sloan[10] suggest, an unintended consequence of **Marr** may be for one of the parties, in what is clearly a purely commercial transaction, to attempt to argue that the context of their commercial relationship gives rise to a common intention constructive trust. In other words, the clarity of the presumption of the resulting trust may now be blurred.

[9]M. George and B. Sloan, 'Presuming too little about resulting and constructive trusts?' [2017] Conv 303.

[10]See note 9.

The rationale for *Marr*

While bemoaning the uncertainty introduced by **Marr** which compounds the messy approach of **Stack** to determining the extent of the beneficial interest in such familial breakdown situations, it does nevertheless attempt to reflect the reality of life. There is often a grey area between property which is acquired as a purely domestic venture and property acquired for commercial purposes. A couple in a relationship may well invest their money jointly. They often view this as part of their future and part of the 'family'. It is not approached in a straightforward contribution of money but is the classic joint venture with a 'what is yours is mine' approach underpinning it. In such circumstances, **Marr** is struggling to engage with reality and produce the result which reflects the intention of the parties, albeit that intention may be vague, unthought, and unformulated. It is the age old dichotomy of 'justice versus certainty' although one may question the chance of judges, years after the events in question, really succeeding in finding justice in any particular case.

LOOKING FOR EXTRA MARKS?

- Lord Neuberger's speech in **Stack**, while coming to the same conclusion, dissented as to the reasoning. This question (because of the publisher's word limit) does not have space to deal with that other than in a brief reference but, if you have time in the exam, this would be worthy of inclusion for extra marks.

- Again, reference to the Law Commission Report is often felt desirable by tutors (even though the chance of it ever being implemented is so remote as to be on the other side of the solar system), so drop that in too (*Cohabitation: Financial Consequences of Relationship Breakdown*, Law Com No. 307, 2007) for extra marks.

TAKING THINGS FURTHER

The following three articles provide commentary on the topics of trusts of the family home and the way in which the courts are considering their application to commercial contexts.

- George, M. and Sloan, B., 'Presuming too little about resulting and constructive trusts?' [2017] Conv 303.
- Mills, M., 'Single name family home constructive trusts: is *Lloyds Bank* v *Rosset* still good law?' [2018] Conv 350–366.
- Piska, N., 'Two recent reflections on the resulting trust' [2008] Conv 441.
- Yip, M. and Lee, J., 'The commercialisation of equity' (2017) 37 LS 647.
  This article discusses what it says on the tin:

Online Resources   www.oup.com/uk/qanda/

For extra essay and problem questions on this topic, as well as advice on revision and exam technique, please visit the online resources.

11 Equitable Estoppel

ARE YOU READY?

In order to attempt the questions in this chapter you will need to have covered the following topics:

- Doctrine of proprietary estoppel
- Remedies
- Basic material on constructive trusts

KEY DEBATES

Debate: the role of unconscionability in proprietary estoppel and its remedies.

Proprietary estoppel remains a contested area with two House of Lords' decisions, *Yeoman's Row Management* v *Cobbe* [2008] UKHL 55 and *Thorner* v *Major* [2009] UKHL 18 following on from the innovative application of estoppel to limit a person's testamentary freedom by the Court of Appeal in *Gillett* v *Holt* [2001] Ch 210. All of these cases have generated an extensive discussion about the criteria and application of proprietary estoppel in academic circles.

The Law Commission Report, which led to the passing of the **Law of Property (Miscellaneous Provisions) Act 1989**, abolished the equitable doctrine of part performance. It was envisaged that the doctrine of estoppel would take its place, and there have now been two or three cases where this doctrine has been applied to prevent a contract or deed from being declared void for failure to comply with statutory formalities. However, each case needs to be carefully examined on its facts as the House of Lords made clear in *Yeoman's Row*. This is a topical and fast-moving area as estoppel seems to be the claim of choice currently where families are fighting over property.

Debate: how to satisfy the equity?

Estoppel cases are necessarily very varied in their results, but there is a helpful judgment of Walker LJ in *Jennings* v *Rice* [2003] (referred to in the questions) suggesting guidelines for the courts as to how they should satisfy an estoppel.

⊙

Because estoppel can give rise to a proprietary interest, it is of considerable importance in land law where it may be necessary to determine whether a third party will be bound or not by an estoppel interest. This chapter has not considered this aspect of the subject as this is usually dealt with in Land Law. Question 4 of Chapter 15 also includes an estoppel interest.

QUESTION | **1**

... once the elements of proprietary estoppel are established an equity arises. The value of that equity will depend upon all the circumstances including the expectation and the detriment. The task of the court is to do justice. The most essential requirement is that there must be proportionality between the expectation and the detriment.

(Aldous LJ in *Jennings* v *Rice* [2003] 1 P & CR 8)

Explain how the courts have sought to do justice in satisfying an estoppel.

⚠ CAUTION!

- Read the question carefully and take care to write about remedies to satisfy an estoppel rather than spending too much time on the doctrine itself.

- A good knowledge of *Jennings* v *Rice* as the leading authority on how an estoppel should be satisfied is required.

- Aim for a PEA approach throughout although bear in mind that you will have several points to make (which correspond with the headings) so the PEA will take place under each heading.

▢ DIAGRAM ANSWER PLAN

> Explain the nature of estoppel and its essential requirements

▼

> Explain the range of remedies which have been given to satisfy an estoppel

▼

> Discuss estoppels where money payments have been awarded instead of a proprietary remedy

▼

> Discuss the judgment of Robert Walker LJ (as he then was) in *Jennings* v *Rice*, where he considers proportionality in relation to expectation and detriment

▼

> Discuss the impact of the House of Lords' decision in *Thorner* v *Major* [2009] UKHL 18

▼

> Conclusions

[1] This introduction to the topic lays out the basics of estoppel. It is a brief introduction into the main topic.

Estoppel is a doctrine of equity[1] which has been applied to a variety of informal dealings in order to do justice. The essential requirements have been that a statement is made by one person as to their intention on which another person acts to their detriment in such a way that it would be unjust to allow the person who has made the statement to renege upon it (*Taylors Fashions Ltd* v *Liverpool Victoria Trustees Co. Ltd* [1982] QB 133).

Remedies

[2] Having briefly established the doctrine this is the **key point**.

[3] The point is followed in this paragraph by **evidence** and then *analysis*.

The doctrine is wide and has been applied to a variety of situations.[2] The interests granted to satisfy an estoppel are usually (although not always) proprietary. They have included[3] a right in the nature of an easement (*E. R. Ives Investment Ltd* v *High* [1967] 2 QB 379), a licence (*Inwards* v *Baker* [1965] 2 QB 29, *Matharu* v *Matharu* (1994) 68 P & CR 93), the full fee simple (*Pascoe* v *Turner* [1979] 1 WLR 431), a long lease (*Griffiths* v *Williams* (1978) 248 EG 947), and where it was applied prospectively to limit a person's testamentary freedom (*Gillett* v *Holt* [2001] Ch 210). However, in *Powell* v *Benny* [2008] P & CR D31, a sum of money was awarded. In *Crabb* v *Arun DC* [1976] Ch 179, Scarman LJ sought, as a remedy for estoppel, 'the minimum equity to do justice'. Estoppel was given proprietary recognition in the **Land Registration Act 2002, s. 116**.

[4] You will have covered promissory estoppel in contract.

Proprietary estoppel, unlike promissory estoppel,[4] may be used to found an action and is not confined to setting up a defence. It is not, like promissory estoppel, limited by the terms of a contract, and the courts have jealously guarded their wide discretion in applying it, taking into account any unconscionability and the circumstances of the parties. The statement giving rise to the estoppel may be vague as to what was actually intended and the detriment may be conduct over a number of years; these factors mean that the courts often have difficulty in finding a just solution. In some cases, it has been impossible to award an interest which exactly achieves what was required to reflect the estoppel, and the courts have awarded an interest which most nearly approxi-

[5] *Evidence* continues here with a good range of cases showing different remedies in different circumstances.

mates to it. Thus, in *Ungurian* v *Lesnoff* [1990] Ch 206[5] a life tenancy under the **Settled Land Act 1925** was awarded to a cohabitee, although it gave her the very wide powers of disposition under the Act, and in *Griffiths* v *Williams* a lease at a nominal rent for life. In other cases, the courts have exercised their discretion to err on the side of generosity because of the possibly difficult behaviour of one of the parties (as in *Pascoe* v *Turner*, where, on expenditure of less than £700 on a house, a cohabitee was awarded the fee simple), or have refused to make any award where the circumstances of the parties had changed so that this would have caused hardship to the party who had made the statement (*Sledmore v Dalby* (1996) 72 P & CR 196—where ten years' rent-free occupation had satisfied the estoppel).

Payments[6]

[6] Monetary payments are unusual (although becoming less so with the flow of cases) given the proprietary nature of the doctrine so worth a separate paragraph.

In some cases, the courts have taken the view that a monetary payment is the best way of satisfying the estoppel (*Guest v Guest* [2019] EWHC 869 (Ch); *Habberfield v Habberfield* [2019] EWCA Civ 890; *Davies v Davies* [2016] EWCA Civ 463). In *Wayling v Jones* (1995) 69 P & CR 170 the promised property had already been sold, so that the only possibility of compensation was by a money payment from the estate. In *Baker v Baker* [1993] 2 FLR 247, the relationship had broken down, so that the only practicable way of satisfying the estoppel was by a money payment. In *Dodsworth v Dodsworth* (1973) 228 EG 1115, where the promisees had spent £700 improving a house where they were told they could live for as long as they liked, they were allowed to remain there until the expenditure had been reimbursed. Money awards were also deemed appropriate in *Campbell v Griffin* [2001] EWCA Civ 990 and *Jennings v Rice* [2003] 1 P & CR 8 where the value of the equity resulting from the estoppel was found to be less than half the value of the house which the plaintiff claimed to have been promised.

Jennings v Rice[7]

[7] Good to link clearly to the quotation in the question.

Given the wide discretion which the courts have applied in the cases,[8] it is hardly surprising that Weeks J remarked in *Taylor v Dickens* [1998] 1 FLR 806 at first instance that one might as well 'issue every civil judge with a portable palm tree', and that equity was in danger again of becoming as long as the Chancellor's foot. Whilst a discretion is desirable to do justice in a particular case, it creates problems for lawyers who have to advise their clients.

[8] This paragraph starts with the *point*.

For this reason,[9] the judgment of Walker LJ in *Jennings v Rice* is to be welcomed as an attempt to lay down some guidelines.[10]

[9] This is part of the *analysis*.

Walker LJ said that the courts cannot exercise a totally unfettered discretion, which might anyway vary from one judge to another. He considered that any strict rules for the application of a discretion would be inappropriate, but that nevertheless, 'The need to search for the right principles cannot be avoided'. He conceded that the search would be difficult because of the unlimited variety of factual situations which could give rise to an estoppel.

[10] Set these out clearly—here your reading of the case will pay off.

Walker LJ observed that in these contractual cases where the promise and the detriment are fairly clearly defined and the arrangement between the parties does not fall far short of a contract, there is not much difficulty as the estoppel can be satisfied by the implementation of the agreement. An extreme example of such a case would be *Yaxley* v *Gotts* **[2000] Ch 162**, where there was an agreement but it was void as it failed to comply with the **Law of Property (Miscellaneous Provisions) Act 1989, s. 2.**

Where, however, the promisee's expectations far exceed what he might have expected as a result of the detriment, then the court should limit the expectations to make them more proportionate. The equity from an estoppel arises from the expectations and detriment and the unconscionable behaviour of the promisor, but the expectations and the detriment must be proportionate in the remedy granted.

Impact of *Thorner*[11]

On the other hand, distinct from cases where the interest is immediate, in other cases the assurance may relate to a future property right[12] (*Thorner v Major* **[2009] UKHL 18**; *Gillett v Holt* **[2001] Ch 210**). These cases present much more difficulty in satisfying the estoppel particularly where the expectation is to receive property on the death of the promisor.

In *Thorner*, the House of Lords acknowledged that an assurance as to an inheritance might well involve a change in the extent of the property between the date of the assurance and the death and that would then be relevant to the relief that the claimant was awarded. However, provided that there was still an identifiable property at the death then the court would be willing to grant the relief.

In *Thorner*, the claimant was granted the beneficial ownership in the whole of the farm and the business although the extent of the farm had changed since the first assurances. But the court was prepared to make an award since the approach is to look back at the time at which the promise should have been carried out and ask whether it would be unconscionable not to give effect to it. As Lord Hoffmann stated in *Thorner*, 'The owl of Minerva spreads its wings at dusk';[13] in other words, the assessment of the equity is retrospective.

The majority in *Thorner* based their view of the claimant's entitlement on the doctrine of proprietary estoppel whereas Lord Scott considered[14] that the nature of the expectation made a claim based on estoppel difficult, preferring the constructive trust as the better mechanism for realising the claimant's expectation. His view, first set out in *Yeoman's Row Management* where equitable relief was denied, was that cases where the expectation which had been disappointed was for a future property right were more appropriately dealt with using the constructive trust. In *Thorner*, albeit the basis for his decision was different from the majority, his view as to the way in which the equity should be satisfied (i.e. the transfer of the farm and the business to the claimant) was the same.

[11] A new heading here is useful to separate out these cases concerning future property rights (typically where a promise to leave property in a will is made).

[12] This is more **evidence** and *analysis*.

[13] See article by Lord Neuberger in 'Taking Things Further'.

[14] This point showing the debate between the majority and minority is worth extra marks.

Gillett concerns a future property right where the expectation was to receive property on death and the effect of the equity was to limit testamentary freedom. The Court of Appeal deemed that the promisor was estopped from denying the promise during his lifetime and undertook an inquiry into the extent of the estate making an award which was consistent with the reasonable expectation the claimant had been led to hold. The satisfaction of the equity there was to make an evaluation of what it was reasonable for the claimant to receive in the light of the promise which had been made and his detrimental reliance.

Conclusion[15]

[15] The conclusion is relatively brief as much of the analysis above incorporates concluding viewpoints.

So, it is clear that although there are some judicial guidelines as to the manner of satisfying the equity, nevertheless there remains much flexibility in the scope available to the courts in providing a particular remedy. The scope of an estoppel appears to be as unlimited as the factual circumstances which may arise.

LOOKING FOR EXTRA MARKS?

- Thoroughly analyse Walker's guidelines in *Jennings*.
- Cover the minority judgment in *Thorner* and analyse the points.
- Explain how proprietary estoppel differs from promissory estoppel.
- Use the full range of cases as evidence of each point.

QUESTION | 2

Luke is the owner of a large agricultural barn which he is using for his pottery business. Two years ago, Luke was approached by Eddy, an old friend from their school days, who had inherited a large amount of money from his father which had been made mainly from buying former agricultural buildings and developing them into high-quality housing. Eddy proposed that they should convert the barn into two large houses. As Luke had no money to invest in this venture, they agreed that Eddy would bear all the costs involved in acquiring planning permission; he would then buy the barn from Luke for £650,000 and undertake the development, and when the work was completed he would recoup his costs out of the sale of the housing and they would share the profits equally.

At some considerable expense, the planning permission was successfully obtained last year. However, Luke has now received an offer from AristoBuild plc to sell the barn to them, with the benefit of the planning permission, for £850,000. He is now refusing to go ahead with the original agreement with Eddy.

Advise Eddy.

⚠ CAUTION

- ▣ You need to know the cases on proprietary estoppel thoroughly.
- ▣ If coursework is set in this area then good knowledge of the journal articles is helpful.
- ▣ Watch out for a recent and topical case—this may well trigger a question in this area.

⬚ DIAGRAM ANSWER PLAN

Identify the issues	▣ Introduction to the context of the question and the doctrine of proprietary estoppel
Relevant law	▣ Discussion of the modern application of the doctrine to include the three elements: representation, reliance, and detriment
Apply the law	▣ Discussion of the circumstances in which the reliance took place and the extent to which it is reasonable for the claimant to have relied on the representation
Conclude	▣ Advise Eddy

Ⓐ SUGGESTED ANSWER

Introduction[1]

[1] The introduction covers the issues and outline of the law.

If the agreement between Luke and Eddy is in respect of an interest in land, the absence of any formalities as required by **s. 2(1) of the Law of Property (Miscellaneous Provisions) Act 1989** means that no action can be brought for specific performance of a contract. The question then remains as to what rights and remedies might be available to Eddy given that he has expended money in obtaining planning permission for the conversion of Luke's barn. Proprietary estoppel and the remedial constructive trust need to be considered. If these fail then Eddy may have to rely on personal claims for damages at common law such as unjust enrichment or *quantum meruit*.

Modern Application[2]

[2] This section and the next outline the development of the law and its modern iteration.

The essentials are threefold: representation, reliance, and detriment. There must be a clear and unequivocal representation whether by words or conduct made by the legal owner on which the claimant reasonably relies (and therefore changes his position) and on which the claimant acts to his detriment or is unconscionably disadvantaged (*Liden v Burton* **[2016] EWCA Civ 275**). Cases relying on the doctrine of proprietary estoppel can rest either on a common expectation, an imperfect gift, or a unilateral mistake (*Yeoman's Row* at para. 47 citing Gray and Gray, *Land Law*, 4th edn at 10.189). The problem posed in the question is one where there is an expectation held in common by both parties that the agreement will be carried through; that is, that Eddy will undertake the acquisition of the planning permission and will then buy the unconverted barn from Luke.

Belief Agreement Binding[3]

One issue which arises, therefore, is the extent to which the parties, and the claimant in particular, believed that the agreement was binding or knew that it was not. In *Ramsden v Dyson* **(1866) LR 1 HL 129**, Lord Kingsdown relied on the fact that the claimant mistakenly believed that the agreement was binding whereas in *A-G of Hong Kong v Humphreys Estate (Queen's Gardens) Ltd* **[1987] AC 114**, there was no question but that the claimant (the Government of Hong Kong) knew that the agreement was binding in honour only. In *Plimmer v Mayor, Councillors and Citizens of the City of Wellington* **(1884) 9 App Cas 699**, when a businessman engaged in an arrangement to provide landing places with the provincial government, it was held wholly inequitable that the government should be allowed to renege on this agreement. In *Taylors Fashions Ltd v Liverpool Victoria Trustees Co. Ltd* **(1979) [1982] QB 133**, Oliver J delivered an important analysis of proprietary estoppel when he stated that 'it would be unconscionable for a party to be permitted to deny that which, knowingly, or unknowingly, he has allowed or encouraged another to assume to his detriment ...' (at pp. 151–152).

Commercial or Family Context?[4]

These cases indicate a different approach between commercial and domestic contexts. Cases such as *Inwards v Baker* **[1965] 2 QB 29**; *Pascoe v Turner* **[1979] 1 WLR 431**; *Windeler v Whitehall* **[1990] 2 FLR 505**; *Gillett v Holt* **[2001] Ch 210**; *Grundy v Ottey* **[2003] WTLR 1253**; *Jennings v Rice* **[2003] 1 P & CR 8**; *Lissimore v Downing* **[2002] 2 FLR 308**, where there is a domestic context, tend to show a greater readiness on the part of the courts to apply the doctrine.

Where a claimant has a mistaken belief, on which they rely to their detriment, that they have a proprietary interest, the courts are more ready to accord them the right under the doctrine than in those cases of a commercial context where the parties are deemed to have been aware of the lack of their formal rights. In **Yeoman's Row**,[5] the House of Lords held that the claimant, a businessman, knew that the agreement was binding in honour only. His claim for enforcement of the agreement based on proprietary estoppel was therefore not upheld. He was only able to claim damages for the expenditure he had committed to the abortive project. The limitations of proprietary estoppel in commercial cases where there is no element of unconscionability was also considered in **Crossco No. 4 Unlimited v Jolan Ltd [2011] EWCA Civ 1619** and **Herbert v Doyle [2010] EWCA Civ 1095**. In **Thorner v Major [2009] UKHL 18**, a case of a familial context, the House of Lords came to an opposite conclusion. Their Lordships held that a representation had been made by the deceased that his cousin would inherit and that it had been reasonable for the claimant to rely on it and conduct himself in a way that was detrimental if the promise was not fulfilled.

[5] This case and **Thorner v Major** are highly dependent on their facts so it is worth setting them out in more detail than usual.

Where Estoppel is Conditional[6]

[6] Next *issue* and *rule*.

Difficulties have been raised about the applicability of proprietary estoppel to cases where the estoppel is conditional. For instance, in cases where the promise will only be implemented on death through inheritance as in **Gillett** then there is an argument that the promise which is conditional on death is uncertain. The property which is left at death may be different from the property which is in existence when the representation is originally made. Lord Scott[7] in **Thorner** at para. 20, argues that the remedial constructive trust is a better route to find a remedy in such cases than estoppel, 'For my part I would prefer to keep proprietary estoppel and constructive trust as distinct and separate remedies'. Lord Hoffmann at para. 8, however, in the same case, found no difficulty in applying estoppel to such cases arguing that certainty is available when the promise is realised and is achieved by ascertaining the form of the relief which equity can grant. The agreement between Eddy and Luke[8] is for a future agreement to convey land to take place. Had the planning permission not been obtained then the question apparently remains open: would the whole agreement have fallen? It would seem unlikely in the circumstances that Eddy would have wanted to go ahead with the agreement had the potential for redevelopment not been attained. In such a case, Lord Scott in **Thorner** expresses the view that the better remedy would be the remedial constructive trust. A constructive trust based on the decision in **Pallant v Morgan [1952] Ch 43** would not be effective because the land was not purchased following an agreement relating to the joint venture (**Banner Homes Group plc v Luff Developments [2000] EWCA Civ 18, [2000] EWCA Civ 3016**).

[7] This is the minority judgment—worth extra marks.

[8] Application of *rule* to *problem* here.

Lord Scott in *Yeoman's Row* (at para. 15) also indicated that a flaw in the claimant's argument in that case was that he was not claiming an interest in land as appeared to have been required by Oliver J in *Taylors Fashions* and Lord Kingsdown in *Ramsden*. Lord Walker at para. 61 in *Thorner*, indicates that the necessary requirement for proprietary estoppel to apply is for the assurance to relate to an identified piece of land owned by the defendant (*Crabb v Arun District Council* **[1976] Ch 179**). This is the case in the current problem—Luke is the owner of the barn. However, the point made by Lord Scott in *Yeoman's Row* is that the agreement was speculative. An 'expectation dependent upon the conclusion of a successful negotiation is not an expectation of an interest having [sufficient] certainty' (Lord Scott at para. 18). In this context, the interest to be granted lacked certainty and both parties knew that the agreement was not legally binding.

Application[9]

[9] These final paragraphs cover the final application of the law to the facts and incorporate the conclusions.

So, could Luke and Eddy's agreement be distinguishable from that in *Yeoman's Row*? There seem to be two possible grounds of distinction: the agreement is clear (the land will be transferred and the net profits split 50:50); and the parties are arguably not operating on a commercial basis (they are old friends and Eddy may not be running a business). The first point is problematic in that the agreement is presumably conditional on obtaining planning permission. That favours an outcome as in *Yeoman's Row*, i.e. estoppel is not available because there is no certainty as to the interest to be obtained. However, the judgment in *Thorner* clearly suggests that estoppel is retrospective—it bites not at the time of the assurance but at the point when the expectation is not realised. Once Eddy has obtained planning permission—as he has—then arguably the estoppel should be realised since there is a clear and unequivocal assurance as to the terms of the agreement.

The second point relating to the argument that the agreement was on a familial rather than a commercial basis where both parties might be considered to have clearly understood the lack of enforceability in their transactions, would rely on further evidence surrounding the capacity of the two parties. In both *Yeoman's Row* and *Thorner* much was made of the evidence surrounding the understanding of the parties. It is likely that that would be relevant again here to determine the context in which Luke and Eddy were operating. Finally, even if proprietary estoppel was not available there remains the possibility of an argument that Luke holds his land on a constructive trust for himself and Eddy to take account of his unconscionable conduct. In any event, the element of unconscionability—not specifically dwelt upon in *Thorner* although clearly acknowledged (albeit unsuccessfully in *Yeoman's Row*)—is plainly in evidence here.

[10] Extra marks here for comprehensive analysis including the common law outcome to the problem.

Failing all else,[10] Eddy would have a personal remedy for compensatory damages on a *quantum meruit* basis at common law for the expenditure he committed in obtaining planning permission.

LOOKING FOR EXTRA MARKS?

▪ Including the 'five *probanda*' is worth extra points to show your knowledge of the development of this doctrine. But it does make for a longer answer than you would normally be expected to produce so you might want to bear it in mind if this topic crops up as coursework.

▪ Dig a little deeper into the cases—discuss the differences between Lords Scott and Hoffmann in *Thorner v Major*. (Again, as before this makes this suggested answer quite long—so don't feel it is necessary to include this—you will still get a reasonable mark.)

▪ Be comprehensive in your use of case law—don't just limit yourself to the leading cases but give other examples in brackets (but don't go into depth on them unless it is coursework).

TAKING THINGS FURTHER

▪ Dixon, M., 'Proprietary estoppel: the law of farms and families' [2019] Conv 89–92.
This editorial provides some interesting commentary on estoppel in farming families—a common context for this area of law.

▪ Dixon, M., 'Confining and defining proprietary estoppel: the role of unconscionability' (2010) 30 LS 408.
An article considering the role of unconscionability after the decisions in **Thorner v Major** *and* **Yeoman's Row Management v Cobbe**.

▪ Gardner, S., 'The remedial discretion in proprietary estoppel' (1999) 115 LQR 438.
This article considers four different hypotheses upon which the remedy for estoppel could be based.

▪ Lord Neuberger, 'The stuffing of Minerva's owl? Taxonomy and taxidermy in equity' (2009) 68 CLJ 537.
This article considers the remedy for satisfying an estoppel and its timing.

▪ Malcolm, R., 'A rural family at war', *Estates Gazette*, No. 0108, 24 February 2001, pp. 162–163.
An article considering the decision in **Gillett v Holt**.

Online Resources

www.oup.com/uk/qanda/

For extra essay and problem questions on this topic, as well as advice on revision and exam technique, please visit the online resources.

Administration of Trusts **12**

ARE YOU READY?

In order to attempt the questions in this chapter you will need to have covered the following topics:

- Administration of trusts
- Powers of trustees
- Investment duties of trustees
- **Trustee Act 2000**

KEY DEBATES

Debate: the general principle that a trustee may not benefit from the trust is an important cornerstone principle. But it is subject to challenge and exceptions have emerged.

Some of these appear in the **Trustee Act 2000**. So the Act sets out circumstances where a trustee of a private trust who acts in a professional capacity may be entitled to receive reasonable remuneration out of the trust funds for any services that he provides to the trust. It is a key debate as to how these statutory exceptions marry up with the case law which is strict on the point.

Trevor is the sole trustee of an exhaustive discretionary trust of income, the objects of which are the nephews and nieces of Sally. Sally has two nephews, Benjy and Damian, and one niece, Caroline. Six months ago Trevor lent Benjy the sum of £20,000 out of his (Trevor's) own money. Caroline and Damian have now learned that Trevor has decided to pay the entire income of the trust for the present year, some £15,000, to Benjy. Caroline and Damian claim that Trevor exercised his discretion under the trust in Benjy's favour only in order that Benjy would be in sufficient funds to repay that loan. Caroline and Damian wish to have the proposed exercise of the discretion prevented, and further wish to compel Trevor to distribute the income for the present year among all three objects equally.

Advise Caroline and Damian.

CAUTION!

- The question concerns review of trustees' decisions. It is based on case law which looks at the context and deals with trustee discretion.

DIAGRAM ANSWER PLAN

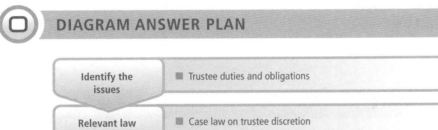

Identify the issues	■ Trustee duties and obligations
Relevant law	■ Case law on trustee discretion
Apply the law	■ Improper exercise of trustee's discretion? Trustee does not have to give reasons for decisions. Inspection by beneficiaries of trust documents. Court's exercising trustee's discretion?
Conclude	■ Advise Caroline and Damian

A

[1] Start by stating in what circumstances it is improper and then explain how and why.

If Trevor has exercised the discretion vested in him in order to ensure that he is repaid the debt Benjy owes him, this is an improper exercise of the discretion.[1] It is improper because the power of selection must be exercised in good faith and for its proper purpose: the trustee must consider the objects' interests, not his own. If Caroline and Damian can prove that the exercise was so motivated, they can apply to the court to have the improper appointment set aside, and Trevor will be personally liable to them for any loss resulting from the breach of trust: *Molyneux v Fletcher* **[1898] 1 QB 648**.

The problem for Caroline and Damian, however, is essentially one of proof. A trustee is not obliged to give reasons for the exercise of his discretions: *Re Beloved Wilkes' Charity* **(1851) 3 Mac & G 440** and *Re Londonderry's Settlement* **[1965] Ch 918, CA**. If, however, a trustee does give reasons, and these are improper, the objects can have the exercise set aside: *Klug v Klug* **[1918] 2 Ch 67**.

In *O'Rourke v Darbishire* **[1920] AC 581**, at pp. 626–627, Lord Wrenbury expressed the view that a beneficial interest under a trust carried with it a proprietary right to see trust documents. On this analysis, it would be important to determine whether objects of a discretionary trust, such as Caroline and Damian, have proprietary rights under the trust, and also whether the documents at issue can be characterised as trust documents: *Re Londonderry's Settlement* **[1965] 1 Ch 918**, at p. 938.

Lord Walker, however, delivering the advice of the Privy Council in *Schmidt v Rosewood Trust Ltd* **[2003] 2 AC 709**, said that the right to seek disclosure of trust documents was not based on any proprietary right, but was rather an aspect of the court's inherent jurisdiction to supervise, and if necessary to intervene in, the administration of trusts. Although not strictly binding in English law, the views expressed by the Privy Council in this case are highly persuasive.[2] Applying the principles there laid down, it would seem that, although an individual object of a discretionary trust (such as Caroline or Damian) does not have any proprietary right under the trust, such object may seek the protection of equity.

[2] Always good to point out the status of a Privy Council decision.

Whether any protection will be awarded to Caroline and Damian, and the nature of any such protection, is at the court's discretion, and will vary with the circumstances. In the *Schmidt* case, Lord Walker said that, in determining whether an object may see trust documents, the court may have to balance the interests of the different beneficiaries or objects, the trustees, and third parties.[3] In performing this balancing exercise, the court will accord greater weight to the claims of an object with a real (as opposed to a mere theoretical) possibility

[3] Shows good knowledge to quote the judge.

of benefit. The fact that Caroline and Damian are members of a very small class of discretionary objects is therefore favourable to their claim.

Lord Walker said[4] that the balancing of the various interests must also take into account any issues of personal or commercial confidentiality. In *Re Londonderry*, the object of a fiduciary power complained of the small amount of capital allotted to her by the trustees. She asked to see copies of the minutes of trustees' meetings and other correspondence in the hope that these would reveal the basis for the trustees' allocation. The Court of Appeal held that the trustees were not bound to disclose the documents: it considered that the disclosure of such confidential information could cause trouble in the family out of all proportion to any resulting benefit. It also said that, if the trustees knew that they could be required to make such disclosure, it might interfere with the proper exercise of their discretion. In *Breakspear v Ackland* **[2008] EWHC 220 (Ch)**, the beneficiaries sought disclosure of a wishes letter provided by the settlor to the trustees in a family discretionary trust. It was held that the confidentiality in the letter was, in the absence of some express term by the settlor, in the trustees, and they were under no obligation to disclose it. The discretion would be exercised in accordance with what was judged to be the best interests of the beneficiaries and the due administration of the trust, and on the basis of an assessment of the objective consequences of disclosure rather than by reference to the subjective purpose for which the disclosure was sought (*Dawson-Damer and Others v Taylor Wessing LLP* **[2015] EWHC 2366 (Ch)**).

As the discretionary trust in the question involves a very small group of family members, there is a real possibility of family strife[5] were Trevor to be compelled to disclose the documents giving the reasons for his decision to pay the entire income to Benjy. This factor might lead the court either to decline to order Trevor to reveal such documents to Caroline and Damian, or to compel them to reveal only such parts of them as do not indicate the reasons for his decision.

The Court of Appeal in *Re Londonderry* commented that the position would be different if an object were to make a case of *mala fides*.[6] The problem for Caroline and Damian, however, is that evidence of *mala fides* might be difficult to obtain without recourse to such documents. Unless Trevor has made statements disclosing bad faith, the objects might find it difficult to prove that the exercise was improper.

In *O'Rourke*, Lord Parmoor did not consider it important to determine whether the right of a beneficiary to inspect trust documents was based on a primary proprietary right, or whether it was a right under the law of disclosure to be enforced in the course of litigation:

[4] This paragraph is an 'extra marks' section. It also adds to the length of the answer and could safely be summarised in exam conditions.

[5] Family strife—the stuff of much litigation.

[6] This is the language used in the cases. You could just say 'bad faith' if you prefer.

O'Rourke, at pp. 619–620. In the light of these and other comments in *Re Londonderry*, it was suggested that where objects have no initial right to ask to see the documents in question, they might circumvent this problem by bringing an action alleging an improper exercise of the trustees' discretions, and then obtaining disclosure of documents in the proceedings: *Megarry* (1965) 81 LQR 196.[7] In *Scott* v *National Trust* [1998] 1 WLR 226, Robert Walker J opined[8] that trustees might be compelled through disclosure to reveal the substance of their reasons for their decision if such decision were directly attacked by legal proceedings. On the other hand, the courts are unwilling to award disclosure in a claim that is merely a 'fishing expedition', i.e. where the substance of the claim depends entirely on what might be revealed by the disclosure itself. In *Re Murphy's Settlements* [1999] 1 WLR 282, Neuberger J said that the absence of any suggestion that the trustees have acted wrongfully is a factor affecting whether the court will compel them to reveal information; and this seems to be consistent with the view of the Privy Council in the *Schmidt* case.

The fact that Trevor exercised his discretion in favour of an object to whom he had lent some of his own money only a short while before, might raise a suspicion that Trevor has not exercised his power for its proper purpose, and this might just weigh the scales in favour of disclosure in an action for breach of trust brought by Caroline and Damian.

Even if Caroline and Damian succeed in having the exercise set aside, they cannot themselves compel Trevor positively to exercise his discretion as they direct. All three objects together, assuming they are all *sui iuris* and form a closed class, could compel the distribution of the income to them under an extension of the rule in *Saunders* v *Vautier* (1841) 4 Beav 115. Caroline and Damian, however, are only two of the three objects of the discretionary trust of income.

It is unclear, however, whether the court would itself be able (or willing) to exercise the trustee's dispositive discretion under a discretionary trust.[9] In *Klug* v *Klug* itself, the court did order the advancement to be made; but it may be that it was merely giving effect to the wishes of the remaining trustee whose decision was not tainted by improper considerations. In *McPhail* v *Doulton* [1971] AC 424, the House of Lords stated that the court would, if called upon to do so, execute a discretionary trust in the manner best calculated to give effect to the settlor's intentions; and, ultimately, where a proper basis for distribution appears, this could be by itself directing the trustees so to distribute. In so holding, it revived the authority of eighteenth-century cases where the court had itself executed a discretionary trust: *Warburton* v *Warburton* (1702) 4 Bro PC 1 and *Richardson* v *Chapman* (1760) 7 Bro PC 318.[10] This jurisdiction will be exercised

[7] A nice academic 'extra marks' point (albeit made by a rather eminent judge). It adds extra words and could safely be cut out in exam.

[8] This is really the correct word as it is quoting the **opinion** of His Lordship.

[9] This point is unclear because of the precedents—so say so.

[10] Always fun to be able to cite a couple of really old cases.

only in the last resort: cf. *Mettoy Pension Trustees v Evans* **[1990] 1 WLR 1587**, where the court exercised the same jurisdiction to execute a fiduciary power. In practice, therefore, where a trustee persistently fails properly to exercise his discretion to appoint amongst the objects, the latter might be better advised to seek such trustee's removal and replacement: *Re Gestetner Settlement* **[1953] Ch 672** admits of such possibility.

LOOKING FOR EXTRA MARKS?

- Using the academic reference from Megarry's article in the LQR (see the answer) will gather extra marks.
- Dealing with the precedents as above—likewise.
- Citing some earlier authority which is relied on in the leading case.
- Discussing the judgments—as the suggested answer does. Note that this does add extra words to the normal length of an exam answer so you might not manage it in the exam—but bear it in mind for coursework questions.

QUESTION | 2

Six months ago, Topaz, a trustee, wished to sell some jewellery which belonged to the trust. He asked Jade, a jeweller whom he knew to have been fined for smuggling stones into the country a few years earlier, to carry out a valuation. Jade valued the jewellery at £100,000. In reliance upon this, Topaz instructed Jade to sell the jewellery for that amount to Sapphire, which he did. A month later, Sapphire sold the jewellery at an auction for five times that amount.

Three months after the sale, Jade had still not accounted to Topaz for the proceeds. Topaz then began to press Jade for payment, but was met with evasive replies. Last week, Topaz learned that Jade lost the entire £100,000 proceeds whilst gambling, and is now insolvent.

a Advise the beneficiaries of the trust as to their rights against Topaz.

b How would your advice differ if the trust had contained a clause excluding the trustee from all liability other than for 'wilful default'?

CAUTION!

- Do be careful to answer only what is asked and no more. Part (a) only asks for you to deal with their rights against Topaz. It earns no marks whatever to consider any rights the beneficiaries may have against any other parties mentioned. Differently worded, it could easily have become a question on tracing and third party receivers or dealers—but it is not. If you know your stuff, your answer should be a little gem.

■ The powers of a trustee to delegate have been considerably extended by the **Trustee Act 2000**; the examiners will expect you to be fully acquainted with the law. It should be noted that the appointment of an 'agent' under the statutory provision is not restricted to the appointment of an agent in the contractual sense, i.e. for entering into agreements with third parties. Thus, although a person appointed to value property is not a contractual agent, the **Trustee Act 1925, s. 22(3)**, expressly permits trustees to have the trust property valued 'by duly qualified agents'. It seems likely that the term 'agent' is used in a similarly wide sense in the **Trustee Act 2000**. A trustee is, for example, under a duty to keep proper accounts (*Pearse* v *Green* **(1819) 1 Jac & W 135**, at p. 140). Such a duty comprises a 'delegable function' (**s. 39(1)**) of a trustee of a private trust, so it seems that an accountant might be appointed to maintain the trust accounts as an agent under **s. 11**.

■ Part (b) concerns the validity of trustee exclusion clauses. Don't forget to answer this part. It is a common technique to add at the end of a question: 'How would your answer differ if …'. It is like the sting in the tail and you would be surprised how many students forget to answer it.

DIAGRAM ANSWER PLAN

Identify the issues	Delegation of trustee powers
Relevant law	**Trustee Act 2000**
Apply the law	(a) Appointment of agent (**Trustee Act 2000, s. 11**) • In compliance with statutory duty of care? • Did T opaz actively consider valuation? • Asset management function • Supervision of agent (**Trustee Act 2000, ss. 21–22**) (b) Meaning of 'wilful default' in earlier Trustee Acts Express exclusion clause • cannot exclude liability for dishonesty • dishonesty in context of solicitor-trustee
Conclude	(a) Advise the beneficiaries of the trust as to their rights against Topaz (b) Advise as to how would your advice differ if the trust had contained a clause excluding the trustee from all liability other than for 'wilful default'

Part (a)

[1] This opening paragraph sets out the key issues and the relevant law.

The sum of at least £100,000 has been lost to the trust as a result of Jade's gambling.[1] It may be that a further £400,000 has been lost through a sale to Sapphire at a considerable undervalue. The beneficiaries have a personal right of action against Topaz to require him to make good this loss if they can establish that Topaz has committed a breach of trust.

[2] You always need to include this caveat.

[3] What follows is the statement of the trustees' powers.

In the absence of any provision in the trust instrument,[2] trustees may authorise[3] any person to exercise any delegable function as their agent; and the appointment of an agent to value and to sell trust assets is a delegable function (**Trustee Act 2000, s. 11(1), (2)**). More specifically, trustees may have trust property valued by duly qualified agents (**Trustee Act 1925, s. 22(3)**). Topaz may nevertheless be liable to the beneficiaries on various grounds.

[4] Now list the points following the answer plan.

First,[4] it could be argued that the appointment of Jade as an agent was wrongful in itself. In appointing a person to act as agent, a trustee is under the statutory duty of care set out in the **Trustee Act 2000, s. 1(1)** and **Sch. 1, para. 3(1)(a)**. In appointing an agent, Topaz must therefore exercise such care and skill as is reasonable in the circumstances, having regard in particular to any special knowledge or experience he holds himself out as having or, if he acts as a trustee in the course of a business or profession, to any special knowledge or experience that it is reasonable to expect such a person to have. A trustee will not be liable for any act or default of the agent unless he has failed to comply with that duty of care (**Trustee Act 2000, s. 23(1)**).

[5] Good to pick up this point (and may be worth a few extra marks too). It is unusual to be able to cite the Law Commission in this way.

In its Report which led to the **Trustee Act 2000**, the Law Commission took the view that the statutory duty of care codified the liability of a trustee in equity: *Trustees' Powers and Duties* (Law Com No. 260, 1999), para. 3.24.[5] Assuming that this is correct, the principles laid down in the case law before the **Trustee Act 2000** continue to apply. The cases establish that a trustee is to be judged by the test of the prudent man of business acting in his own affairs: *Speight* v *Gaunt* (1883) **9 App Cas 1**. A prudent man of business would employ an agent only in his proper field (*Fry* v *Tapson* (1884) **28 ChD 268**); and in appointing a jeweller to value and sell jewellery, Topaz has probably satisfied this requirement. A prudent man of business, however, would probably not appoint as his agent to value and sell jewellery belonging to the trust a person whom he knows to have been convicted of a crime involving dishonesty. It is therefore likely that the choice of Jade as agent was itself a breach of trust, so that Topaz is personally liable for the loss to the trust.

Secondly, whilst the **Trustee Act 2000** permits a trustee (subject to specified exceptions) to delegate discretions as well as duties, on the facts of the problem Topaz initially asked Jade merely to value the jewellery. The decision to instruct Jade to sell would therefore have needed to be made on the basis of that valuation. If Topaz simply accepted Jade's valuation without himself considering it, this would itself be a breach of trust.

Thirdly, a trustee may not appoint an agent to exercise any 'asset management function' as his agent, except by an agreement which is in, or is evidenced in, writing and on terms that the agent will comply with a policy statement which the trustee has prepared (**Trustee Act 2000, s. 15(1), (2)**). An asset management function includes the acquisition of property which is to be subject to the trust (**s. 15(5)(b)**). If Jade was appointed to deal with the sale of the jewellery on the basis that the proceeds of sale would be paid to him, his appointment involved the exercise of an asset management function. Topaz will therefore be liable if his appointment of Jade did not meet the requirements of **s. 15**.

Fourthly, when a trustee has appointed an agent, he must keep under review the arrangements under which the agent acts, and must consider if there is a need to exercise any power of intervention (which includes giving the agent directions, and revoking the appointment) (**Trustee Act 2000, ss. 21, 22**). The trustee is therefore effectively under a duty to supervise the agent after appointment, in respect of which he is again subject to the statutory duty of care (**s. 2** and **Sch. 1, para. 3(1)(e)**). It might therefore be argued[6] that Topaz was in breach of his duty as trustee to protect the trust assets, in that he left a large sum of money (the sale proceeds) in Jade's hands for an undue length of time. Three months is surely longer than a prudent man of business would allow. It is likely that Topaz's inaction amounts to a breach of trust.

[6] Brief conclusion.

Part (b)

[7] A nice historical note. It shows breadth of reading and study.

An exclusion of liability for wilful default first appeared in trust instruments in the eighteenth century; but the exclusion of liability was put on a statutory footing in various Trustee Acts of the nineteenth century,[7] where the phrase was construed objectively, i.e. so as not to derogate from the principle laid down in *Speight v Gaunt* (1883) **9 App Cas 1** that a trustee must act as a prudent man of business would act in his own affairs: *Re Brier* (1884) **26 ChD 238, CA**. The same phrase was used in the Trustee Act 1925, s. 30(1) (now repealed), which Maugham J in *Re Vickery* [1931] **1 Ch 572**, however, interpreted literally, i.e. as requiring consciousness of wrongdoing. Maugham J reached this conclusion by relying upon *Re Equitable*

City Fire Insurance Co. Ltd [**1925**] **1 Ch 407**, a case which concerned the liability of auditors, not trustees. Maugham J's view conflicted with earlier cases such as *Re Brier*, and effectively made the section a fool's charter. Nevertheless, in *Armitage v Nurse* [**1998**] **Ch 241**, Millett LJ expressed support for Maugham J's interpretation.

[8] Another point showing depth and understanding.

The Trustee Act 1925, s. 30(1) was repealed by the **Trustee Act 2000**, so that a trustee no longer has the benefit of the statutory exclusion of liability.[8] A trustee may, however, have the benefit of an exclusion of liability clause contained in the trust instrument. The **Trustee Act 2000** does not invalidate trustee exclusion clauses; indeed, it effectively provides that the statutory duty of care may be restricted or excluded by the trust instrument (**Sch. 1, para. 7**). An exclusion clause in the trust instrument may be very wide in scope: the Court of Appeal held in *Armitage v Nurse* that such a clause may exclude the liability of a trustee for acts and defaults in carrying out his functions as trustee except those which involve dishonesty. This principle applies even if the trustee is a solicitor and himself prepared the trust instrument: *Bogg v Raper*, *The Times*, 22 April 1998, CA. The principle in *Armitage v Nurse* was slightly qualified in *Walker v Stones* [**2000**] **4 All ER 412, CA**, where it was said that, at least where the trustee is also a solicitor, the test for honesty is not purely subjective. Thus a solicitor-trustee who deliberately acts in breach of trust may be dishonest for this purpose, regardless of his subjective belief, if no reasonable solicitor-trustee could have thought that what he did was for the benefit of the beneficiaries (at p. 443, per Sir Christopher Slade).

[9] A summarising conclusion.

The exclusion clause[9] in the trust instrument in the problem will therefore be effective to protect Topaz from liability for breach of trust according to its terms for all acts except those involving 'wilful default' or dishonesty. The question does not state whether Topaz was a solicitor-trustee, but it does not seem that he deliberately acted in breach of trust. In any event, it would not appear from the facts given that he was dishonest, and it may well be that he was not conscious of any wrongdoing. In these circumstances, it seems likely that he will be able to rely on the clause to exclude his liability.

⊕ LOOKING FOR EXTRA MARKS?

▪ Trustee exclusion clauses are quite common in trust instruments nowadays, and it seems generally to be accepted that the **Unfair Contract Terms Act 1977** does not apply to trustee exclusion clauses: Goodhart, 'Trust law for the twenty-first century' (1996) 10(2) TLI 38. Since the Court of Appeal in *Armitage v Nurse* [**1998**] **Ch 241** upheld the validity of a very wide exclusion clause, however, such clauses have been a matter of concern, being the subject of a Consultation Paper, *Trustee Exemption Clauses*, produced by the Trust Law Committee in 1998. Dealing with this point would be worth extra marks.

▨ During the passage of the **Trustee Act 2000** through the House of Lords, some of their Lordships expressed concern that professional persons acting for a settlor in drawing up a trust instrument are effectively free to insert an exclusion clause protecting them from liability, whilst at the same time charging for their professional services to the trust. The Lord Chancellor agreed that the matter needed to be looked into and referred it to the Law Commission, which subsequently published a Report, *Trustee Exemption Clauses* (Law Com No. 301, 2006). The Report indicates that the Law Commission retreated from the view expressed in its earlier Consultation Paper (Consultation Paper No. 171, 2002) which had favoured legislation; instead the Law Commission recommended only the introduction of rules of practice. Reference to this could be worth extra marks.

QUESTION | 3

By his will, Edward, who died earlier this year, gave £500,000 to his trustees, Sam and Giles, in trust for Edward's daughter, Daphne, for life, remainder to Edward's nephew, Norris. The will gave the trustees an express power to invest in shares quoted on the London Stock Exchange, 'except in shares of Maropet plc'. Sam is a solicitor; Giles is a farmer and an old friend of Edward. Sam and Giles would like to invest part of the trust fund in Old Masters. Norris is a keen environmentalist, and he has written to the trustees asking that they do not make investments in companies which engage in the emission of greenhouse gases.

In the light of these circumstances, advise Sam and Giles:

a   of their powers of investment;

AND

b   as to their duties in selecting investments.

CAUTION!

▨ The law relating to trustee investment was considerably altered and simplified by the **Trustee Act 2000**. This question covers what qualifies as an investment, and the equitable and statutory duties of trustees relating to the selection and review of investments.

DIAGRAM ANSWER PLAN

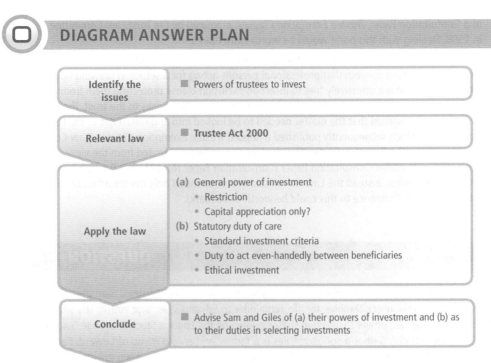

Identify the issues	■ Powers of trustees to invest
Relevant law	■ Trustee Act 2000
Apply the law	**(a)** General power of investment • Restriction • Capital appreciation only? **(b)** Statutory duty of care • Standard investment criteria • Duty to act even-handedly between beneficiaries • Ethical investment
Conclude	■ Advise Sam and Giles of (a) their powers of investment and (b) as to their duties in selecting investments

A) SUGGESTED ANSWER

Part (a)

[1] First paragraph sets out the key issue and the law.

Subject to any provisions in the trust instrument, a trustee may make any kind of investment that he could make if he were absolutely entitled to the trust assets (**Trustee Act 2000, s. 3(1)**).[1] This power is called 'the general power of investment' (**s. 3(2)**). The general power of investment does not itself give trustees a power to make investments in land (other than in loans secured on land) (**s. 3(3)**); trustees are, however, given a separate power to acquire as an investment freehold or leasehold land in the United Kingdom (**s. 8(1)(a)**).

The general power of investment is additional to any express powers of investment, but is subject to any restriction or exclusion that the trust instrument may contain (**s. 6(1)**). Had the investment clause

[2] Start here applying the law to the problem.

in the question provided that the trustees were to be empowered to invest *only* in shares quoted on the London Stock Exchange, the general power of investment would have been effectively excluded.[2] The positive inclusion of a power to invest in shares quoted on the Stock Exchange is not, however, to be treated as an exclusion of the general power of investment. Sam and Giles therefore have the general power of investment, subject only to the restriction on investing in shares in

Maropet plc. That this is the intended effect of the statute is apparent

from an explanatory note which the Law Commission attached to the clause of its Draft Bill which later became **s. 6 of the Trustee Act 2000**: Law Commission, *Trustees' Powers and Duties* (Law Com No. 260, 1999).[3]

The older view of an investment is that it is the purchase of property from which interest or income is expected to accrue: *Re Wragg* [1919] 2 Ch 58.[4] More recently, however, it has been accepted that an investment includes any laying out of money with a view to obtaining a return, which suggests that even the purchase of an asset which can produce a return only on sale is included: *Re Lilly's Will Trusts* [1948] 2 All ER 906. The modern view is that investment may include a capital, as well as an income, return: *Cowan v Scargill* [1985] Ch 270; *Harries v Church Commissioners for England* [1992] 1 WLR 1241, at p. 1246. On this basis, the purchase of Old Masters, which do not themselves produce an income, could today be regarded as an investment. The risk for the trustees, however, is that if such paintings were sold soon after purchase, it might be argued that they were acquired not for investment but for purposes of trading, with the result that the profits of the sale could be liable to income tax.

Part (b)

The **Trustee Act 2000**[5] subjects trustees to a statutory duty of care, which applies when a trustee is exercising the general power of investment or any other power of investment, however conferred, or when carrying out his statutory duties in relation to the exercise of a power of investment or to the review of investments (under **ss. 4** and **5**) (**Trustee Act 2000, ss. 1** and **2** and **Sch. 1, para. 1**).

The duty of care requires a trustee to exercise such care and skill as is reasonable in the circumstances, having regard in particular to any special knowledge or experience that he has or holds himself out as having, and (if he acts as a trustee in the course of a business or profession) to any special knowledge or experience that it is reasonable to expect of such a person (**Trustee Act 2000, s. 1(1)**). It would appear that this puts into statutory form a distinction which had been previously drawn in the case law, under which a professional trustee (namely a trust corporation) is treated as subject to a higher standard of care than an unpaid (lay) trustee: *Re Waterman's Will Trusts* [1952] 2 All ER 1054; *Bartlett v Barclays Bank Trust Co. Ltd (No. 1)* [1980] Ch 515, at p. 534 and *Pitt v Holt* [2011] EWCA Civ 197, [2011] 3 WLR 19. It would appear from the question that Giles is a lay trustee; he will therefore be judged by the standard of care established in the case law, namely that of the prudent man of business investing for the benefit of persons for whom he feels morally bound to provide: *Re Whiteley* **(1886) 33 ChD 347**, at p. 355 (Lindley LJ). In investing, therefore, Giles may not take more than a prudent degree of risk: *Learoyd* v *Whiteley* **(1887) 12 App Cas 727**, at p. 733; *Bartlett* v *Barclays Bank Trust Co. Ltd (No. 1)* **[1980] Ch 515**, at p. 531. Although he is not a professional trustee, Sam is a professional person, so that it would seem that he will be required to exercise a higher degree of skill in relation to the legal work which he performs for the trust.

In exercising any power of investment, whether under the **Trustee Act 2000** or otherwise, a trustee must have regard to the standard investment criteria, and must from time to time review the investments of the trust and consider whether, having regard to such criteria, they should be varied (**Trustee Act 2000, s. 4(1), (2)**). The standard investment criteria require the trustee to have regard to the suitability of the investment to the trust and to the need for diversification so far as is appropriate to the circumstances of the trust (**s. 4(3)**). The statutory duty to select suitable investments is twofold: if, for instance, trustees are considering investing in shares in X plc, they must consider both whether investment in shares is suitable for the trust, and whether shares in X plc are a suitable investment within that class. Diversification is important in order to spread the risk of investment. Sam and Giles might therefore be in breach of trust were they to invest the entire trust fund, for instance, in the shares of one company. The trustees are not, however, guarantors of the success of their investment policy, and so are not liable merely because the investments do not, in the course of time, turn out to have been the most profitable that could have been made: *Nestle* v *National Westminster Bank plc* **[1993] 1 WLR 1260, CA**.

Both duties effectively require the trustees to have regard to the particular trust; and the trustees must act even-handedly between the beneficiaries. In the problem, therefore, the investments should be selected so as to provide, so far as possible, both a reasonable income for Daphne for her life, and reasonable capital growth for the remainderman, Norris. The trustees would therefore probably be in breach of trust were they to invest the entire trust fund in Old Masters, since, apart from breaching the duty to diversify, they would be investing in a way that would produce no income for Daphne.

In selecting investments, and having regard to the above, the trustees' duty is to secure the maximum financial return for the trust: *Harries* v *Church Commissioners for England* **[1992] 1 WLR 1241**, at p. 1246. The consequence is that, in a private trust (such as that in the question), the trustees may not have a policy of ethical investment which would be likely significantly to reduce financial returns. The only exception to this in the case of a private trust is where all the beneficiaries are *sui iuris*, form a closed class, and unanimously agree to such a policy: ***Cowan v Scargill* [1985] Ch 270.** Therefore, even assuming Norris is at least 18 years of age, the trustees would probably be in breach of trust in pursuing the ethical policy he proposes unless Daphne expressly agrees to it.[6]

[6] This last concluding sentence is probably as far as you can go in presenting a firm conclusion.

 ## LOOKING FOR EXTRA MARKS?

▨ Including some development of the law to show how it stands today and how it has travelled is worth marks as showing depth of study and understanding of the topic.

 ## TAKING THINGS FURTHER

▨ Hayton, D., 'The irreducible core content of trusteeship', in *Trends in Contemporary Trust Law* (A. J. Oakley, ed.), Oxford University Press, 1996, chapter 3.
This chapter provides some highlights for your revision.

▨ Luxton, P., 'Trustee exclusion clauses: lost in the heather?', in *Modern Studies in Property Law: Volume 1: Property 2000* (E. Cooke, ed.), Hart Publishing, 2001, chapter 3.
This chapter provides a good critique of trustee exclusion clauses.

 ## Online Resources   www.oup.com/uk/qanda/

For extra essay and problem questions on this topic, as well as advice on revision and exam technique, please visit the online resources.

Debate: the role of tracing for breach of trust and the change in position defence.

Cases such as *Re Diplock* [1948] Ch 465, CA, *Lipkin Gorman* v *Karpnale Ltd* [1991] 2 AC 548, HL, *Westdeutsche Landesbank Girozentrale* v *Islington LBC* [1996] AC 669, HL, and *Foskett* v *McKeown* [2001] AC 102, HL form part of this debate.

QUESTION | 1

The only restriction on the ability of equity to follow assets is the requirement that there must be some fiduciary relationship which permits the assistance of equity to be invoked.

(Per Millett J, *Agip (Africa) Ltd* v *Jackson* [1990] Ch 265)

Discuss, in the light of this quotation, the requirement that there must be some fiduciary relationship before tracing in equity is permitted.

CAUTION!

- The central issue in this question is the requirement of a fiduciary relationship, so the answer requires a thorough discussion of the case law on this point. The crucial thing is to ensure that the answer does not deteriorate into one of the 'write all you know' type. Related ideas can therefore be explored, but only to the extent that they throw light on the central issue.

DIAGRAM ANSWER PLAN

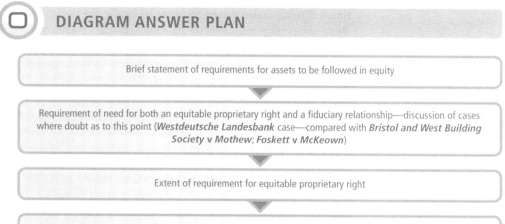

Brief statement of requirements for assets to be followed in equity

Requirement of need for both an equitable proprietary right and a fiduciary relationship—discussion of cases where doubt as to this point (*Westdeutsche Landesbank* case—compared with *Bristol and West Building Society v Mothew*; *Foskett v McKeown*)

Extent of requirement for equitable proprietary right

Discussion of types of fiduciary relationship and the courts' flexible approach

SUGGESTED ANSWER

[1] Set out the legal context.

There are certain requirements which must be satisfied before a claimant may follow assets in equity.[1] These are: there must be an equity to trace; the property must be traceable; and the result must not be inequitable. The issue in the question is whether the first of these requirements, the equity to trace, imports the need for a fiduciary relationship.

[2] Brief discussion of development of tracing to show current status.

Before the **Judicature Acts 1873** and **1875**,[2] the courts of common law and the Court of Chancery applied their own distinctive rules relating to tracing. Just as tracing at common law was available only to a person who had a proprietary right at law, so tracing in equity was available only to a person who had a proprietary right in equity. Following those Acts, it might have been thought that equitable tracing would be available to a beneficial legal owner where common law tracing proved inadequate. This indeed appears to have been recognised in *Banque Belge Pour L'Etranger v Hambrouck* [1921] 1 KB 321, CA. In *Re Diplock* [1948] Ch 465, however, the Court of Appeal expressed the view that, in order to be able to trace in equity, it was

[3] An important point which mustn't be missed with supporting cases.

not sufficient for the claimant merely to have an equitable proprietary right, there also had to be a fiduciary relationship.[3] In *Westdeutsche Landesbank Girozentrale v Islington LBC* **[1996] AC 669**, the House of Lords seemed to accept the correctness of this proposition. Other cases, however, reveal some judicial reluctance to accept such a requirement. Doubts were expressed by Millett LJ in *Bristol and West Building Society v Mothew* **[1998] Ch 1**, at p. 23; and in *Foskett v McKeown* **[2001] 1 AC 102**, Lord Millett (then in the House of Lords) stated that he could see no logic in the requirement. These observations may indicate that the Supreme Court might at some future time wish to reconsider *Re Diplock*. The requirement for a fiduciary relationship in order to trace in equity remains, however, for the present at least.[4]

[4] Shows you recognise the possibility of change in the future.

[5] Explain how fiduciary relationship arises.

Where the claimant has an equitable proprietary right, there will be a fiduciary relationship.[5] The classic example of this is, of course, the trust, whether express, implied, or constructive. A trust is not, however, a prerequisite: a person who entrusts property to a fiduciary, for instance, will retain an equitable proprietary interest sufficient to enable her to trace. Thus, in *Re Hallett's Estate* **(1880) 13 ChD 696**, one Mrs Cotterill paid money to her solicitor to invest on her behalf; instead he paid part of this into his personal bank account. It was held that, in these circumstances, Mrs Cotterill was entitled to trace her money in equity. The same principles apply to all fiduciary relationships, such as those between a company and its directors, between a principal and agent, and between partners in a business *inter se*.

[6] Explain need for proprietary right.

It is clear, however, that a fiduciary relationship is not itself sufficient to enable the claimant to trace.[6] Tracing is, after all, the process of identifying the claimant's property or its product in a third party's hands, so there can be no right to trace if the claimant has no proprietary right to the assets in question. In the *Westdeutsche Landesbank* case, the House of Lords held that the bank retained no proprietary interest in money which it had paid to the defendant local authority under an interest rate swap arrangement which was *ultra vires* the local authority. The claimant would therefore have had no right to trace such money in equity. On the other hand, it may be that the requisite proprietary right need not be equitable. In *Aluminium Industrie Vaassen BV v Romalpa Aluminium Ltd* **[1976] 1 WLR 676**, it was held that, where a fiduciary relationship existed, even a legal owner (with no distinct equitable proprietary right) could trace in equity.

Because no fiduciary relationship exists in respect of property vested in a beneficial legal owner, it might appear that tracing is not available to such owner if the property is stolen from him by a thief. If the property stolen is money and is mixed by the thief in his own bank account, the victim, whilst possessing a personal remedy against the thief, cannot claim any legal proprietary remedy against the money in the account. In such circumstances, however, the House of Lords accepted that, once the victim's legal title to the money passes (upon mixing in the account), a constructive trust is imposed upon the thief, and it is this trust which gives rise to a fiduciary relationship enabling the victim to trace in equity into the mixed fund: see *Lipkin Gorman* v *Karpnale Ltd* **[1991] 2 AC 548** (Lord Templeman); and the *Westdeutsche Landesbank* case (Lord Browne-Wilkinson).

The case law provides other illustrations of the courts' willingness to interpret the requirement for a fiduciary relationship flexibly.[7] It does not, for example, matter that such relationship does not exist between the claimant and the person against whom the tracing claim is brought. In *Re Diplock* itself, money was wrongfully distributed by the executors of a will to a number of charities. It was held that the next of kin, who should have been entitled to such money, were entitled to trace into the hands of the money's innocent recipients. The right of the next-of-kin to trace arose from their equitable right against the executors to have the estate properly distributed. In that case, therefore, the fiduciary relationship was between the next-of-kin and the executors.

Another example of the courts' flexible approach is in relation to payments made under a mistake.[8] A fiduciary relationship, giving rise to a right to trace in equity, can also arise where the defendant receives the claimant's property as a result of a mistake. In *Chase Manhattan Bank NA* v *Israel-British Bank (London) Ltd* **[1981] Ch 105**, the plaintiffs, as a result of a bookkeeping error, wrongly made a double payment of $2 million into the account of the defendant bank. At that time, the common law action of money had and received did not apply to money paid as a result of a mistake of law, which that was (but this is no longer so: see *Kleinwort Benson Ltd* v *Lincoln City Council* **[1999] 2 AC 349, HL**). The plaintiffs therefore needed to be able to trace in equity. It was held that the mistaken second payment gave rise to a fiduciary relationship, which gave the plaintiffs a right to trace. The House of Lords in the *Westdeutsche Landesbank* case has since doubted that the fiduciary relationship arose at the time of the mistaken second payment; rather, their Lordships considered that it arose only when the defendant's conscience was affected, i.e. when it became aware of the mistake two days later. In *Angove's Property Ltd* v *Bailey* **[2016] UKSC 47**, the Supreme Court suggested that where money is transferred with the intention of transferring the entire beneficial interest then a constructive trust will only arise where that intention is vitiated by a fundamental mistake or where the money has come into the wrong hands through fraud or theft or other

[7] Illustrate with case law.

[8] More examples given here with cases to illustrate.

like actions. A fundamental mistake is a narrow concept only arising where the payment is made to the wrong person or where the wrong item is transferred. This casts further doubt on *Chase Manhattan* although the comments in *Angove's Property* are only obiter. So the decision in *Chase Manhattan* nevertheless remains good law insofar as it illustrates that the fiduciary relationship needed to trace does not need to be a pre-existing one.

LOOKING FOR EXTRA MARKS?

- Further detail on the cases could be added for extra marks.

QUESTION | 2

Brown is a solicitor and a trustee of the Rainbow Trust. His co-trustee, Grey, is not a solicitor, but is a member of the Rainbow family. Grey is content to leave the entire management of the trust to Brown. Under the terms of the trust, Leone has a life interest, and the capital is held for Azure and Grey in equal shares.

In 2004, Brown invested half of the trust fund in the family company, Rainbow Ltd, which he understood to be an authorised investment within the terms of the trust deed. In fact, the trust deed expressly prohibited the trustees from investing more than one-fifth of the trust fund in Rainbow Ltd. When Rainbow Ltd went into insolvent liquidation in 2015, the trust's total investment in that company was lost. All the other investments which Brown made have been very successful, however, and during the period he has been administering the trust a healthy capital growth has been achieved.

Between 2004 and 2015, Brown made advances of capital sums out of the trust to Leone, which comprised breaches of trust. Brown did not realise that these payments were in breach of trust, as he did not check the terms of the trust deed, which he kept in his office safe.

Advise Azure.

CAUTION!

- The question is not difficult but requires a knowledge of the statutory provisions imposing liability and providing defences. Discussion of the case law dealing with the possibility of setting off a profit made by successful investments against losses sustained by an improper investment is required, however, to achieve a good mark.

- There is only one devious point hidden in the question and that relates to the limitation period. The clue to look out for is the careful use of dates. If they are not relevant, the examiner would probably have simply set the events in the previous year.

DIAGRAM ANSWER PLAN

Identify the issues	▦ Liability of trustee for breach of trust
Relevant law	▦ **Trustee Act 1925, s. 61** and case law including *Target Holdings v Redferns*; *AIB v Redler*; *Dimes v Scott*; etc.
Apply the law	▦ Establishing the breaches of trust in the problem and the nature of the liability of the trustees • Effect of breach which results in enhancement of profits for beneficiaries (rule in *Dimes v Scott*) • Reversal of rule where gain and loss made in single transaction (*Fletcher v Green*) • Effect of limitation in the **Limitation Act 1980, s. 21(3)** on problem • Relief for trustee acting honestly and reasonably and who ought fairly to be excused (**Trustee Act 1925, s. 61**) • Distinction between status of professional trustee (Brown) and lay trustee (Grey) • Unjust enrichment of Leone; tracing and the defence of change of position • Partial indemnities
Conclude	▦ Advise Azure

A **SUGGESTED ANSWER**

¹Introduction setting out the law with reference to facts of problem.

The basic principle is that trustees who commit a breach of trust which results in a loss to the trust estate are personally liable to the beneficiaries to make good the loss.¹ Brown's excessive investment in Rainbow Ltd and the wrongful advances of capital were both in breach of the terms of the trust deed. Brown is therefore prima facie liable to make good such losses to the trust fund. The liability of trustees is personal, not vicarious: *Townley v Sherborne* **(1643) J Bridg 35**. Grey is not therefore vicariously liable for Brown's breaches of trust. Grey may be personally liable for his own breach, however, in failing to participate in the management of the trust and merely leaving matters in the hands of his co-trustee: *Bahin v Hughes* **(1886) 31 ChD 390**. Equity does not, after all, countenance a sleeping trustee.

[2] Establish the breaches of trust in the problem and the nature of the liability of the trustees.

The investment in Rainbow Ltd is a breach of trust to the extent that the amount invested exceeded the one-fifth limit imposed by the trust instrument.[2] The measure of the trustees' liability is the loss caused to the trust. In this instance, the onus would be on Azure to establish that there is a loss which would not have occurred but for the breach: *AIB Group (UK) plc v Mark Redler & Co Solicitors* [2014] UKSC 58; *Target Holdings Ltd v Redferns* [1996] 1 AC 421, HL, at p. 440. Unless there are circumstances which indicate that the trustees were in breach of trust in investing in Rainbow Ltd at all, it would seem that the trustees' liability would be limited to the loss of the excess over one-fifth only.

Brown has, however, invested the remaining assets profitably. Normally, a gain made in one transaction may not be set off against a loss suffered in another. This is the rule established in *Dimes v Scott* (1828) 4 Russ 195,[3] where the trustees retained an unauthorised investment for longer than the prescribed period. When the investment was eventually sold, the trustees were able to invest extensively in Consols, as the price had dropped. This resulted in a greater gain for the remaindermen. The trustees were nevertheless held liable for the loss caused by the retention of the unauthorised investment without being allowed to set off the gain.

[3] Set out the rule then deal with the circumstances when it is reversed.

[4] Here comes the reversal of the rule.

If the gain and the loss were made in a single transaction, though, then the rule is reversed.[4] In *Fletcher v Green* (1864) 33 Beav 426, the proceeds of sale of an unauthorised investment were invested in Consols, the value of which then rose. It was held that the trustees were entitled to take advantage of such rise. The difficulty, as these cases illustrate, is often in determining whether the gains and losses occur in the same or in separate transactions. In *Bartlett v Barclays Bank Trust Co. Ltd (No. 1)* [1980] Ch 515, the trustees had engaged in a sequence of speculative investments. One of these, the Guildford project, was successful; but another, the Old Bailey project, was a disaster. The bank pleaded that it should be permitted to set off the profit from one against the loss on the other. Brightman J allowed them to do so, expressing the view that it would be unjust to deprive the bank of the element of salvage in assessing the cost of the shipwreck. In the question, Brown and Grey would be able to set off the gains only if they could show that the activities which produced such gains were so connected to the losses as to form part of one transaction. On the facts as stated, there is no evidence of such connection, and so the trustees are unlikely to succeed.

[5] Deal here with the devious limitation point.

A claim brought by a beneficiary against a trustee for breach of trust must be brought within six years from the date on which the right of action arose (**Limitation Act 1980, s. 21(3)**).[5] There is a proviso to the sub-section that time does not start to run against a remainderman until his interest falls into possession. As the advances made by Brown were in breach of trust, they would not cause Azure's interest to fall into possession for the purposes of the **Limitation Act**: *Re Pauling's Settlement Trusts* **[1964] Ch 303, CA**. Azure's interest falls into possession only on the death of Leone, and as the question suggests that Leone is still alive, it would appear that time has not yet even started to run against Azure. He will not, however, be permitted to bring any claim against the trustees if it is shown that he participated in, or consented to, the breach, or if it can be shown that he later acquiesced in the breach: *Re Pauling's Settlement Trusts*.

[6] Legal position of trustee acting reasonably etc.

A trustee who would otherwise be liable for breach of trust may be relieved if he can show that he acted honestly and reasonably and ought fairly to be excused (**Trustee Act 1925, s. 61**).[6] It is unlikely that the court would grant relief under this section to a person who is professionally involved with the management of trusts, such as Brown (*Santander UK plc v RA Legal Solicitors* **[2014] EWCA Civ 183**). It is the trustee who has the onus of showing that he acted honestly and reasonably: *Re Stuart* **[1897] 2 Ch 583**. There are no general principles in applying the statute; every case turns on its own

[7] Application to problem.

circumstances: *Re Turner* **[1897] 1 Ch 536**. Nevertheless, it might be surmised that if Grey left everything to Brown and never asked for explanations,[7] he would probably not be considered to have acted reasonably, and he might not even count as honest for this purpose: *Re Second East Dulwich Building Society* **(1899) 79 LT 726**. A trustee may also be able to escape liability by relying on an express exclusion clause in the trust instrument; the question does not indicate, however, whether the Rainbow Trust contained any such clause.

[8] From hereon application to problem continues.

The fact that Brown is a solicitor and Grey apparently a layman[8] may be a relevant factor in determining the liability of Brown and Grey *inter se*: if it can be shown that Brown exercised a controlling influence over Grey, the latter might be entitled to an indemnity from the former (*Re Partington* **(1887) 57 LT 654**). It seems unlikely, however, that an indemnity could be claimed by a non-participating trustee. Apart from this, it might be possible for Grey to claim a contribution from Brown under the **Civil Liability (Contribution) Act 1978**, although there is no reported case law as yet to indicate what the attitude of the courts might be where such a claim is brought by a passive trustee. Rights of indemnity or contribution between the trustees do not, however, affect the personal liability of each to Azure; so that if each of the trustees is personally liable, Azure could recover the full amount of the loss from either of them, leaving it to that trustee to make a claim against his co-trustee.

Leone received the advances in breach of trust. Leone has therefore been unjustly enriched, and she will be liable to repay to the trust the sums advanced to her if they can be traced into her hands, unless she can rely on the defence of change of position. The trustees' personal liability will be reduced to the extent of any sums so recovered from her. If, however, Leone can establish such a defence (so that she can show that she is an innocent volunteer who has, for example, spent the money so that it cannot be traced), *Re Diplock* **[1948] Ch 465** suggests that she will not be personally liable to repay the advances, since she did not receive the money from the personal representatives of an estate in the course of administration. The modern principle of unjust enrichment nevertheless suggests that she should remain personally liable, since she has still had the benefit of the sums she received (as where she spent them on a holiday). If Leone is held personally liable to repay, her liability is reduced to the extent that such sums can be personally recovered from the trustees (*Re Diplock*, at p. 503). If, on the other hand, Leone instigated or requested the breach, the trustees are entitled to impound her beneficial interest by way of indemnity: *Chillingworth* v *Chambers* **[1896] 1 Ch 685**; **Trustee Act 1925, s. 62**. The trustees will also be entitled to withhold payments of income from Leone in order to repair the breach: cf. *Re Balfour's Settlement Trusts* **[1938] Ch 928**.

If it were to be shown that Grey had participated in the breach of trust, he will be required to indemnify Brown to the extent of his beneficial interest under the trust, which would effectively give Brown a partial indemnity: *Chillingworth* v *Chambers*.

 ## LOOKING FOR EXTRA MARKS?

- Further discussion of the cases would earn extra marks. The impact of *AIB* v *Redler* on the decision in *Target Holdings* could be examined in further detail and the academic commentary (seeing 'Taking Things Further') and especially P. Turner, 'The new fundamental norm of recovery for losses to express trusts' (2015) 74 CLJ 188) incorporated in the answer.

- The point doesn't expressly arise in the question but look out for possible limitation points further to *Creggy* v *Barnett* **[2016] EWCA Civ 1004** where the question of an acknowledgement which could restart the limitation period was discussed (obiter) in relation to claims for breach of trust or where a fiduciary had misapplied funds. On this limitation point, see the Law Commission Report, *Limitation of Actions* (Law Com No. 270, 2001), paras 3.146–3.155 and this case commentary: D. Whayman, 'More clues as to the nature of the remedy for breach of trust' [2017] Conv 139.

George was appointed the sole executor of Harriet's will. Harriet died last year leaving her entire estate, worth £130,000 after payment of debts, to her cousin Albert in Australia. George died recently. Albert has only just learned of this and has discovered that George, believing that as executor he was entitled to the estate beneficially and knowing that he was terminally ill, has made the following dispositions of the estate:

a £40,000 of the estate was contributed to the purchase of a house by George's daughter, Peggy. The house was purchased for £60,000 and Peggy contributed the remaining £20,000. The house is now worth £80,000.

b George settled £40,000 on trust for his son Felix as part of a marriage settlement on the occasion of his marriage to Matilda.

c George used £20,000 to buy a valuable antique Grecian urn which he gave to his service club.

d George used £20,000 to finance his gambling habits and this has all been lost at the Spend Casino.

e George gave the remaining £10,000 to his housekeeper May. May paid this into her current account, in which there was a balance of £5,000, but has since drawn out £10,000.

Advise Albert whether he has any claim against the recipients of Harriet's estate.

! CAUTION!

- This problem raises a number of different permutations of the tracing remedy. Most problems raised in this field relate to the issue of tracing in equity. You will need to know the limitations of the remedy of tracing at common law.

- The issue of the defence of change of position is also raised so you should discuss the important House of Lords' decision in *Lipkin Gorman* v *Karpnale Ltd* [1991] 2 AC 548, although this case is concerned with tracing at common law.

DIAGRAM ANSWER PLAN

Identify the issues	■ Tracing

Relevant law	■ Case law such as *Sinclair* v *Brougham*, *Re Diplock*, *Boscawen* v *Bajwa*, *Lipkin Gorman* v *Karpnale Ltd*, *Clayton's Case*, *Barlow Clowes (in liquidation)* v *Vaughan*

Apply the law	(a) Position of Peggy as innocent volunteer; equitable proprietary interest of Albert; mixing of funds; inequitable results and the loss of the tracing remedy; equitable claims *in personam*
	(b) Marriage consideration and status of Felix with an equitable interest; Felix not 'equity's darling'; claim *in personam*
	(c) Status of club as volunteer; equitable tracing into volunteer's hands; identifiable proceeds of trust money
	(d) Position where trust money dissipated; tracing into hands of the casino which is a volunteer; defence of change of position; claim *in personam*
	(e) Mixing of trust money with that of innocent volunteer; rule in *Clayton's Case*; position where money used to buy investment

Conclude	■ Advise Albert

SUGGESTED ANSWER

[1] It is important to dispose of the common law position and this brief explanation by way of introduction does just that.

Introduction[1]

The right to trace is available at common law if the claimant retains the legal title to the property. Here, tracing at law is not available because George, the legal owner, has disposed of the property and the legal title has passed. It is necessary, therefore, to consider the availability of the remedy in equity.

Part (a)

[2] Position of Peggy as volunteer.

Peggy is presumably an innocent volunteer.[2] The trust funds have been mixed with her money. The mixed funds have been used to purchase a house. The value of the house has now risen.

[3] State Albert's interest.

Albert is the true beneficiary, and therefore has an equitable proprietary interest.[3] £40,000 of the trust property is in the hands of an innocent volunteer and has been used for the acquisition of property. An equitable proprietary remedy may be available which will enable Albert to trace the property.

4 Deal here with the mixing of funds.

In equity, where the trust property has been transferred in breach of trust to an innocent volunteer who has mixed it with her own,[4] the trust and the volunteer share *pari passu* in the property purchased with the mixed fund: *Sinclair* v *Brougham* **[1914] AC 398, HL**, *Re Diplock* **[1948] Ch 465, CA**. They will share the profits and the capital in the proportions in which they contributed.

5 Right to trace lost comes next.

The right to trace may be lost where it would produce an inequitable result.[5] In *Re Diplock*, it was held that where trust money was spent on altering or improving land then it would be inequitable to force the innocent volunteer to sell the land to satisfy a charge on it. Peggy has used the money to buy land. It might be argued, therefore, that her circumstances have changed as a result of the receipt of the trust money, thus rendering it inequitable for the remedy to be enforced against her. This would, however, mean that Peggy would be unjustly enriched. In the light of *Boscawen* v *Bajwa* **[1996] 1 WLR 328**, the most appropriate solution would be for the court to defer Albert's right to enforce the equitable charge until Peggy has had a reasonable opportunity to raise and pay the amount due, e.g. by mortgaging the house.

6 Final point is the equitable claim *in personam*.

If the proprietary claim fails, then an equitable claim *in personam* can be brought for the principal sum of £40,000 without interest.[6] However, Peggy will only be liable to the extent that the money cannot be recovered directly from George's own estate. The claim in these circumstances is limited to claims arising out of the administration of estates and is subject to the primary liability of the executor: *Re Diplock*.

Part (b)

7 Explain marriage consideration.

£40,000 was settled on trust under a marriage settlement for Felix. He is within the marriage consideration and, therefore, not a volunteer.[7] Where trust property has been transferred to a bona fide purchaser of a legal estate for value and without notice of the equitable interest, the property is taken free from the claims of the beneficiaries.

8 Explain here why he is not 'equity's darling'.

However, Felix has acquired merely an equitable as opposed to a legal interest and does not receive the protection of 'equity's darling'.[8]

Alternatively, and especially if the tracing remedy does not satisfy Albert's loss, he may recover the loss (or the balance) in a claim *in personam*.

9 Again final point is about personal remedy.

In this case, Albert should look to the personal remedy against George's estate in the first instance,[9] but may recover the balance from Felix in a claim *in personam*.

Part (c)

10 Explain volunteer status of club.

The service club is a volunteer[10] as it has given no consideration for the urn. Presumably it is also innocent.

11 Explain equitable tracing here.

Equitable tracing is,[11] however, available against an innocent volunteer if the property can be traced into the volunteer's hands. The trust money has been exchanged for the urn with no mixing of other funds. The club have the identifiable proceeds of the trust money. Albert can therefore trace in equity[12] into the urn and obtain an order to restore the urn, being property acquired with the £20,000.

Part (d)

£20,000 of trust property was dissipated by George on gambling at the Spend Casino.

The right to trace is lost where the property has ceased to be identifiable. Where the money has been dissipated, therefore, it can no longer be identified and cannot be traced. However, the money has passed into the hands of the Spend Casino, which is a volunteer, as no valuable consideration is given: *Lipkin Gorman* v *Karpnale Ltd* **[1991] 2 AC 548**. However, a casino stands the risk of losing or winning when it permits someone to place bets. The defence of change of position[13] was considered in *Lipkin Gorman* v *Karpnale Ltd*, a case which was concerned with legal tracing only. In *Lipkin Gorman* v *Karpnale Ltd*, it was held by the House of Lords that a casino was entitled to set off any winnings made by the gambler on the basis that it had changed its position by paying such winnings to him. Change of position was not a complete defence and the club was held liable in an action for money had and received for the net amount he had lost gambling at the club. It was stated, *per curiam*, by the House of Lords, that it is right to recognise the defence of change of position in good faith in restitution claims, based on the unjust enrichment of the defendant. The House of Lords, however, left the development of this doctrine to future cases. So, although it is likely that future courts will develop this doctrine, there is presently no direct authority for this defence to be raised by the Spend Casino in a claim to trace in equity.

[13] The defence of change of position is the big point here.

The Spend Casino will also be subject to a claim *in personam* under *Re Diplock*, as confirmed on appeal in *Ministry of Health* v *Simpson* **[1951] AC 251, HL**. This will be for the amount which Albert has been unable to claim from George's estate and will be limited to the principal sum without interest.

Part (e)

£10,000 of trust money has been mixed in May's current account with £5,000 of her own money.[14] Where trust money is mixed with that of an innocent volunteer, tracing in equity is available. However, May has withdrawn £10,000. As the account is a current account, the rule in *Clayton's Case* **(1816) 1 Mer 572**, first in, first out applies.[15] The rule in *Clayton's Case* is a rule of convenience and applies unless it is impracticable or would result in injustice (*Barlow Clowes International Ltd (in liquidation)* v *Vaughan* **[1992] 4 All ER 22**).

[14] Mixing again but this time with innocent volunteer (so tracing available).

[15] The rule in *Clayton's Case* is the big point here.

If the prima facie rule is to apply here, then, as May had £5,000 of her own money in the account, she is presumed to draw that out first, followed by £5,000 of trust money. The remaining money is, therefore, trust money.

If the £10,000 withdrawn has been used to buy an investment, Albert will be able to claim a charge on the investment and rank *pari passu* with May. If, however, the £5,000 trust money cannot be traced (if, for example, it has been dissipated), Albert will be left to pursue a claim *in personam* as discussed previously.

LOOKING FOR EXTRA MARKS?

- You could aim to get some more academic discussion in especially on the change of position defence. But the facts are complex and the question is quite long so you would be pushing it to get much more in (unless it was for coursework).

QUESTION | 4

On 1 January 2019, Tonto, who was trustee of the Una Charitable Trust, in breach of trust paid into his bank account £10,000 of the charity's money. There was already £6,000 of his own money in his account. One week later he bought shares to the value of £5,000 and withdrew this amount from his account. The next day, he drew out £3,500 which he used to buy a boat. On 1 March 2019, he paid into the account in breach of trust £5,000 belonging to the Duo Trust Fund, of which he was also trustee. The next day he drew out £5,000 which he used to pay debts which he had incurred in his business. The following day he withdrew a further £5,000 which he gave to his daughter, Dora, which she used as a deposit on a house she was buying.

The boat has now been destroyed in a hurricane. The shares are now worth £6,000.

Tonto has just been declared bankrupt.

Advise the beneficiaries of the two trusts.

CAUTION!

- This question deals with the mixing of monies in a bank account. Once money or other property has been mixed, it is not possible to trace at common law. The question therefore requires an application of the rules for tracing in equity. The answer takes account of the significant decision of the Court of Appeal in *Boscawen* v *Bajwa* [1996] **1 WLR 328**.

- It is important to be aware that different rules apply to the mixing of trust monies with a trustee's own money, and the mixing of the monies of two trusts that are both treated as innocent volunteers.

- Where there is a series of transactions involving payments into and out of a bank account, as here, it is essential to work the transactions through in draft form first, calculating the amounts remaining in the bank account and to whom they belong after each transaction.

- Also be sure to apportion the rights to any property purchased from the mixed account according to whose money has been used for its purchase.

- You should, of course, explain which rule you are applying in each transaction, so that a kind-hearted marker will be able to give you credit for legal knowledge even if you slip up on your arithmetic!

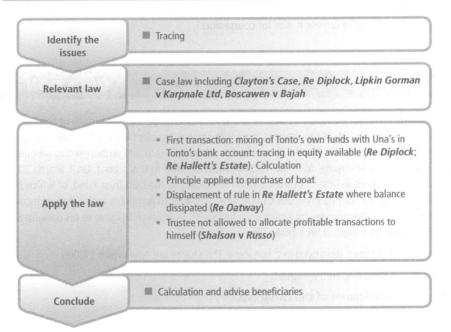

DIAGRAM ANSWER PLAN

Identify the issues
- Tracing

Relevant law
- Case law including *Clayton's Case*, *Re Diplock*, *Lipkin Gorman* v *Karpnale Ltd*, *Boscawen* v *Bajah*

Apply the law
- First transaction: mixing of Tonto's own funds with Una's in Tonto's bank account: tracing in equity available (*Re Diplock*; *Re Hallett's Estate*). Calculation
- Principle applied to purchase of boat
- Displacement of rule in *Re Hallett's Estate* where balance dissipated (*Re Oatway*)
- Trustee not allowed to allocate profitable transactions to himself (*Shalson v Russo*)

Conclude
- Calculation and advise beneficiaries

SUGGESTED ANSWER

As Tonto is bankrupt, a personal claim against him for breach of trust is likely to be of little value to the Una Charitable Trust ('Una') or to the beneficiaries of the Duo Trust ('Duo'). Una and Duo should therefore first try to trace their funds into the property to which the funds have been applied.

The first transaction¹ involves the mixing in Tonto's bank account of Tonto's own money and money belonging to Una. Tracing at law is not possible as the money has been applied by its legal owner, Tonto; and, in any event, money or other property cannot be traced at law once it has been mixed. Tracing is, however, possible in equity, as Tonto is a trustee and therefore in a fiduciary relationship (*Re Diplock* **[1948] Ch 465**), and property can be traced in equity even after it has been mixed.

The shares which Tonto buys for £5,000, paid for from the account, are prima facie deemed to have been purchased out of his own £6,000 in the account, on the basis that a trustee is deemed not to be acting in breach of trust: *Re Hallett's Estate* **(1880) 13 ChD 696**. If this is the case, the shares belong to Tonto, and the money remaining in the account belongs as follows:

Tonto: £1,000
Una: £10,000

If the same principle is applied on the purchase of the boat, then the boat represents £1,000 of Tonto's money and £2,500 of Una's money. The bank account then has no money of Tonto's left in it, and there is £7,500 of Una's money remaining.

The rule in *Re Hallett's Estate*, however, is displaced where the trustee,² having purchased an investment, subsequently dissipates the balance in the account, which, on the application of *Re Hallett's Estate*, would mean that the beneficiary's money would have been dissipated. In such circumstances, *Re Oatway* **[1903] 2 Ch 356** held that the beneficiary is entitled to treat the investment as having been purchased first out of the trust monies, so as to enable the beneficiary to trace into the investment. The underlying principle may be that a trustee should not be permitted to allocate profitable transactions to himself, as this would allow him to benefit from his own wrongdoing: *Shalson v Russo* **[2005] Ch 281** (Rimer J). But the notion that it is the beneficiaries who may 'cherry pick' opposed to the trustee may go too far the other way: *Turner v Jacob* **[2008] WTLR 307**. The fact that some money of Una's remains in the bank account should not, therefore, affect Una's right to trace into the shares, which, in view of the boat's destruction, it would obviously be better advised to do.

The remedy granted in *Re Oatway* itself was an equitable charge over the investment to the value of the trust monies used in its purchase. That case did not deal with the position in the event of the investment's increasing in value. It would, however, appear to follow from dicta in *Re Tilley's Will Trusts* **[1967] Ch 1179** (where trust money had been mixed with the trustee's own), that Una should be able to benefit from the entire increase in value, i.e. to claim that the shares are held for it upon a constructive trust.

If the view in **Shalson v Russo** is applied, the money remaining in the bank account immediately after the shares have been purchased belongs as follows:

Una: £5,000

Tonto: £6,000[3]

The rule in **Re Hallett's Estate** is then applied to the purchase of the boat,[4] which is therefore bought entirely from Tonto's own money. After the purchase of the boat, the money remaining in the bank account is as follows:

Una: £5,000

Tonto: £2,500

The rest of this answer proceeds on the basis that the view expressed in **Shalson v Russo** applies to the application of **Re Oatway**.

Tonto's payment into the account of £5,000 belonging to Duo[5] means that there is then £12,500 in that account. When Tonto subsequently withdraws the first £5,000 from the account, the withdrawal first comprises £2,500 of Tonto's own money (**Re Hallett's Estate**). As between innocent volunteers, the appropriation of withdrawals from an active bank account is governed by the rule in **Clayton's Case (1816) 1 Mer 572**, whereby withdrawals are treated as made in the same order as payments in, i.e. first in, first out. As Una and Duo are both innocent volunteers, the balance of £2,500 withdrawn is treated as Una's money. The second withdrawal of £5,000 therefore comprises the remaining £2,500 of Una's money, and £2,500 of Duo's. This leaves £2,500 in the bank account which can be traced by Duo.

Assuming that the creditors are bona fide purchasers without notice, Una cannot trace its £2,500 applied in the discharge of Tonto's debts into their hands.[6] Una can, however, claim to be subrogated to the creditors' claims against Tonto: **Boscawen v Bajwa [1996] 1 WLR 328, CA**. If the creditors' claims were secured, e.g. by a mortgage over Tonto's assets, Una would be able to claim an equitable charge over those assets to the extent of £2,500. If, however, the creditors' claims were unsecured, there is no advantage to Una, as a personal claim would not give it priority over Tonto's creditors in Tonto's bankruptcy.

Assuming that Dora is an innocent volunteer,[7] Una and Duo can prima facie trace the monies which she has received into the house she has bought. In **Re Diplock**, however, the Court of Appeal held that where an innocent volunteer had applied trust monies in building an extension to its existing premises, tracing would not be permitted as this would produce an inequitable result, i.e. the plaintiff could compel a sale of the entire premises. That principle, however, seems to be giving way to a broader principle that tracing will be permitted unless the defendant can establish the defence of change of position. In *Lipkin Gorman* v *Karpnale Ltd* **[1991] 2 AC 548**, the House of Lords held that such a defence was available to a tracing claim; *Lipkin Gorman* itself concerned tracing at common law, but it has been suggested by Millett J that such a defence is also available in equitable tracing: *Boscawen* v *Bajwa*. However, in *Foskett* v *McKeown* **[2001] 1 AC 102** Lord Millett suggested that the defence of change of position is available only where the basis of the claim is unjust enrichment. Where the claimant uses the tracing process to vindicate a property right, by contrast, the only defence is that of the bona fide purchaser for value.

[8] The appropriate remedy.

The most appropriate remedy might be for the court[8] to grant Una and Duo an equitable charge over the house, but to defer their right to enforce it for a reasonable time in order to enable Dora to raise (e.g. by mortgaging the house) the amount necessary to satisfy the equitable charge. If the house has increased (or fallen) in value, Dora, Una, and Duo, all being innocent volunteers, share the increase (or the loss, as the case may be) rateably: *Sinclair* v *Brougham* **[1914] AC 398, HL**; *Re Diplock*.

If Dora is indeed an innocent volunteer, no personal claim will lie against her: *Ministry of Health* v *Simpson* **[1951] AC 251**. If, however, she receives the £5,000 with constructive notice that it is trust money, she will be personally liable as a constructive trustee to account for it under the principle of knowing receipt: *Agip (Africa) Ltd* v *Jackson* **[1990] Ch 265** (Millett J).

LOOKING FOR EXTRA MARKS?

- Further discussion of the restitution point and reference to the literature on unjust enrichment would gain extra marks.

TAKING THINGS FURTHER

- Chambers, R., 'Liability', in *Breach of Trust* (P. Birks and A. Pretto, eds), Hart Publishing, 2002, chapter 1.
- Lowry, J. and Edmunds, R., 'Excuses', in *Breach of Trust* (P. Birks and A. Pretto, eds), Hart Publishing, 2002, chapter 9.
- Payne, J., 'Consent', in *Breach of Trust* (P. Birks and A. Pretto, eds), Hart Publishing, 2002, chapter 10.
- Smith, L., *The Law of Tracing*, Clarendon Press, 1997.

■ Turner, P., 'The new fundamental norm of recovery for losses to express trusts' (2015) 74 CLJ 188.

*This article discusses the decision in **AIB Group (UK) plc v Mark Redler & Co Solicitors**.*

■ Whayman, D., 'Obligation and property in tracing claims' [2018] Conv 157–174.

This article discusses the basis of the tracing claim, that is, should it be property-based or obligation-based. This is an article which could be useful if you are undertaking coursework which requires you to analyse the basis for the tracing claim.

The following references provide a discussion of liability issues for breach of trust:

Online Resources

www.oup.com/uk/qanda/

For extra essay and problem questions on this topic, as well as advice on revision and exam technique, please visit the online resources.

Equitable Remedies

14

ARE YOU READY?

In order to attempt the questions in this chapter you will need to have covered the following topics:

- Injunctions
- Interim injunctions and the *American Cyanamid* principles
- Freezing orders and search orders
- Specific performance

KEY DEBATES

Debate: claims brought based on the Human Rights Act 1998 in respect of the right to respect for private and family life and breach of confidence actions may be the basis for equitable intervention.

As in, for example, *Venables and Thompson* v *News Group Newspapers* [2001] 1 All ER 908, [2001] 2 WLR 1038, and *Douglas and Zeta-Jones* v *Hello! Ltd* [2001] 2 WLR 992, [2001] 2 All ER 289. This is a developing area and one to watch out for with new cases emerging. The widespread use of non-disclosure agreements and injunctions to prevent them being broken under breach of confidence actions are also topical (*Arcadia & ors* v *Telegraph* [2018] EWCA Civ 2329).

Debate: the problem of using equitable remedies in such a way that they would amount to contracts of slavery.

This arises in older cases such as *Lumley* v *Wagner* and in the modern context the question is should equitable remedies be used to enforce the carrying on of a business? *Cooperative Stores* v *Argyll* is an excellent example of this point.

QUESTION | 1

The Draconian and essentially unfair nature of [search] orders from the point of view of respondents against whom they are made requires, in my view, that they be so drawn as to extend no further than the minimum extent necessary to achieve the purpose for which they are granted, namely the preservation of documents or articles which might otherwise be destroyed or concealed.

(Per Scott J in *Columbia Picture Industries Inc.* v *Robinson* **[1987] Ch 38**)

Discuss critically.

CAUTION!

- A quotation of this sort can be followed by various commands: 'comment', or 'examine', or, as in this question, 'discuss'. Sometimes, as here, you are required to perform the test 'critically'. Whatever the form adopted by your examiner you are required to do two things for a degree-level answer to this question. First, you must show you know what the procedure entails. So, in this question you must explain what the search order is all about. You will be expected to cite the relevant authorities. Secondly, you must be critical. The key is to read the quotation. This may seem obvious, but there is a great temptation in the exam room to read and digest only key words. In this question the key words are 'search orders'. An answer which simply describes the search order procedure will achieve a pass, but little more. What is required is a critical analysis of the current use of the procedure.

- The quotation gives the lead. You should explain in what respects the procedure is considered by the judge to be 'Draconian'. The quotation is provocative so your answer can be argumentative, even bullish. Give both sides of the argument, then come down on one side and give reasons for your decision. Provided you have argued your case well, you will not lose marks if your examiner happens to disagree with your verdict.

- As with all discussion questions, beware of losing your way. Plan your arguments in advance. Prepare a checklist of the points to be made, then tick them off as you make them. A question of this sort gives you the opportunity to show off your skills in arguing a case, provided you have a sound knowledge of the law involved.

DIAGRAM ANSWER PLAN

> Search orders and **Civil Procedure Act 1997, s. 7**

> Problems regarding the abuse of search orders

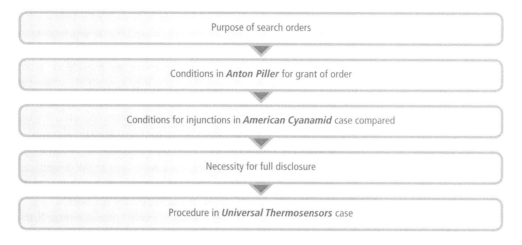

Purpose of search orders

Conditions in *Anton Piller* for grant of order

Conditions for injunctions in *American Cyanamid* case compared

Necessity for full disclosure

Procedure in *Universal Thermosensors* case

A | **SUGGESTED ANSWER**

[1] Start by establishing the legal basis.

Search orders have sometimes been described as civil search warrants, enabling the applicant to enter on the respondent's premises, search, and take relevant evidence.[1]

Since their initial use, originally in *EMI Ltd* v *Pandit* [1975] 1 WLR 302, and subsequently in *Anton Piller KG* v *Manufacturing Processes Ltd* [1976] Ch 55 from which they derived their previous name '*Anton Piller* orders', these orders have been extensively used. They now have a statutory basis in **s. 7 of the Civil Procedure Act 1997**, and are also governed by the **Civil Procedure Rules 1998**.

[2] Establish the reason for their use but also the concomitant problems.

Their popularity has ensured that the injustice which they were created to remedy has been ameliorated.[2] However, applicants have not always been entirely honest when seeking this remedy; they have not always come to equity with clean hands. Concern has been expressed, both on the Bench and by academic writers, that such orders are being abused. In *Universal Thermosensors Ltd* v *Hibben*, Nicholls V-C laid out a series of guidelines for the use of these orders. He recognised that they can be both a virtue in eliciting evidence which would otherwise not have seen the light of day, and a vice in that the procedure is open to abuse. These guidelines are now laid out in Practice Direction [1996] 1 WLR 1552.

[3] Explain when they are sought.

Search orders are sought where there is a risk that vital evidence may be lost or destroyed.[3] Their use has been particularly appropriate in cases where the defendant is suspected of infringing the claimant's intellectual property rights or of breaching trade secrets. They have also been used in one reported case within the field of family law

(*Emanuel* v *Emanuel* [1982] **1 WLR 669**), to enable the wife's solicitors to enter the husband's home and inspect documents relating to his financial means.

In order to bring such a case, a claimant needs evidence which might be in the hands of the defendant. It might consist of confidential documents or material such as videotapes. In the *Anton Piller* case, the defendants were the plaintiffs' selling agents. The plaintiffs believed that the defendants were selling confidential information about their electrical equipment and plans to their competitors. However, to prove this they needed access to documents kept at the defendants' premises. The Court of Appeal granted an order which permitted them to enter the defendants' premises and inspect the documents.

It is crucial that the application is made without notice. If the other side knew of the application the risk is that the evidence would be destroyed forthwith. Surprise is a key element of the procedure. Herein lies the danger. The judge, at the hearing without notice, must rely exclusively on the word of the applicant.

In the first place, the judge may be required to determine to what extent any particular scientific or technical knowledge is the subject of patent or copyright, or is merely legitimately accepted scientific research. As Hoffmann J said in *Lock International plc* v *Beswick* [1989] **1 WLR 1268**, 'It may look like magic but turn out merely to embody a principle discovered by Faraday or Ampère'.

Secondly, an unscrupulous applicant might abuse the power in a commercial situation by seeking to crush a competitor by the use of oppressive tactics. In *Lock International plc* v *Beswick*, the *Anton Piller* order was carried out by five representatives of the applicant. These were solicitors or employees of the applicant. They were, however, accompanied by 11 or 12 police officers who were armed with a search warrant in respect of alleged criminal activities of the respondent.

On appeal (noted (1990) 106 LQR 173), it was said that what had happened was regrettable, and it was unfortunate that the judge had not been informed of the involvement of the police.

[4] Set out the conditions for grant.

Three conditions for the grant of the order were laid down[4] in *Anton Piller KG* v *Manufacturing Processes Ltd* by Ormrod LJ:

(i) there must be a very strong prima facie case;

(ii) there must be actual or potential damage of a very serious nature; and

(iii) there must be clear evidence that the defendant has in his possession incriminating documents or things and a real risk that they might be destroyed before an application with notice can be heard.

Lord Denning MR added to these the condition that the order must do no real harm to the defendant. It would seem, however, that the fact that disclosure might expose the defendant to the risk of violence from his associates is not a defence (*Coca-Cola Co. v Gilbey* [1995] 4 All ER 711).

[5] Compare conditions with those under *American Cyanamid*.

These conditions are more onerous than the conditions laid down in *American Cyanamid Co. v Ethicon Ltd* [1975] AC 396[5] for the issue of interim (formerly known as 'interlocutory') injunctions. This reflects the concern of the courts to protect the respondent from an abuse of process. The procedure should not be used as a means of finding out what proceedings can be brought (*Hytrac Conveyors Ltd v Conveyors International Ltd* [1983] 1 WLR 44). In other words, the material sought should be specific and should support the cause of action proposed by the claimant for the trial of the main claim. Fishing expeditions are not permitted. The orders are not, in fact, search warrants. They are precisely limited.

When applying for the order, the applicant must make a full disclosure to the court. There is clearly a potential weakness in a procedure which only hears one side of the case. Therefore, there is a particularly strict duty for a full and frank disclosure of all relevant facts. As Scott J pointed out in *Columbia Picture Industries Inc. v Robinson* [1987] Ch 38, the procedure constitutes an apparent breach of the rule of natural justice that citizens should not be deprived of their property without a fair hearing.

In carrying out the order the applicant should be accompanied by a solicitor. Documents or other evidence may be inspected and removed according to the terms of the order. They may not be used for any other purpose unless the respondent has consented or the court has so ordered. If damage is caused to the respondent then the applicant may be obliged to pay damages which could be exemplary in nature.

Two cases have sought to limit the scope of search orders: *Tate Access Floors Inc. v Boswell* [1991] Ch 512 and *Rank Film Distributors Ltd v Video Information Centre* [1982] AC 380. The former case emphasises a requirement for the claimant to make a full disclosure. In the latter case it was held that the privilege against self-incrimination could be raised by a defendant. This decision was abrogated by the **Senior Courts Act 1981, s. 72**, in cases relating to intellectual property.

[6] Human Rights points.

Since the decision, the **Human Rights Act 1998** has adopted the **European Convention on Human Rights**, of which **Art. 8(1)** states that everyone has the right to respect for his private and family life, his home, and his correspondence.[6] **Article 8(2)** states that there shall be no interference by a public authority with this right except in the interests of the society to which that person belongs and makes it clear that the domestic courts are to balance the rights of the individual under the Article with protection of the society in which he lives. In *C plc* v *P* **[2006] EWHC 1226 (Ch), [2007] EWCA Civ 493, CA**, C obtained a search order against P and took his computer in pursuance of the order. It was subsequently discovered that P had downloaded child pornography. This was a pre-existing document to which the defence of privilege from self-incrimination (PSI) does not apply under the Convention. The Court of Appeal found (for different reasons) that the case was not an 'exceptional case' requiring departure from the **Human Rights Act 1998**, that the material had been found in the course of execution of a valid court order, and was therefore not protected by PSI. The protection afforded by the PSI rule had previously been criticised (see, e.g., Lord Templeman in *Istel (AT&T)* **v** *Tully*) and the court in *C plc* v *P* was in something of a dilemma as to how the offending material should be disposed of as it is an offence to be in possession of such material.

In ***Universal Thermosensors Ltd* v *Hibben***, Nicholls V-C set out seven points of procedure. The defendant must have the opportunity to get legal advice, so the order should be served at a time that enables this to happen. If the defendant is a woman alone in a private house, the claimant's solicitor must be a woman, or accompanied by a woman. A detailed list of items removed should be prepared at the premises and checked by the defendant. The defendant should be restrained from communicating with others, apart from a lawyer, only for a limited period of time; a week is too long. Orders at business premises should be executed in the presence of an officer or employee. The claimant should not use the opportunity for a general search of the defendant's papers. The order should be served and supervised by an experienced solicitor independent of the claimant, who should submit a written report to the defendant and to the court at a subsequent hearing with notice.

[7] Give here some concluding comments.

The courts are clearly concerned to ensure that the procedure is not abused.[7] As an equitable remedy, the search order has shown the willingness of the courts to adapt well-established remedies to new situations. The maxim that equity will not allow a wrong to be without a remedy is still valid today, yet the dangers of the procedure are acknowledged by the courts that developed it. Concern over abuse of search orders has been expressed both by the judges and the legal profession as a whole. While such orders provide a valuable remedy, the balance must be maintained between the potential parties to a claim. Although it is unlikely that this remedy will disappear, it is likely that, in future, judges will need very cogent evidence before granting search orders.

+ **LOOKING FOR EXTRA MARKS?**

■ This type of question may also occur as a coursework assessment which would require a deeper analysis of the literature. For example, more should be made of the article by Dockray and Laddie (1990) 106 LQR 601 and the judgment of Nicholls V-C in *Universal Thermosensors Ltd* v *Hibben* [1992] 1 WLR 840. The application to the European Court of Human Rights in *Lock International plc* v *Beswick* [1989] 1 WLR 1268, noted in the article by Dockray and Laddie, should also be considered in the light of the implementation of the **Human Rights Act 1998**. There is a decision of the Court of Appeal (*C plc* v *P* [2007] **EWCA Civ 493**) on the effect of the **Human Rights Act 1998** and the applicability of the privilege against self-incrimination (PSI) under the Convention.

Q **QUESTION** **2**

Lex Ltd produces videos and tapes of lectures and accompanying notes for the purpose of teaching law to overseas students by distance learning. Ten staff are employed on a full-time basis. Portia, a senior member of staff, and author of a leading textbook on European law, is employed on a five-year contract to develop new materials within her field. Her contract requires her not to work for any other firm of law tutors during the period of her contract and for one year thereafter. Portia is a member of the National Union of Law Teachers (NULT).

Negotiations over conditions of service between Lex Ltd and its staff have now broken down. The following circumstances have occurred:

a Portia, who has three years left to run on her contract, has written a letter of resignation to Lex Ltd. She has accepted an offer of employment at the Cambridge base of the tutorial firm, Law sans Larmes, which has its headquarters in Brussels.

b All the materials that Portia had been working on have disappeared from the office, and Lex Ltd fears that they may now be in the possession of Law sans Larmes. The company has also discovered that its current students have received advertisement material from Law sans Larmes, and believes that Portia took a list of clients with her. It also believes that Law sans Larmes have bank accounts in Cambridge and Brussels, and that fees received are transferred on a regular basis to the Brussels account.

Advise Lex Ltd of any equitable remedies it may have in these circumstances.

! **CAUTION!**

■ This problem question has a variety of points in it and mixes both specific performance and injunctions. They are, however, quite straightforward and not too difficult to spot.

DIAGRAM ANSWER PLAN

Identify the issues	■ Specific performance and injunctions
Relevant law	■ Case law including (a) *Lumley v Wagner* (1852) 1 De GM & G 604; *Warner Bros Pictures Inc.* v *Nelson* [1937] 1 KB 209; *Warren v Mendy* [1989] 1 WLR 853; *Page One Records Ltd* v *Britton* [1968] 1 WLR 157; Trade Union and Labour Relations (Consolidation) Act 1992; (b) *A-G* v *Guardian Newspapers Ltd (No. 2)* [1990] 1 AC 109; *Anton Piller KG* v *Manufacturing Processes Ltd* [1976] Ch 55; *Mareva Compañia Naviera SA* v *International Bulkcarriers SA* [1975] 2 Lloyd's Rep 509
Apply the law	(a) Contracts of service; claim for injunction to enforce express negative stipulation (cases); problem where effect to prevent employee working at all (cases); difficulties in reconciling *Warner Bros* case with later case law. (b) Injunction to restrain abuse of confidential relationship; confidential information; maxim that equity will not act in vain; use of search orders
Conclude	■ Advise Lex Ltd

SUGGESTED ANSWER

(a)

[1] Here the key issue is set out then the law.

Portia is in breach of her contract of employment with Lex Ltd.[1] An employment contract, that is, a contract *of* service, cannot be enforced specifically against an employee (**Trade Union and Labour Relations (Consolidation) Act 1992**). This statutory provision stems from the equitable principle that such contracts should not be turned into 'contracts of slavery' (per Fry LJ in *De Francesco* v *Barnum* **(1890) 45 ChD 430** at p. 438). A claim for damages would provide an adequate remedy since, although Portia is a leading author etc., it is likely that she could be replaced.

[2] Restraint of trade point.

Lex Ltd may, however, wish to enforce the express negative stipulation in her contract restraining her from working for anyone else during the remaining contractual period.[2] Earlier case law indicates that a claim for an injunction to this effect would be successful.

[3] Early cases.

In *Lumley* v *Wagner* (1852) 1 De GM & G 604,[3] an opera singer broke her contract which required her to sing at the plaintiff's theatre for three months. The remedy of specific performance was refused but an injunction preventing her singing at any other theatre during the contractual period was granted. This was followed in *Warner Bros Pictures Inc.* v *Nelson* [1937] 1 KB 209 where the actress, Bette Davis, was prevented from working for a rival film company in breach of a no-competition clause.

[4] Cases restricting application.

However, these cases have been modified where it appears that to grant the remedy would mean that the defendant was prevented from working in any capacity[4] (*Whitwood Chemical Co.* v *Hardman* [1891] 2 Ch 416). In *Rely-A-Bell Burglar and Fire Alarm Co. Ltd* v *Eisler* [1926] Ch 609, an injunction was refused which would have enforced compliance with a stipulation by an employee not to enter into any other employment during the term of his contract. In effect, the defendant would be required to work for the plaintiff or starve. It is considered unrealistic to expect an individual with a particular talent to work in an entirely different capacity. *Warner Bros Pictures* was disapproved in *Warren* v *Mendy* [1989] 1 WLR 853, a case where an injunction preventing a boxer from seeking financial services from anyone other than his manager was refused. The principle was stated that an injunction will not be granted if its effect is to prevent a person from working for anyone other than the claimant. In *Page One Records Ltd* v *Britton* [1968] 1 WLR 157, 'The Troggs', a group of musicians, appointed the plaintiff company to act as their agent for five years, and agreed not to engage any other person to act in that capacity. An injunction enforcing the negative stipulation was refused since the practical effect would have been to oblige the group to continue to employ the plaintiff company.

[5] Don't shirk the point. If it is difficult to reconcile then say so.

The case of *Warner Bros Pictures* is difficult to reconcile[5] with the later cases of *Page One Records* and *Warren*. One significant difference is the length of the contracts: in *Warner Bros Pictures* the term of the contract was for not more than 20 weeks, while in *Warren* it was for two years. Issues of mutual trust and confidence are also relevant. So, where mutual confidence continues to exist between employer and employee, the court may be ready to grant an injunction (*Hill* v *Parsons & Co. Ltd* [1972] Ch 305). However, in this problem there is no mutual trust or confidence left.

The negative stipulation in Portia's contract is that she has expressly agreed not to work for any other firm of law tutors in the UK during the contractual period. If an injunction were to be granted, then, in effect, she would be obliged to resume employment with Lex Ltd, notwithstanding that a decree of specific performance would be

unlikely to be available. Such a result is contrary to the principles expressed in the later cases and an injunction is, therefore, likely to be
refused.⁶

The principle would remain the same whether the injunction was
sought against either Law sans Larmes or Portia.

(b)

⁷ The key issue followed by the
statement of the law.

Lex Ltd may seek an injunction to prevent Portia taking its latest
teaching materials.⁷ There is a right in equity to restrain an abuse of
confidential information. This does not necessarily rely on an employment relationship.

⁸ Application of the law to the
problem.

Knowledge of the list of customers is critical to Lex Ltd's commercial enterprise and would also amount to confidential information.⁸
An interim injunction could have been sought to prevent this information being divulged (*Robb* v *Green* **[1985] 2 QB 315**). However,
the information has already been acted upon, and equity will not act
in vain. In *Spycatcher*, (*A-G* v *Guardian Newspapers Ltd (No. 2)*
[1990] 1 AC 109), the final injunction was refused. The information
had already been published worldwide and the injunction would have
been futile. A claim for damages against Law sans Larmes might be
appropriate if a profit has been made (*Seager* v *Copydex Ltd (No.
2)* **[1969] 1 WLR 809**).

⁹ **Human Rights Act** point.

It is unlikely that either party will be able to rely on the **Human
Rights Act 1998**.⁹ Under that Act, freedom of expression is guaran-
teed subject to qualifications, under **Art. 10**, but the nature of the
publication of the teaching materials is not likely to fall under this
protection. Any potential dissemination of these materials by Portia
would be to the rival company and for personal profit. The information which Portia has taken is not material which is likely to be made
available to the public or where publication would be in the public
interest. Likewise, reliance on **Art. 8**, which guarantees protection
of the family and home, would not be appropriate in respect of any
claim by Lex Ltd (*Douglas and Zeta-Jones* v *Hello! Ltd* **[2001]
2 WLR 992, [2001] 2 All ER 289**) since the nature of the material
is commercial.

If Lex Ltd fears that the teaching materials have also been taken,
it may seek a search order against both parties (*Anton Piller KG* v
Manufacturing Processes Ltd **[1976] Ch 55**). This would permit the
company's agents to inspect the evidence at the premises of Law sans
Larmes and at Portia's home. The application is made without notice
where there is a risk that the evidence might be destroyed before a
claim could be brought. The application must be made, and the order
served, in accordance with the procedures established in *Universal
Thermosensors Ltd* v *Hibben* **[1992] 1 WLR 840**. In particular, as

the defendant is a woman, the order must be served by, or in the presence of, a woman.

[10] Set out here the conditions for the grant.

Lex Ltd must show a very strong prima facie case and actual or potential damage of a very serious nature.[10] It already has evidence that the information is in the hands of Law sans Larmes and the damage to its business could be irreparable.

Lex Ltd is clearly concerned that if it sues Law sans Larmes for damages the latter may be unable to satisfy the claim if assets are transferred abroad. It may, therefore, consider seeking a freezing injunction under the procedure established in *Mareva Compañía Naviera SA* v *International Bulkcarriers SA* **[1975] 2 Lloyd's Rep 509**. This is an order which prevents the defendant from transferring assets abroad. It is usually obtained without notice and could be sought at the same time as the search order.

[11] *American Cyanamid* principles.

The principles in *American Cyanamid Co.* v *Ethicon Ltd* **[1975] AC 396** must be satisfied.[11] Further to the **Senior Courts Act 1981, s. 37(3)**, the injunction may be granted to prevent the defendant removing the assets from the jurisdiction of the court or dissipating them in some way.

Lex Ltd must show that it has a good arguable case and will be required to give an undertaking in damages in the event that it is unsuccessful at trial. In addition, it must comply with the guidelines originally established in *Third Chandris Shipping Corp.* v *Unimarine SA* **[1979] 2 All ER 972**. The remedy will only be available where there is good reason to believe that assets will be moved out of the jurisdiction or otherwise disposed of so as to defeat the claim.

[12] Raise here the issue about the protection of assets.

Some of the assets of Law sans Larmes appear to be in Brussels.[12] Lex Ltd may consider the possibility of seeking a freezing injunction which covers not only the English bank account, but also the Brussels account. The Court of Appeal have affirmed in the cases of *Babanaft International Co. SA* v *Bassatne* **[1990] Ch 13**, *Republic of Haiti* v *Duvalier* **[1990] 1 QB 202**, and *Derby & Co. Ltd* v *Weldon* **[1990] Ch 48**, that there is no geographical limit to the jurisdiction of the court. However, an injunction in this form would not be available where it may adversely affect third parties and where its effect may be oppressive to the defendant.

LOOKING FOR EXTRA MARKS?

- You should be able to score a good 2(i) if you work methodically through the various remedies, explaining their availability in each instance. For a first-class answer, some critical analysis of their usage is necessary.

a Amelia, a sculptress, agrees with Belinda to make a bust of Belinda, a world-renowned child actress, for £500. When the bust is completed, Cindy, a film buff and fan of Belinda, offers Amelia £1,000 for it. Amelia, who is in severe financial difficulties, accepts Cindy's offer.

Advise Belinda on the availability of any equitable remedies for breach of contract in these circumstances.

b Delia took a long lease of the top flat on the 14th floor of a tower block being built two years ago. The service contract requires Easimoney Ltd, the freeholder, to undertake external building repairs, to have the outside of the windows cleaned once a month, and to install a lift within a reasonable period of time.

A recent gale has dislodged some tiles from the roof, and rain now leaks into Delia's flat. Despite Delia's repeated requests, the roof has not been repaired. The windows are never cleaned and the lift has not been installed.

Advise Delia of any equitable remedies that might be available to her.

! CAUTION!

- This is a straightforward question requiring a knowledge of the rules relating to specific performance. It is a good illustration of the need to read the question. For example, the claimant in part (a) is a child. This is not simply to add local colour to the question but is designed to raise the issue of mutuality. If you miss this point, your marks go down.

- The second part of the question requires you to know the application of specific performance to contracts requiring supervision and construction contracts. You have to know the case law. Of particular importance is the decision of the House of Lords in *Co-operative Insurance Society Ltd* v *Argyll Stores (Holdings) Ltd* **[1998] AC 1**. (See also P. Luxton [1998] Conv 396.) If you can answer the first part, but know nothing about the cases relevant to the second, then it is too risky to tackle this question. A superb answer to the first part but zero on the second will barely earn you a pass. But if you have specific performance at your fingertips, then this question is fairly uncomplicated if you pick up all the points.

DIAGRAM ANSWER PLAN

Identify the issues	■ Specific performance

Relevant law	(a) **Sale of Goods Act 1979, s. 52** and cases such as *Cohen v Roche* [1927] 1 KB 169 (b) *Co-operative Insurance Society Ltd v Argyll Stores (Holdings) Ltd* [1998] AC 1 and other case law

Apply the law	■ Part (a) • Discretionary nature of remedy of specific performance • Contracts for personal property • Effect of hardship • Equity will not act in vain • Need for mutuality ■ Part (b) • Specific performance of landlord's covenants • Problem where need for constant supervision and exceptions • Case law examples including *Co-operative Insurance Society Ltd v Argyll Stores (Holdings) Ltd*

Conclude	■ (a) Advise Belinda; (b) advise Delia

(A) SUGGESTED ANSWER

(a)

[1] Set out your store by explaining how this remedy is discretionary.

The equitable remedy of specific performance is discretionary.[1] It will not be available where damages provide an adequate remedy, or where the claimant has acted in an inequitable manner. Neither will the court grant the remedy unless it can be enforced; equity will not act in vain. If it is unjust to the defendant to grant the remedy, it will not be awarded.

[2] Then deal with contracts of personal property explaining why they are not normally subject to the remedy of specific performance (SP).

Normally, contracts for the transfer of personal property will not be specifically enforced.[2] They can usually be compensated for adequately by an award of damages. However, if the item of property has some particular rarity, or beauty or uniqueness, such as King Canute's hunting horn (*Pusey v Pusey* (1684) 1 Vern 273), then specific performance may be granted.

There is statutory authority for the remedy contained in the **Sale of Goods Act 1979, s. 52**. This enables the court to grant specific performance of a contract to deliver specific or ascertained goods where it is just to do so.

The contract between Amelia and Belinda is for personal property, a bust of Belinda. In order for the remedy of specific performance to be granted there must be something unique about the property. In *Cohen v Roche* **[1927] 1 KB 169**, a contract for the sale of eight Hepplewhite chairs was not specifically enforceable. The chairs were not considered to be of any special value or interest. On the other hand, a contract for the sale of a ship was enforced in *Behnke v Bede Shipping Co. Ltd* **[1927] 1 KB 649**, where the ship was of 'peculiar and practically unique value to the plaintiff'.

The bust of Belinda is unique: there is only one in existence. It is a case which falls within the ancient jurisdiction of cases such as *Pusey v Pusey*, where the goods are distinguishable because of their rarity, rather than *Cohen v Roche*, where the goods, though rare and valuable, are still no more than ordinary commercial articles.

[3] Deal next with the effect of hardship.

However, Amelia is in severe financial difficulties and, for that reason, accepts the offer from Cindy.[3] Since the remedy is discretionary, the court would consider whether it is equitable in the circumstances to grant Belinda specific performance of the contract against Amelia. Where a hardship would amount to an injustice (if Amelia could show that it would put her out of business) then the court may be reluctant to award specific performance of the contract (*Patel v Ali* **[1984] Ch 283**).

[4] Then the principle that equity will not act in vain.

Neither will the court act in vain.[4] An equitable remedy will be granted only if it can be complied with by the defendant. In *Jones v Lipman* **[1962] 1 WLR 832**, the defendant attempted to defeat a contract for the sale of land by transferring the land to a company he had set up for this express purpose. The court awarded specific performance because the company was a sham. Normally specific performance would not be granted against a defendant who no longer owned the property. If Amelia has already delivered the bust to Cindy, then Cindy will take free of Belinda's claim to specific performance, assuming Cindy is a bona fide purchaser without notice. In these circumstances, Belinda will have to rely on the remedy of damages for breach of contract.

[5] This point may get missed—but not by you if you have spotted the point about a minor.

For specific performance to be awarded, it must be available to either party.[5] If there is a lack of mutuality, there is a discretion to refuse the remedy. In *Flight v Bolland* **(1824) 4 Russ 298**, a minor was refused specific performance as it would not have been available against him. There is judicial authority for the viewpoint that the time to determine mutuality is at the time of the trial, not the contract.

In *Clayton* v *Ashdown* **(1714) 2 Eq Ab 516**, it was held that where a minor attained majority at the time of the trial the remedy would be available. This principle was confirmed by the Court of Appeal in *Price* v *Strange* **[1978] Ch 337**.

[6] Concluding sentence.

There are, therefore, various grounds on which the court may refuse to exercise its discretion to award specific performance in favour of Belinda.[6]

(b)

[7] Specific performance of landlord's covenants—problem where need for constant supervision and exceptions.

Delia is seeking specific performance of her landlord's covenants.[7] The general principle is that the court will not grant specific performance of a contract where constant supervision would be required: 'Specific performance is inapplicable where the continued supervision of the court is necessary in order to ensure the fulfilment of the contract' (Dixon J, *J. C. Williamson Ltd* v *Lukey and Mulholland* **(1931) 45 CLR 282**, at pp. 297–298). Equity will not act in vain and the court is unable constantly to supervise the performance of a contract. In practice, this means that if the court might have to give 'an indefinite series of rulings in order to ensure the execution of the order', the court will not grant the remedy (*Co-operative Insurance Society Ltd* v *Argyll Stores (Holdings) Ltd* **[1998] AC 1**). It will not, therefore, enforce a contract where such supervision would be necessary.

There are, however, exceptions to this principle and the courts, in some of the modern cases, are more willing to grant specific performance even where there are potential problems relating to supervision.

The earlier case of *Ryan* v *Mutual Tontine Westminster Chambers Association* **[1893] 1 Ch 116** shows the application of the general principle. The lessor of a flat covenanted to appoint a caretaker who would be in constant attendance and would undertake cleaning and general portering duties. A caretaker was appointed but he was frequently absent. The Court of Appeal refused to grant specific performance as it would be unable to supervise the performance of the covenant. It awarded damages instead.

However, in *Posner* v *Scott-Lewis* **[1987] Ch 25**, specific performance of a similar covenant to employ a resident porter was awarded. The court held that if the obligation was sufficiently defined and the degree of supervision was not unacceptable, then, if the plaintiff would suffer greater hardship, the equitable remedy would be awarded.

Similarly, if the order can be defined with precision, so that the defendant knows exactly what is to be done, then the court will be more likely to grant the discretionary remedy (*Morris* v *Redland Bricks Ltd* **[1970] AC 652**, at p. 666, per Lord Upjohn).

The strength of the claimant's case is also a relevant factor given the equitable nature of the remedy (see Spry, *Equitable Remedies*, 8th edn, Thomson Reuters, 2009).

[8] This is the unmissable case—House of Lords and very important authority.

In *Co-operative Insurance Society Ltd v Argyll Stores (Holdings) Ltd* [1998] AC 1,[8] a case concerning the enforcement of a covenant in a commercial tenant's lease to continue running the business, Lord Hoffmann distinguished between orders which require a defendant to carry on an activity and orders which require him to achieve a result. In the former case, which might involve an order to carry on running a business over an extended period of time, the possibility of repeated applications for rulings on compliance with the order may arise. Whereas in the latter case, where a result is to be achieved, however complicated, the court may simply look at the finished result and rule on whether compliance has been effected. So cases such as *Wolverhampton Corp. v Emmons* [1901] 1 KB 515, concerning a building contract, and *Jeune v Queens Cross Properties Ltd* [1974] Ch 97, concerning repairing covenants, are exceptions to the general principle because they involve the achievement of a result—a building, or specific repair.

[9] Application to the problem here.

The terms in Delia's lease are threefold.[9] The first is to install a lift. In *Wolverhampton Corp. v Emmons* [1901] 1 KB 515, the Court of Appeal established three requirements: the building work must be clearly defined; damages would be an inadequate remedy; and the defendant has possession of the land. It would seem that these requirements are satisfied. The building work is clearly defined except that the time limit is vague. However, the court is unlikely to be unwilling to specify what would constitute a reasonable time. Since the work would have to be undertaken on part of the block of flats which is in the landlord's possession, it would be impossible for Delia to carry out the work herself. Damages would, therefore, be an inadequate remedy.

This exception was extended to landlords' covenants to repair in *Jeune v Queens Cross Properties Ltd* [1974] Ch 97. The **Landlord and Tenant Act 1985, s. 17**, now provides that specific performance of a landlord's repairing covenant may be granted. This overrides any equitable principles restricting the remedy. Delia would therefore be able to seek specific performance of the covenant to repair in respect of the damage to the roof caused by the gale.

The covenant to have the windows cleaned highlights the problem of supervision. Clearly, such a contractual obligation is ongoing and would require constant superintendence. However, applying *Posner v Scott-Lewis*, the work is clearly defined. If an order is issued requiring the landlord to appoint a firm of window cleaners to carry out the work, then the supervision required is no more than the appointment of the porter *in Posner* v *Scott-Lewis*. This falls into the category defined by Lord Hoffmann in the *Co-operative Insurance Society* case, as the achievement of a result. Damages might be an adequate remedy in that they would enable Delia to employ a window cleaner herself. However, to employ a window cleaner to clean the exterior of the windows on the 14th floor is not practicable and the court would no doubt take the view that it would cause greater hardship to Delia than to the landlord. Therefore, Delia has a reasonable prospect of success in enforcing this covenant.[10]

[10] And the conclusion.

LOOKING FOR EXTRA MARKS?

- Including the range of cases across the remedies will earn extra marks especially as it covers more than one of the equitable remedies. Some discussion on the merits of specific performance versus a common law remedy of damages might be introduced. Take a look at the Luxton (1998) and Davies (2018) articles ('Taking Things Further') for some interesting approaches on this point.

TAKING THINGS FURTHER

- Davies, S. P., 'Being specific about specific performance' [2018] Conv 324–338.
  This article discusses the various merits of the availability of specific performance and considers the Canadian approach.
- Dockray, M. and Laddie, H., 'Piller problems' (1990) 106 LQR 601.
  This article deals with the search order.
- Gray, C., 'Interlocutory injunctions since *Cyanamid*' (1981) 40 CLJ 307.
  *A broader article dealing with the post-***Cyanamid*** principles and the changes made by that case.*
- Luxton, P., 'Are you being served? Enforcing keep-open covenants in leases' [1998] Conv 396.
  *This is a useful discussion on specific performance and the ***Co-operative Argyll*** case.*

Online Resources   www.oup.com/uk/qanda/

For extra essay and problem questions on this topic, as well as advice on revision and exam technique, please visit the online resources.

15 Mixed Topic Questions

INTRODUCTION

Your examination paper may contain one question which mixes a number of different topics. This may be upsetting at first sight. You may have carefully revised several topics which are covered in the question only to discover that it includes one topic which you thought safe to leave out. Assuming that each section in the question bears equal marks (and that is a reasonable assumption unless there is any contrary indication), then it is probably unsafe to tackle it in these circumstances. Most (if not all) questions in the paper will be discrete and you will find the question on charities or administration of trusts or whatever your favourite topic may be, without any difficulty. Once you have identified it then you are away.

However, the possibility of a mixed topic question is another reason why you should read the questions carefully before starting to write. A question might include two sections on charities, then a section on a private purpose trust with a question mark over its validity, and a concluding section on a gift to an unincorporated association. One question spotted in a university exam paper contained four problems: a secret trust; certainty of objects; certainty of intention; and wound up with the doctrine of election—not a pretty sight. If you glance at the question, think 'charities', and plough into it, only to discover 20 valuable minutes later that you have to deal with a subject about which you know nothing, you have wasted a great deal of effort and lost, probably, a class or worse.

Needless to say, if you know each of the topics then you do not have a problem. In fact, if your luck holds and you are thoroughly familiar with the case law for each point, this question may be a dream ticket.

Four questions have been selected to illustrate these points. Question 1 mixes charitable trusts, discretionary trusts, and covenants to settle. Question 2 mixes constitution of trusts, *donationes mortis causa*, and certainty of words and objects. Question 3 mixes the three certainties, secret trusts, and trusts of imperfect obligation. Question 4 covers mutual wills and estoppel.

(Q) QUESTION | 1

Four years ago Alpha transferred £100,000 to Beta 'upon trust to provide, at his discretion, grants for law students in the United Kingdom, absolute preference to be given to my relatives'.

One year ago, Alpha covenanted with Beta to transfer to Beta, upon the same trusts, any property he (Alpha) might subsequently acquire under the will of Gamma. One month later Gamma died, and in his will he bequeathed 10,000 shares in Delta Ltd to Alpha.

Alpha died last month, without having taken steps to transfer the shares in Delta Ltd to Beta. In his will Alpha gave all his property to his niece, Omega.

Discuss.

(!) CAUTION!

- Do not be taken by surprise by a pick 'n' mix question. Suspend disbelief: just because part (a) is on secret trusts does not mean the other sections must also be on the same theme. Read the questions carefully. Note that the instruction is: 'discuss'. So, that is a clue that it is not confined to one single topic.

- The separate parts of the question are not intrinsically difficult, but the higher marks will be obtained by a student who can show how the different areas interact.

DIAGRAM ANSWER PLAN

> Entitlement to shares in Delta Ltd

> Constitution of trust
> Breach of covenant to transfer and remedy of damages
> Rights of third parties
> Validity of trust for charitable purposes?
> Validity of trust as a private discretionary trust?

(A) SUGGESTED ANSWER

[1] You could start by considering the validity of the trust or the transfer of the shares into the trust.

It will first be considered who is entitled to the shares in Delta Ltd.[1] As sole beneficiary of Alpha's will, Omega is entitled to the shares if they formed part of his estate at his death. They will not comprise part of such estate if they are the subject-matter of a fully constituted charitable trust. Alpha, however, never transferred the legal title to the shares to the trustee, Beta, as he had covenanted to do. Furthermore, there is no evidence that he did everything necessary to be done by him in order to perfect the transfer in equity: see *Milroy v Lord* **(1862) 4 De GF & J 264** and *Re Rose* **[1952] Ch 499, CA**. The trust therefore remains incompletely constituted in respect of the shares. There is no evidence that valuable consideration has been supplied for the creation of the trust. As regards the shares, therefore, the trust is an incompletely constituted voluntary settlement. Equity will not compel Alpha's estate to transfer the shares to Beta, since equity will not assist a volunteer: *Re Plumptre* **[1910] 1 Ch 609**.[2]

[2] This establishes the starting position.

The decision in *Pennington v Waine* **[2002] 1 WLR 2075**, is unlikely to assist in this case. In *Pennington v Waine*, a share transfer form had been executed but not delivered to the beneficiary. The beneficiary needed to hold shares in the company in order to be appointed as one of its directors, and, despite non-delivery of the share transfer form, he was still appointed. It was held that it was sufficient that the shares had been transferred by an instrument in writing in accordance with **s. 1(1) of the Stock Transfer Act 1963** and that it would be unconscionable for the transfer not to be effected.

The test of unconscionability is difficult to apply because of uncertainty—and that is a criticism of the decision. But it is arguable that *Pennington v Waine* is distinguishable from the current problem since no steps at all have been taken to transfer the shares and there appears to be no detrimental conduct undertaken on the basis of the promise which might render it unconscionable not to allow equity to assist the volunteer. In that case, the person entitled to the shares would be Omega.[3]

Nevertheless, even though the shares are not themselves bound by the trust, it is still necessary to consider whether Beta can sue Alpha's estate for damages for breach of covenant.[4] It has been argued that a covenantee of a voluntary covenant should be able to sue for damages for its breach and hold such damages in trust for the volunteers: see Elliott (1960) 76 LQR 100. The courts, nevertheless, are opposed to such a claim. In *Re Pryce* **[1917] 1 Ch 234**, the court would not direct the covenantees to sue, and in *Re Kay's Settlement* **[1939] Ch 329** it positively directed them not to sue. There is no objection to such a claim if the covenantee is suing in respect of her own loss as beneficiary, as in *Cannon v Hartley* **[1949] Ch 213**; but this is not the situation in the problem. By contrast, in *Fletcher v Fletcher* **(1844) 4 Hare 67**, the court held that there was already a perfect trust of a chose in action: viz., the benefit of the covenant itself. This suggests that if Alpha intended the benefit of the covenant to comprise trust property, Beta will be obliged to sue Alpha's estate for damages for breach of covenant and to hold the substantial damages which he will recover upon the trusts declared. There is, however, no evidence that this was Alpha's intention.

[4] This is the next point.

An alternative explanation was proffered in *Re Cook's Settlement Trusts* **[1965] Ch 902** by Buckley J. He considered that, whilst it might be possible to create a valid trust of the benefit of a covenant concerning property in existence and owned by the settlor at the date of the covenant, it is not possible to create a trust of the benefit of a covenant which relates to after-acquired property. If this view is followed, there can be no trust of the covenant in the problem.

Since the covenant was entered into only one year ago, it is enforceable by a third party whom the covenant purports to benefit, unless it appears that the parties intended otherwise (**Contracts (Rights of Third Parties) Act 1999**). If the specified purpose is charitable, this raises the question whether such a covenant is enforceable by the Attorney General. This seems unlikely, since he is not a person who is intended to benefit from the covenant. It also seems unlikely that the persons who might benefit under a charitable trust would have a personal right of action under the 1999 Act, since such persons do not have a beneficial interest under a charitable trust. The conclusion must be that the 1999 Act does not operate in relation to voluntary covenants to transfer property in favour of charity.[5]

Even if a trust of a chose in action has been created, Beta will not hold it upon the trusts declared unless these are valid trusts.[6] The **Charities Act 2011, s. 3(1)** lists 13 descriptions of purposes which will be charitable if they satisfy the 'public benefit' test which is set out in **s. 4**. The thirteenth category (**para. (m)**) includes all purposes previously recognised as charitable. It also preserves the ability of the courts to develop charity law by enabling new purposes to develop by analogy with, or within the spirit of, any of the purposes listed in **paras (a) to (l)**. The limiting factor that the purpose be beneficial to the community is now apparently subsumed within the broader 'public benefit' test contained in **s. 4**. However, if a purpose has already been held to be for the public benefit then that requirement will already have been satisfied. New purposes under **para. (m)** will have to be shown to be for the public benefit.

Applying **s. 3(1)**, clearly the primary purpose here (providing grants for law students in the United Kingdom) would be charitable under **para. (b) of s. 3(1)**. It would also be charitable under **para. (m)** as education has always been a charitable purpose and was Lord Macnaghten's second category of charitable purposes in **Pemsel's Case [1891] AC 531**. Under the previous law, the requirement for public benefit excluded from charitable status a trust for a group of beneficiaries defined by a personal nexus (**Oppenheim v Tobacco Securities Trust [1951] AC 297**; **Re Compton [1945] Ch 123**), and this appears to be imported into the current law by **s. 4 of the Charities Act 2011**. Under the previous law, there was a qualification in that, provided that the primary class of beneficiaries was a sufficient section of the public, the courts allowed preferences for a class of beneficiaries which was not (**Re Koettgen [1954] Ch 252** where a 75 per cent preference was allowed). **Re Koettgen** was much criticised (see **IRC v Educational Grants Association Ltd [1967] Ch 993**) and it remains to be seen whether the preference cases will survive the new public-benefit test. Although a preference of 75 per cent of the fund was accepted as a charity in **Re Koettgen**, a priority class on whom the whole of the fund can be spent is not: **Caffoor v ITC [1961] AC 584**. The words 'absolute preference' in the disposition may suggest a priority, in which case it will fail.

[7] And now the last point.

If it is not charitable, can the trust be valid as a private discretionary trust?[7] It would probably satisfy the test for certainty of objects, since it would appear to be possible to say of any given person whether or not they are a law student in the United Kingdom: **McPhail v Doulton [1971] AC 424, HL**. It would probably also not fail for administrative unworkability, since the description of objects probably does form something like a class: **McPhail v Doulton**. Nevertheless, unless (which is unlikely) it can be construed as a trust for immediate distribution of capital, it would be void for perpetuity. Assuming this to be so, the benefit of any chose in action would be held by Beta on a resulting trust for the benefit of Alpha's estate. In practice, this means that the covenant is simply unenforceable.

[8] Don't forget to deal with this point—if it is not valid, where does it go?

If the purported trust is void, the money which Alpha transferred to Beta is also held on a resulting trust for Alpha's estate. Omega is therefore entitled to it.[8]

LOOKING FOR EXTRA MARKS?

▧ Picking up all the points is the key here to extra marks.

▧ For a few more, discuss the correctness of the decision in ***Pennington*** v ***Waine***.

QUESTION | 2

Discuss, with reference to decided cases, whether any of the following words create a valid trust. Indicate any problems which may have to be overcome before a trust can be imposed in these cases.

a Look, I am giving this cheque to our baby.

b The money in my deposit account is as much yours as mine.

c I hereby give to my executors and trustees £500,000 on trust to apply the said sum at their absolute discretion for the maintenance and support of red-haired women in London.

d It is my dying wish, Marjorie, that you should have my London flat. Here are the deeds and the keys, put them in your bag. My solicitor will sort out the details when I am dead.

! CAUTION!

▧ This question contains a mixed bag of problems relating to the constitution of a trust. It draws heavily on particular cases, which can make it very unattractive if you are not familiar with the exact case. In that sense, it is not a very sporting question. Many examiners try to avoid questions which rely on the student's knowledge of a particular case, preferring to test the understanding of general principles. However, if you are faced with a question of this type, and you know the relevant cases, then it can be a gift.

▧ Avoid the temptation of starting your answer with an immediate reference to the case. For example, do not start with: 'This is a ***Jones*** v ***Lock*** problem …'. Instead, state the issue raised by the question, then the general rule with exceptions, and then illustrate your answer with cases. Some questions of this sort can subtly vary the facts of the case. Watch out for those!

DIAGRAM ANSWER PLAN

Identify the issues	■ Constitution of trust; certainty of objects
Relevant law	**(a)** Case law such as *T. Choithram International SA v Pagarani*; *Jones v Lock* **(b)** Case law such as *Paul v Constance*; *Re Vandervell's Trusts (No. 2)* **(c)** *McPhail v Doulton* and other case law **(d)** *Sen v Headley* and other case law
Apply the law	■ Declaration of trust ■ Imperfect gifts as evidence of intention to create a trust ■ Necessity of intention to create trust ■ Intention manifested by conduct ■ Intention manifested by words and conduct ■ Certainty of objects ■ Test for certainty in a discretionary trust ■ Problem of capriciousness ■ Deathbed gifts ■ Principle of *donatio mortis causa* ■ Whether land can be the subject of a deathbed gift
Conclude	■ Discussion of the problems each scenario has in relation to the establishment of a valid trust

A **SUGGESTED ANSWER**

Part (a)

[1] Setting out the law.

In order for a trust to be created there must be a clear manifestation of an intention to create a trust.[1] Where the settlor makes a declaration of self as trustee, the trust is fully constituted. Where the settlor is to be one of co-trustees, the declaration constitutes the trust and it is not necessary for the property to be transferred into the names of all the trustees to give effect to it (*T. Choithram International SA* v *Pagarani* [2001] **1 WLR 1, PC**).

[2] Applying the law to the facts.

The statement made implies a gift not a trust.[2] The gift is imperfect since a cheque is merely an order to a banker; therefore, even if the cheque is handed to a baby when the words are spoken, no property right is thereby transferred beyond the paper on which the cheque is written. In *Jones* v *Lock* (1865) **LR 1 Ch App 25**, an attempt was made to argue that, in effect, the donor had made a declaration that he was a trustee of the cheque for the beneficiary. It was held that a failed gift will not be construed in equity as evidence of an intention to declare a trust. Likewise, in *Pappadakis* v *Pappadakis* [2000] **WTLR 719**, it was held that an invalid assignment which did not identify the assignee who was to hold on trust could not operate as a declaration of trust.

Although there is present an intention to benefit the donee, there is no intention present to hold the property as trustee. This was confirmed in *Richards* v *Delbridge* (1874) **LR 18 Eq 11**, where words written on a lease which indicated an intention to give the lease to the grandson of the leaseholder were held ineffective at common law to effect the transfer. Since they were words indicating a gift, they were ineffective in equity to operate as a declaration of trust.

[3] Now the conclusion.

The gift will be perfected only when, and if, after presentation of the cheque, the funds are transferred to the credit of the payee's account.[3]

Part (b)

[4] This starts by going straight into the application combined with the identification of the key issue (you can refer back to the previous answer).

This statement again raises the issue of certainty of intention to create a trust.[4] In this situation the holder of the deposit account has not made an attempt to transfer the account into joint names. It may be arguable, according to the circumstances of the case, that the account holder has manifested an intention to hold the account on trust by conduct. The words are not sufficient in themselves but, coupled with the conduct of the parties, they may be. For example, in *Paul* v *Constance* [1977] **1 WLR 527**, where money was put into an account in the sole name of Mr Constance, his assurances to Mrs Paul that the money in the account was owned jointly were held sufficient to indicate an intention by him to hold the account on trust for them jointly. In *Re Vandervell's Trusts (No. 2)* [1974] **Ch 269**, where money from a settlement was used to purchase shares in exercise of an option, it was held that the conduct of the trustees in using this money and paying dividends into the settlement constituted sufficient evidence of an intention to create a trust even though no specific words had been used. Compare *T. Choithram International SA* v *Pagarani* [2001] **1 WLR 1**, where words which indicated an outright gift were construed in the context of the case as words of a gift to be held on the trusts of a settlement already constituted by the donor.

The decision in *Paul v Constance* was applied in *Rowe v Prance* **[1999] 2 FLR 787**, where a boat, which was held in the sole legal ownership of the defendant, was considered to be held on trust for the claimant and defendant in equal shares. The defendant had always referred to the boat as 'our boat' and had assured the claimant (his partner in an extramarital affair) that her interest in the boat was her security.

There must, however, be a clear intention evinced, whether by words and/or conduct, to create a trust. In *Re B (Child: Property Transfer)* **[1999] 2 FLR 418**, where a house, further to a consent order, was transferred to the mother 'for the benefit of the child', no trust was created for the child. The relationship between mother and child had broken down.

[5] And the conclusion.

Therefore, although it is difficult to state that the words are sufficient on their own to create a trust, coupled with other conduct there may be sufficient certainty of the requisite intention.[5]

Part (c)

[6] Point this out then jump to the key issue.

In this gift there is a clear intention to create a trust.[6] However, the issue is whether a gift to red-haired women in London is sufficiently certain to be carried out by the trustees. The trust appears to be discretionary. The test for certainty of objects in a discretionary trust was

[7] The law.

outlined in *McPhail v Doulton* **[1971] AC 424, HL**,[7] where it was held that the test was the same as that established for powers in *Re Gulbenkian's Settlements* **[1970] AC 508, HL**. The test is, 'Can it be said with certainty that any given individual is or is not a member of the class?' The question is concerned with whether the concept is clear, rather than with any evidential difficulties. So, in *Re Baden's Deed Trusts (No. 2)* **[1972] Ch 607**, the question was whether the words 'relatives' and 'dependants' were conceptually certain.

The problem of definition arises, therefore, in respect of red-haired women. Can it be said whether any given person is or is not a member of the class? The problem is not, in this case, in proving evidentially whether a person is or is not within the class. Instead, the difficulty lies in defining the term 'red-haired'. Whereas all people may agree whether certain individuals are red-haired, there may be some borderline cases where the trustees could not decide. The concept of what constitutes red hair may, therefore, be so unclear that it is impossible to carry out the trust.

Another problem might arise in relation to the width of the class. If a discretionary trust is so wide that it is administratively unworkable, this may invalidate it. In *McPhail v Doulton*, Lord Wilberforce suggested that a discretionary trust for the residents of Greater London might be so wide that it was unworkable. This was followed in *R* v *District Auditor, ex parte West Yorkshire Metropolitan County Council* **(1986) 26 RVR 24 (QBD)**, where a discretionary trust was purportedly created for the inhabitants of the county of West Yorkshire. The description of objects was considered to be so large that the trust was invalidated for administrative unworkability. This would be different if the gift was construed as a mere power (see *Re Manisty's Settlement* **[1974] Ch 17**).

The difficulties inherent in validating this gift to red-haired women indicate a capriciousness in the mind of the donor. While there is no general principle that a donor may not act capriciously (*Bird* v *Luckie* **(1850) 8 Hare 301**), where the gift involves the exercise by a trustee of a fiduciary obligation, the position is different. The difficulties, in the first instance, of defining red hair, and, secondly, in the potential width of the class, indicate an element of caprice which may cause a court to invalidate a gift on that ground alone (see *Re Hay's Settlement Trusts* **[1982] 1 WLR 202**).

Part (d)

[8] Identify issue.

It appears from the wording that this is a deathbed gift.[8] In order to effect a transfer of land at common law, there should be a deed (**Law of Property Act 1925, s. 52**). There would appear to be no deed transferring legal ownership in this case. Neither does there appear to be any consideration given. Marjorie is, therefore, a volunteer. The normal principle is that equity will not assist a volunteer in enforcing an imperfect gift.[9]

[9] Set out the maxim.

[10] And then the exception and go on to develop this as the key point.

However, there are some exceptions to this and one in particular, the principle of *donatio mortis causa*, may assist Marjorie.[10] There are three conditions which must be satisfied before this exception will be allowed. The gift must be conditional on death, it must be made in contemplation of death, and the donor must give the donee control over the gift (see *Cain* v *Moon* **[1896] 2 QB 283**).

Here, the question indicates that the gift is made in contemplation of death and it is not difficult to raise the presumption that it is, therefore, conditional on death (*King* v *Chiltern Dog Rescue and Redwings Horse Sanctuary* **[2015] EWCA Civ 581**; *Wilkes* v *Allington* **[1931] 2 Ch 104**). The donor states that the formalities will be dealt with after death. The subject-matter of the gift is land. Until recently, it was thought that it was not possible for land to be the subject of a *donatio mortis causa* (*Duffield* v *Elwes* **(1827) 1 Bli (NS) 497**). However, the Court of Appeal decision in *Sen* v *Headley* **[1991] Ch 425** dispelled these doubts. In that case, someone who already had the keys of a house was given a bunch of keys including one to a steel box in the house containing the title deeds. It was held that the donor had parted with dominion over the house and the title deeds in circumstances otherwise satisfying the conditions for a *donatio mortis causa* and the gift was completed. This has subsequently been followed in the High Court decision in *Vallee v Birchwood* **[2013] EWHC 1449 (Ch)**. It would, therefore, seem that as Marjorie has the keys, giving her physical control, and the deeds, this would be sufficient to give rise to the application of the rule that gifts made in contemplation of death are enforceable despite a lack of the appropriate formalities.

 LOOKING FOR EXTRA MARKS?

- You could develop a number of areas here. For instance, you could discuss the certainty of objects question in discretionary trusts and set out the different approaches of their Lordships in *McPhail v Doulton*.

 QUESTION | **3**

Sam, who died recently, appointed Tick and Tack as the executors and trustees of his will and made the following dispositions:

a   £50,000 to my sister Doris absolutely, feeling sure that she will give her son a reasonable amount.

b   £30,000 to Tick and Tack for purposes of which I will inform them.

c   My freehold property 'Dunroamin' to Tick and Tack upon trust to sell and to hold the net proceeds of sale for such worthy causes as they shall think fit.

Sam left his residuary realty to his son Percy and his residuary personalty to his daughter Mavis.

Advise Tick and Tack as to the validity of these dispositions, and as to who should benefit if any of them fail.

 CAUTION!

- This is a question which requires a fairly detailed knowledge of different parts of an equity and trusts syllabus. You may be lucky and find that you remember the relevant law and cases, but unless you feel fairly confident of doing well on two of the three parts, you might be wise to leave it alone. It is a question on which you might scrape a pass if you know some law, but would find it difficult to score well.

- Examiners like to be able to see clearly which part of a question they are marking. It will help the examiner, therefore, if you number each part of your answer and leave a space between the different parts.

○ DIAGRAM ANSWER PLAN

Identify the issues	▨ Certainty of intention; half-secret trusts; trusts of land

Relevant law	▨ Case law; **TLATA 1996**

Apply the law	▨ Issue: precatory words and certainty of intention to create a trust
	▨ Certainty of subject-matter
	▨ Application to problem
	▨ Issue: Half-secret trust if sufficient element of obligation present
	▨ Application to problem: problem regarding future communication
	▨ Problem regarding inconsistency on the face of the will
	▨ Issue: trust of land under **TLATA 1996**
	▨ Power of sale under **s. 4(1)**
	▨ Application to problem: invalid purpose trust as objects not charitable and infringes perpetuity rule

Conclude	(a) Goes beneficially to Doris if no certainty of intention; if certainty of intention still goes to Doris as uncertainty of subject-matter
	(b) Fails completely and results back to testator's estate for Mavis who is entitled to residuary personalty
	(c) Fails completely and results back to testator's estate for Percy who is entitled to residuary realty

Ⓐ ⟩ SUGGESTED ANSWER

Part (a)

[1] Precatory words and certainty of intention.

It is unlikely that the words in the disposition to Doris are sufficiently obligatory to attach a trust to the property in the hands of Doris.[1] Such words are precatory words and, since *Lambe* v *Eames* (1871) 6 Ch App 597 and the **Executors Act 1830**, the courts will not lean in favour of a trust: they simply construe the words in the context of the instrument to ascertain if a trust obligation is imposed. In *Mussoorie*

Bank v *Raynor* (1882) 7 App Cas 321, the words 'feeling confident' were held to be precatory and failed to impose a trust, and the words 'feeling sure' used here would probably similarly fail. Doris would therefore take the gift beneficially.

[2] Certainty of subject-matter.

Even if the words were sufficiently certain to impose a trust, a 'reasonable amount' would be too uncertain as regards subject-matter.[2] Although the court held in *Re Golay's Will Trusts* [1965] 1 WLR 969, that a 'reasonable income' was capable of objective determination by reference to a person's lifestyle, a reasonable amount in this case would not seem to have any objective criteria by which it could be assessed, and it would therefore fail.

Part (b)

[3] Half-secret trust if sufficient element of obligation present.

This disposition could be an attempt to create a half-secret trust if it is found to have the necessary element of obligation.[3] Although the words 'upon trust' are not used, it seems fairly clear from the face of the will that Tick and Tack are not intended to take the disposition beneficially.

[4] Problem of communication.

In the case of a half-secret trust, the half-secret trustees must accept the trust before the execution of the will.[4] This does not appear to have happened, as Sam refers to a future communication. Although communication of the identity of the beneficiary at any time before death would be sufficient for a fully-secret trust, there are dicta in *Blackwell* v *Blackwell* [1929] AC 318, HL, and it was accepted in *Re Bateman's Will Trusts* [1970] 1 WLR 1463, that this must be before the execution of the will in the case of a half-secret trust. The reason given for this is that a communication after the will would allow the testator to change his mind and effectively make testamentary dispositions without complying with the **Wills Act 1837**. This is criticised as failing to take account of the fact that the secret trust arises from its acceptance by the trustees quite independently of the will. Further, since the courts may now order the disclosure of letters of wishes as in *Breakspear* v *Ackland* [2008] EWHC 220 (Ch) then this is a point about which care needs to be taken.

[5] Problem if inconsistency on face of will.

Even if there has already been a communication of the purposes which Tick and Tack have accepted, it will still be invalid as there would then be an inconsistency on the face of the will,[5] which is fatal to a half-secret trust: *Re Keen* [1937] Ch 236. The will clearly refers to a future communication and evidence of a prior communication would be inconsistent with it.

Part (c)

[6] Establish the issue relating to trust of land under **TLATA**.

This will impose a trust of land under the **TLATA 1996**.[6] Even where the trust is expressed as a trust for sale, the power to postpone sale cannot be abrogated (**s. 4(1)**).[7] It is a matter for Tick and Tack whether

[7] Power of sale.

they decide to sell 'Dunroamin' or keep it for the beneficiary under the trust. There would appear to be a discretionary trust as regards the proceeds of sale, but the trust is a purpose trust. There are no objects of the trust who can, if necessary, enforce it against Tick and Tack. Moreover, a trust must be sufficiently certain for a court to enforce it if necessary and 'worthy causes' would be too vague. In *Re Atkinson's Will Trusts* **[1978] 1 WLR 586**, it was held that it would be impossible to confine worthy objects to charitable objects, so there is no possibility of this taking effect as a charitable trust. Although charitable trusts are purpose trusts, they are valid as they are enforceable by the Attorney General. A non-charitable purpose trust fails, however, for certainty of objects, and also if it infringes the rule against perpetual trusts. This trust will therefore fail.[8]

[8] Invalid purpose trust.

[9] This sums it up and sets out where everything goes.

Conclusion[9]

The disposition in (a) will go to Doris beneficially if there is no certainty of intention to create a trust. If there is such certainty, but the purported trust in favour of Doris's son fails for uncertainty of subject-matter, Doris similarly takes the entire legacy beneficially as it is only the trust grafted onto it which fails (*Curtis* v *Rippon* **(1820) 5 Madd 434**). The dispositions in (b) and (c) fail completely, however, and will result back to the testator's residuary estate on failure.

The pecuniary legacy in (b) is personalty and will go as residuary personalty to Mavis. The doctrine of conversion, which applied to a trust for sale under the **Law of Property Act 1925**, was abolished by **s. 3 of the TLATA 1996**, and 'Dunroamin' would go to Percy, who is entitled to the residuary realty.

+ LOOKING FOR EXTRA MARKS?

- Extra marks could be gained by discussing the case law in more detail.

Q QUESTION 4

Five years ago Olga, a spinster, married Clive, a widower with three children. They agreed to make wills in identical terms leaving their property to each other and then to Clive's two daughters, Amy and Bea. Wills in accordance with this agreement were executed by both of them shortly after they married. Clive had quarrelled with his son Nigel and did not want him to benefit from his estate.

About three years ago Clive became seriously and terminally ill. Amy was a nurse and Clive told her that if she would take unpaid leave to go and live with him to look after him, as Olga was not strong enough, he and Olga would ensure that his house 'Greensleeves' would be left to her. Amy took unpaid leave and nursed her father for nine months before he died. While living at the house, she paid for the modernisation of the kitchen and bathroom.

Some three months before he died, Clive and Olga executed identical codicils to their wills, both signed on the same day, varying the ultimate disposition of 'Greensleeves' so that Amy should receive it from the survivor of them and the remainder of their property should ultimately be divided between Amy and Bea.

After Clive died, Olga gave away considerable property which had belonged to Clive to charity. She also won £500,000 on the football pools. Nigel, who lived near to Olga, visited her regularly and did small jobs for her. Olga died recently and a will was found among her papers, dated a few days before she died, revoking all previous wills and testamentary dispositions and leaving all her property 'to my wonderful stepson Nigel'.

Advise Amy and Bea.

CAUTION!

- This question raises some of the unresolved difficulties relating to mutual wills. You should be aware of these problems and also of the necessary requirements to establish mutual wills. Apart from this, however, the question is fairly straightforward.

- The facts of the question disclose two possible causes of action available to one of the parties (Amy) whom you are asked to advise. If you come to the conclusion that Amy is likely to succeed on one ground, you should of course nevertheless go on to consider the other ground also. *Real* cases are often pleaded in the alternative!

DIAGRAM ANSWER PLAN

Identify the issues	▦ The basis of mutual wills is a contract the consideration for which is executory until the first person dies
Relevant law	▦ *Olins* v *Walters* and related case law
Apply the law	▦ Is there sufficient evidence of such a contract (*Re Hagger*)? • If disposing of land, does the contract have to comply with the **Law of Property (Miscellaneous Provisions) Act 1989, s. 2**? Even if it does not, it may be enforceable under a constructive trust (*Yaxley* v *Gotts*) • Does a constructive trust arising from mutual wills attach only to the property the survivor receives from the first to die, or to all the survivor's property? If so, to what extent can the survivor use the capital of such a trust? • Clive's agreement with Amy, upon which Amy acts to her detriment, gives rise to an estoppel under which Amy might claim 'Greensleeves'
Conclude	▦ Advise Amy and Bea

SUGGESTED ANSWER

¹ The first issue is mutual wills.

The enforceability of mutual wills depends upon an agreement between the parties making them: *Olins* v *Walters*.[1] The agreement is that they will both make wills in substantially the same form, leaving property in accordance with the agreement, and they agree not to revoke the wills. It will be an unenforceable agreement until such time as the first of the parties dies, as it will not be supported by consideration until then. However, when the first party dies, the consideration is the benefit which the survivor receives under their will, and the agreement then becomes binding on the conscience of the survivor, who has received a benefit.

It is often difficult to find sufficient evidence of the agreement to establish that the parties did intend to make mutual wills. The fact that the wills are identical is some evidence but is not in itself sufficient (*Re Oldham* [1925] Ch 75) as there should also be an agreement not to revoke the wills. In the case of *Re Goodchild* [1996] 1 WLR 694, the Court of Appeal held that identical wills made by a husband and wife on the same date were not mutually binding as the necessary contractual obligation not to revoke the wills was lacking. However, in *Re Cleaver* [1981] 1 WLR 939, where two sets of wills were made by a husband and wife in identical form and a further will by the surviving wife consistent with her second identical will, this was held to be sufficient evidence of an agreement. In a High Court decision, *Legg and Others v Burton and Others* [2017] EWHC 2088 (Ch), it was held that an agreement for a mutual will could be based on equitable estoppel even where the wills contained contrary wording and in *Fry v Densham-Smith* [2010] EWCA Civ 1410, the existence of an agreement was based on extrinsic evidence. Further, in *Olins v Walters* [2009] Ch 212, where reference to an agreement to enter into mutual wills was made in a codicil, the Court of Appeal held that this was sufficient to establish clear and satisfactory evidence of a contract between the testators. The identical wills made here, together with identical codicils giving effect to identical changes, would probably be sufficient evidence to establish the necessary agreement as in *Re Cleaver*.[2]

A further problem with regard to the disposition of 'Greensleeves' to Amy under mutual wills is whether any such agreement is caught by the **Law of Property (Miscellaneous Provisions) Act 1989, s. 2**.[3] In *Healey v Brown* [2002] EWHC Ch 1405, the judge decided that it was, and as there was no contract in writing signed by both parties (as here), the agreement was void. He held, however, that the agreement for mutual wills was nevertheless enforceable as it was a contract for a constructive trust which arose under the wills, and so, like *Yaxley v Gotts* [2000] Ch 162, was exempted from the formality requirement of s. 2(1) by s. 2(7). Presumably the agreement as to the mutual wills disposing of 'Greensleeves' might similarly be enforceable as the wills would give rise to a constructive trust.

It is probable, therefore, that Amy and Bea will be able to challenge Olga's will leaving all her property to Nigel, and require her estate to be administered according to the terms of her will and codicil made shortly before Clive died. The decision in *Goodchild* suggests that even if there is no legally binding obligation not to revoke a will, the moral obligation ensuing on the death of the first testator to die binds that person's property in the hands of the second testator, who is therefore under an obligation to deal with it as agreed.

There are a number of vexed questions with regard to the property which is subject to any trust created by mutual wills and there do not seem to be any very satisfactory answers.[4]

Does any trust arising attach only to the property which the survivor receives from the other party to the agreement, or does it attach to all the survivor's property on death?[5] If the latter, then the £500,000 which Olga won on the football pools would also be subject to any trust arising. As the survivor entered into an agreement to leave all their own property to the same third party too, this would seem to be a tenable argument. In *Re Dale* [1994] Ch 31, it was

---

[2] Sufficient evidence of contract?

[3] Problem of land.

[4] The big debate—and one of the problems with mutual wills.

[5] Where it is debatable, ask it in question form.

held that the trust attached to all the property held by the survivor at the date of the survivor's death. In *Re Hagger* **[1930] 2 Ch 190**, also a first instance decision, it was considered that the trust should at least attach to all the property held by the survivor at the date of the first death. In *Re Green* **[1951] Ch 148**, it was held that the trust attached only to the property received under the will of the first party to die, but this intention was clear from the terms of the will.

Does the trust arising prevent the survivor from disposing of any property they receive under the will of the first to die?[6] If so, it would effectively be only a life interest in that property which the survivor has. In the Australian case of *Birmingham* v *Renfrew* **(1937) 57 CLR 666**, Dixon J said that the survivor could enjoy the property as if an absolute owner, subject to restrictions on his rights of alienability, but that on his death this 'floating obligation' crystallised and attached to the property. If this is correct, presumably an action could have been brought during Olga's lifetime to prevent her from disposing of any very large sums of money. This point did not arise and was not considered in *Re Dale*.

Additionally, Amy may have grounds to claim the house under the equitable doctrine of estoppel.[7] This could apply to the circumstances of the question in two ways. First, it could apply to make the oral agreement between Clive and Amy enforceable notwithstanding the absence of the requisite formality for a contract for the disposition of land. Secondly, Amy's acting to her detriment in reliance upon a promise made by her father could found a claim in proprietary estoppel.

An oral agreement for the disposition of land will be void as it does not comply with **s. 2 of the Law of Property (Miscellaneous Provisions) Act 1989**, which requires any such agreement to be in writing and signed by both parties. Before 1989, such an agreement had to comply with the formality requirements of s. 40 of the Law of Property Act 1925, but equity would enforce a purely oral agreement if there was a sufficient act of part performance by the party seeking to enforce it, and in *Wakeham* v *Mackenzie* **[1968] 1 WLR 1175** a housekeeper was able to enforce an oral agreement to leave the house to her in return for work she had done. Section 40 was repealed by the 1989 Act and the Law Commission envisaged that the equitable doctrine of part performance would be replaced by estoppel. In *Yaxley* v *Gotts* **[2000] Ch 162**, an oral agreement that a builder who converted a building into flats should have one of the flats in return for his work was held to be binding not only on the person with whom he agreed, but also on his son who knew of the agreement and adopted it. The Court of Appeal applied estoppel, although Robert Walker LJ felt that the situation could also give rise to the imposition of a constructive trust. The agreement between Amy and Clive,

[6] And again state the query here as a question.

[7] Is there an estoppel?

whereby she gave up work to go and look after him, might therefore be enforceable against Olga and her estate.

Amy has also acted to her detriment by spending money on the house in modernising the kitchen and the bathroom. The doctrine of estoppel is much wider in its scope than the doctrine of part performance and may be used to enforce a promise upon which the promisee has acted to their detriment.

The promisor is then estopped from going back on the promise and an equity attaches to the property to which it relates, not only in the hands of the promisor himself but also in the hands of a volunteer acquiring the property from him. Thus in *Inwards* v *Baker* **[1965] 2 QB 29, CA**, a son who was persuaded by his father to build a bungalow on a plot of land belonging to the father was able to remain there after the father died and the land passed to his mistress. In *Pascoe* v *Turner* **[1979] 1 WLR 431**, a man who told a cohabitee with whom he lived that his house and contents all belonged to her, and was aware that she was spending her frugal savings on repairing and redecorating the house after he had left, was estopped from denying this and was obliged to convey the fee simple in the property to her.

Moreover, estoppel is not restricted by the fundamental premise of testamentary freedom (*Gillett* v *Holt* **[2000] 2 All ER 289**). The acquiescence relied upon to found a claim of proprietary estoppel should relate to the property. Amy has acted to her detriment in modernising the property and, if this was in reliance upon her father's promise, this may well be sufficient. Both Olga and Nigel are volunteers, so that Amy's claim to the house, which is necessarily equitable and not registrable under the **Land Charges Act 1972** (per Denning LJ in *E. R. Ives Investment Ltd* v *High* **[1967] 2 QB 379**), might succeed on this ground also.

LOOKING FOR EXTRA MARKS?

▪ If you get all the points in this complex question you will be heading for high marks.

TAKING THINGS FURTHER

▪ Luxton, P., '*Walters* v *Olin*: uncertainty of subject matter—an insoluble problem in mutual wills?' [2009] Conv 498–505.
  This article deals with the problems created by mutual wills.

Online Resources

www.oup.com/uk/qanda/

Go online for extra essay and problem questions and a podcast with advice on revision and exam technique.

In coursework this is even more important that in exams because, as you have time to get it right, then that will be the expectation. In the heat of the exam room there is leeway for some infelicities of style—not in coursework.

Planning

- You have time to plan your coursework assignment and that is time well spent. Coursework is about research and here is an opportunity to demonstrate your research skills. But how good are they? Before you get to this point you need to ensure that you have grasped how to use the law databases and the printed word. Much of research nowadays can be done online but do not assume that everything is available online. While what is produced today is (almost) always put on online immediately as well as being in print, that does not apply to historical material. For instance, the Conveyancer is not available online before the 1980s and there may be important articles which you need to use from that era. A question on fusion of common law and equity may require you to read Maitland in the original—definitely not online. So, don't ignore the advantage of having learned your way around the library and the stock held in print there.

- Next, are you actually competent at using the databases? Ensure you go to the sessions arranged by your library for learning how to use these databases. They are all a bit different and can be idiosyncratic. You may also find that some of the journals you are used to finding in one place are no longer available there. That is for commercial reasons—publishers negotiate with the online databases and can pull out of one set and join another. If you can't find a journal article in one place then hunt around and usually there is an invaluable person who can help you—the law librarian. Make their acquaintance.

- Having done the hard work of learning research skills, use them. Read all the primary (cases, statutes, etc.) and secondary material (books, journal articles, policy documents, guidance, Law Commission reports, etc.) you have been given and go a bit further for that first class answer.

- Take notes as you read of the points which link back to your coursework question. Your notes should consist of the following:

  Citation (book, article, etc.)

  Page number where you read the key point you want to use (that's called a pinpoint)

  Any verbatim quotation in quotation marks

  Any argument, point on which you wish to rely (or dispute, etc.)

You think you will remember these key things—but you won't. It is also the way to avoid an allegation of plagiarism (more on that later).

- As you do this reading (your research) start to develop your argument for the assignment. If you are asked to critique something, e.g. the role of public benefit in the law of charities, use the key points from your reading to make a case about public benefit. For example, this article argues that public benefit is elastic; the Charity Commission have produced guidance showing that public benefit in education cases is down to the trustees to demonstrate, and so on. Build your coursework from your research.

- Write a plan for your coursework. If it is an essay, then you have an argument to make. Think of it as a thread which needs to link all the points you are going to make. For example, if the question asks you to consider whether the rules for interim injunctions fairly balance the interests of the parties, then think through what your answer is going to be. Do you agree that the rules do achieve this or not? Or do you think there are some points either way? Set out your points in a way so that each sets out to answer the question. Keep the thread going to the end.

- If it is a problem question, then list out the issues and jot down in your plan all the cases etc. that are relevant then the secondary material. If asked to advise, decide what your advice is going to be and ensure your conclusion deals with that.

Read, Research, then Reference

- Use OSCOLA (the Oxford Standard Citation of Legal Sources). Download and print a copy of it and keep it beside you as you do your research. In your notes write down the OSCOLA-proof citation. You only need to do it once—do it at the start.

- Make sure you reference any statement, opinion, argument, or statistic that you give. It is about giving credit where it is due and about enabling a reader to go and check for themselves what that author said. For example, 'as Lord Denning states . . .' Then in your footnote to this, put the source of this reference (in the correct OSCOLA format). It is a good news story for you as it shows you have been going about your research in a diligent and profitable manner. Your feedback will mention that there has been good research undertaken. You will be rewarded for reading, researching, and referencing.

● If you are going to quote verbatim then use the appropriate punctuation marks and cite (it is called pinpointing) the exact page numbers where that is to be found.

Practical Points

● Keep within your word limit.
● Footnotes and bibliography must be included and done in OSCOLA fashion. Note that (rather irritatingly) OSCOLA has different rules for footnotes and bibliography. Read OSCOLA and follow the rules.
● Proofread not once but twice. Once when you have just finished; then go away for a few days and proofread again. On each occasion proofread twice—once for sense (does that sentence/paragraph) make sense; is that sentence too long? Then proofread again for typographical errors. If you use a spellchecker still go back and make sure it has chosen the correct word.

Last Word

● Enjoy the research involved and the writing, and most of all making the argument. It is what being a lawyer is all about.

COURSEWORK QUESTION

Critically[1] examine the extent to which the Privy Council in *Marr* v *Collie (Bahamas)* [2017] UKPC 17[2] has settled the debate as to the proper approach[3] to establishing the beneficial ownership of a jointly-held asset, even one acquired as an investment, rather than as a home for the legal co-owners.[4]

[1] Usual suspect—this requires a critical analysis of this decision not a description.
[2] Reading the case is not optional here.
[3] There's a clue here—there is a debate. So you need to engage with that.
[4] Here's the key issue—the difference in treatment of a commercial investment to a family home.

ANSWER POINTERS

1   KEY ISSUE:

Explain the issue: initial presumption of resulting trust or **Stack v Dowden** *approach?*

Explain how the legal dispute centred over whether the correct approach was that set out by Lady Hale in **Stack v Dowden** **[2007] 2 AC 432**, that a conveyance into joint names creates a presumption of equal beneficial ownership, or whether, as held by Lord Neuberger in **Laskar v Laskar** **[2008] EWCA Civ 347** (and following his dissenting judgment in **Stack**), that principle was restricted to the domestic context, in a narrow sense, and so where a property was purchased as an investment, the traditional presumption that property is held on resulting trust for the parties according to their contributions to the purchase price applied, in the absence of evidence to the contrary.

2   THE LAW

Critically analyse the reasoning in cases such as **Stack v Dowden**, **Laskar v Laskar**, and **Jones v Kernott** [2011] UKSC 53. Show how **Marr v Collie** prefers the **Stack v Dowden** approach to the initial presumption of resulting trust.

3   CRITICAL ANALYSIS OF EFFECT OF JUDICIAL AUTHORITY LEADING TO **MARR V COLLIE**:

- What is the 'context' of the acquisition; purely commercial transaction? (falls outside **Stack**).

- Not purely commercial? Joint legal ownership equals equal beneficial ownership; presumption of equal shares unless evidence to the contrary or of some other positive intention can be found.

- Intention not fixed at the date of purchase, but may change and should be determined by evidence from the whole course of dealings between the parties, i.e. by considering the same factors applicable in the case of a couple's home given at para. 69 of Lady Hale's judgment in **Stack**.

- Where evidence that the parties did not acquire property in joint names to give effect to an intention to share co-owned property equally, and no other intention as to sharing can be established by the evidence (including by inference or imputation, see **Jones v Kernott**)—then resulting trust presumption.

Here you will need to refer to some of the proliferation of academic articles prompted both by the earlier cases and by **Marr v Collie**. Examples of such literature following the **Marr v Collie** decision include: J. Roche, 'Returning to clarity and principle: the Privy Council on Stack v Dowden, Case Comment' (2017) 76 CLJ 493–496; M. George and B. Sloan, 'Presuming too little about resulting and constructive trusts?' [2017] Conv 303–312. No doubt more will follow so a current literature review is essential for this (and any) topic.

4   CONCLUSION:

Critique the conclusion of the case and argue about the certainty versus justice point. (Are you a Lady Hale person or a Lord Neuberger person—Is this a divide between property lawyers and family lawyers?)

Online Resources   www.oup.com/uk/qanda/

Go online for extra essay and problem questions and a podcast with advice on revision and exam technique.

Index

D

E

G

H

I

U

V

W